Physical Evidence

Wesleyan Film

A series from Wesleyan University Press
Edited by Jeanine Basinger

The new Wesleyan Film series takes a back-to-basics approach to the art of cinema. Books in the series will deal with the formal, the historical, and the cultural—putting a premium on visual analysis, close readings, and an understanding of the history of Hollywood and international cinema, both artistically and industrially. The volumes will be rigorous, critical, and accessible both to academics and to lay readers with a serious interest in film.

Series editor Jeanine Basinger, Corwin-Fuller Professor of Film Studies at Wesleyan University and Founder/Curator of the Wesleyan Cinema Archives, is the author of such landmark books as *The World War II Combat Film: Anatomy of a Genre, A Woman's View: How Hollywood Spoke to Women, 1930–1960,* and *Silent Stars.*

ANTHONY MANN
by Jeanine Basinger

PHYSICAL EVIDENCE
Selected Film Criticism
by Kent Jones

ACTION SPEAKS LOUDER
Violence, Spectacle, and the American Action Movie
Revised and Expanded Edition
by Eric Lichtenfeld

Physical Evidence

SELECTED FILM CRITICISM BY KENT JONES

Wesleyan University Press MIDDLETOWN, CONNECTICUT

791.4
Jones
2007

Published by
Wesleyan University
Middletown, CT 06459
© 2007 by Kent Jones
Printed in United States of America

5 4 3 2 1

Library of Congress Cataloging-in-Publication Data
Jones, Kent.
Physical evidence : selected film criticism / Kent Jones.
    p.   cm. — (Wesleyan film)
Includes bibliographical references and index.
ISBN-10 0–8195–6844–9 (cloth : alk. paper)
ISBN-13 978–0–8195–6844–1 (cloth : alk. paper)
    1.   Motion pictures.   I. Title.
PN1994.J59 2007
791.43—dc22   2007012626

for Darezhan Omirbaev,
who still believes in cinema
on the other side of the world

Contents

Acknowledgments

The cinema—my cinema—is intimately connected with my life and the people with whom I've shared it: my mother Marcia, who started taking me to the movies in Pittsfield, Massachusetts, in five glorious theaters that are no more; my grandmother Verna Lucia Angelo, born in a log cabin on the Canadian border just as Griffith was making his first Biograph shorts; Maria Hodermarska, who taught me whatever I know about acting; my sons Ethan and Andrézj, who've helped me to see the beauties of Batman and the Flash, to rediscover the wonders of *North By Northwest*, and to understand that *Stagecoach* doesn't have much of a story. And then there's my father, Dana Jones, who passed away on a day in late November of 2005. He was, as they say, a difficult man—stoic, terrified of change, and even more terrified of betraying his emotions, and he spent his private life living with his experience of combat in the Pacific, his public life on the radio as the much loved "Voice of the Berkshires." I was drawn to the movies for many reasons, but a great deal of it had to do with my father, with trying to understand him without intruding on his resolute privacy. I saw him in the faces of Humphrey Bogart, Dana Andrews, Fredric March, Lee Marvin, and other actors. And I still do.

I'm fortunate to have many good friends, all of whom have played some part in this collection: Jonathan Rosenbaum, Alex Horwath, Nicole Brenez and Adrian Martin (pen pals), Robert Walsh, John Gianvito, Manohla Dargis, Howard Hampton, Frederic Bonnaud, Richard Schickel, Pierre Rissient, Fred Wiseman, Rick Linklater, Matt Steigbigel, Elisabeth Lequeret, Michael Almereyda, Sandra den Hamer, Stefan Grisseman, Gary Palmucci, Alan Franey, André Téchiné, Nick James, Meredith Brody, Alla Verlotsky, Olaf Moeller, Nathan Lee, Dominique Paini, Jake Perlin, Luc Dardenne, Richard Pena, Michael Koresky, Raffaele Donato, Violeta Bava, Margaret Bodde, Peggy Chiao, Chris Chang, Thierry Frémaux, Bertrand Tavernier, Flavia de Fuentes, David Thompson, Sarah Finklea, Michael Gizzi, Regina Schlagnitweit, and Sebastien Lemercier.

I need to thank a series of thoughtful, encouraging, and very patient editors: Richard Jameson, Raymond Bellour, Abby Nolan, Thierry Jousse, Serge Toubiana, Rob White, Giulia d'Agnolo Vallan, Dennis Lim, Liz Helfgott, Heather Shaw, Charles Tesson, Mark Peranson, Eric Banks, Jean-Michel

Frodon, James Quandt, Jean-Marc Lalanne, and last but far from least, the editor of this volume, Eric Levy.

I've spent a lot of time talking movies and many, many other things with Jean-Pierre Gorin, Paul Schrader, Greg Ford, Quintín, Mark McElhatten, Benoit Jacquot, Bruce Goldstein, Geoffrey O'Brien, Jim Hoberman, Amy Taubin, Sherri Wolf, Nicolas Saada, Rachel Reichman, Claire Denis, and Thelma Schoonmaker. I always learn something, and I treasure their companionship.

Peter Gizzi, Gavin Smith, Olivier Assayas, Phillip Lopate, and Arnaud Desplechin have offered me encouragement and support, not just in matters relating to this book but throughout some of the most difficult periods of my life. Their friendship means everything to me.

Martin Scorsese, Manny Farber, and Patricia Patterson have been central to my life and my relationship to movies—from the screen, the page, the canvas (in Manny's case, the board), and in person. I honestly don't know who or where I'd be without them.

Bruni Burres would probably prefer that her name go unmentioned here, but she's out of luck. She's a barometer of truth when it comes to movies and everything else, and she's played a much more important role in this book than she knows or would care to admit.

What exactly are we doing when we write about cinema? Are we sizing up an art form? A business? A hybrid of the two? A transitory blip in the history of the visual arts? If the last option is correct, and I have a feeling it is, then we are still obliged to describe it—those of us who remain sufficiently interested, that is. And yet, there's a tendency to slip and slide all over the place in film criticism, between the populist and the exclusive (or "esoteric," which is to movie culture as "liberal" is to politics), the aesthetic and the practical (meaning: the financial), the sacred and the profane. It's as if no one wants to look directly at movies, for fear that they'll dry up and blow away or *be* blown away. The flip side is a tendency to mercilessly weigh down the medium and its individual products with extravagant pronouncements, both negative (the "inherent vulgarity of the medium" idea, trumpeted by everyone from Gore Vidal to David Thomson) and positive (the devotional stream of cinephila in which every movie is a potentially transformative experience). This is a lot to pin on any art form, let alone any single work of art, and it runs directly against the grain of good criticism.

It was once common to hear stories from viewers who detested John Cassavetes's films the first time they saw them, only to realize that those same films had gotten under their skin weeks if not months or years later. Today, when judgments are everything, such delayed reaction times seem unthinkable. The apparent extinction of this type of slow circle around the movie is attributable to a number of factors, including the fire-and-brimstone moral edicts handed down by the sons of Godard (and by the High Priest himself), who see cinematic mortal sins anywhere and everywhere; the example of the aggressively clever and undeniably winning Quentin Tarantino, whose films appeared to make good on an impossible promise of fun-filled art, challenging and easy at the same time; magazine and newspaper editors with a mounting fear of offending their dwindling readerships; the formidable influence of Pauline Kael, a brilliant writer and a self-proclaimed purveyor of single-take judgments, a practice carried on by many writers with only a fraction of her talent; and, finally, the cultural climate around us, in which nothing is allowed to make an appearance until it has been prepackaged and presold and in which the term "popular" has been rendered effectively meaningless. We've been alternately lulled, bullied, sweet-talked, and fatigued into looking askance at anything other than yes or no, liked it or hated it, and we now take it for granted that we come first and the movie comes second. Did we get our money's worth? Was it worth the time we spent or might we have better spent it on something else?—"spent" being the operative word.

On top of everything else, American movies have never been worse. Or, to put it another way, they have become bad in the worst way imaginable. It is not uncommon to go to the multiplex and see three or four coming attractions in a row (following twice as many commercials) either hissed to death or laughed off the screen. The collective sentiment always seems to be: why are you subjecting us to this? Why indeed. The thought that we have been willing participants, that we have contributed to the climate that allowed all this crap to be created in the first place, never enters into the game. Why are we getting more and more and more of the same whizzing music-saturated action, heavy character typing, pop cultural droppings, and junior high scenarios of lessons learned and difficulties overcome through perfunctory chases or "really good talks"—all fixtures in American moviemaking since Ghostbusters? Because we never really complained, that's why. Not to slight the scurrilous nature of marketing departments, which now have a death grip on filmmaking, but they are only able to function in a society in which everyone has either agreed on or quietly acquiesced to the centrality of market-driven thinking. It's a wonder the movies aren't worse.

Thomas Schatz's celebrated "genius of the system" has given way to its obverse, a situation in which you have to be some kind of genius to transcend the system and actually make a good movie. Indeed, the current "system"—more cybernetic than industrial—all but ensures that the movie will turn out as blandly inoffensive as possible, since the dominant idea (perfectly understandable from a business standpoint) is that individuality and artistry are foreign agents, which only gum up the smooth flow of product and consumer appreciation. The situation makes for many alibis, thus allowing mediocrity to flourish. Meanwhile, every murmur of individuality, no matter that the sensibility in question is that of an exciting, sprawling talent like P. T. Anderson, a smooth operator in the guise of a sharp-eyed misanthrope like Todd Solondz, a mildly talented art-school conceptualist with a good ear for nasty dialogue like Todd Haynes, or a wondrously poetic, dangerously private artist like Wes Anderson, is trumpeted to the skies in critical raves, magazine profiles, and guest appearances. The unlucky recipient of such hoopla is more or less compelled to become his or her own brand name and is self-typed right out of the box. It's difficult if not impossible, for instance, to imagine M. Night Shyamalan moving even a little out-side of his heavily strategized narratives and glacial Lewtonisms. And he's only thirty-five.

If there's a worldwide running theme in today's cinema, it is an under-current of extreme anxiety about each individual film's potential stake in the popular imagination, an all-or-nothing proposition given the fact that audi-ences have become accustomed to being grabbed by the throat. I suppose that there's a corresponding anxiety about the future of the medium, and rightly so. The pietistic strain in movie appreciation that makes a fetish out of moviegoing itself (and that consequently gets movies and the experience of watching them on big screens hopelessly confused) is doomed to a bitter-sweet finale, judging from the decreasing attendance figures and relative disinterest in the intellectual currents around cinema. Many writers are des-perate for movies to mean something in the "national conversation" that they simply don't anymore and probably never will again. Kael, as Louis Menand correctly pointed out, was the one who led this conversation, and more than a few critics are now trying to fill her shoes. This is an impossible task, be-cause the relatively broad filmgoing community that read her writing has disappeared and given way to a plurality of enclaves and brotherhoods—avant-gardists, documentary specialists, historians, pop culture mavens, film festivalgoers, academics, etc.—chattering away amongst themselves and occasionally to one another in the shadow of a seemingly monolithic con-sumer culture. Meanwhile, the movies themselves will undoubtedly get big-ger and bigger and smaller and smaller, and the lovely idea of cinema that begins with Griffith and moves through Murnau, Ford, Renoir, Rossellini, Godard, and on through Hou and Wong will, I believe, become more and more a matter of choice, a rigidly defined aesthetic school.

One could feel these shifts taking effect over the last ten years, the period during which these pieces were written—call it The Tarantino Decade. In-evitably, this book is a reflection on and of those years. We saw the wide-spread introduction of digital technology in every corner of moviemaking—shooting, editing, color correcting, sound recording, special effects, ani-mation, and exhibition. We saw the death of the seemingly immortal Stan-ley Kubrick, the collapse of the Canal Plus funding machine in France, and the demise or marginalization of several key small distributors in the United States. We also saw the unstoppable ascendancy of the internet, the school shootings of the late 1990s, the Clinton impeachment, the virtual disappearance of trade barriers, two terms of George W. Bush, the second intifada, the destruction of the Twin Towers, the invasions of Afghanistan and Iraq, the de-stabilization of the Middle East, and the shattering of America's greatest city. These events and shifts have affected moviemaking and moviewatching in all ways: subtly, obliquely, overtly, rashly, on every imaginable level.

The theorist David Bordwell recently said that he was bored with criticism that did nothing but attempt to catch the zeitgeist, and well he should be. On the other hand, I find it impossible to imagine being a responsible critic and *not* doing so. Whenever these pieces step away from the movie itself and make way for references to contemporary events, autobiographical reflections, citations of assorted trends, artists and artworks from other disciplines and areas of culture, the intention is to simply describe the movie itself or to enlarge that description by including the circumstances under which it was made or exhibited; in other words, to describe the territory of and around and within and without the movie. Many of the films and filmmakers discussed here emerged during the last decade, and the ones that didn't are included for the simple (though easily forgotten) reason that the past is always present. Anyone who cares about movies would probably agree with Peter Bogdanovich that there's no such thing as an old movie— that there are only good movies and bad movies, movies we've seen and movies we haven't seen.

More than ever, the good movies are the ones that go against the grain. What was once possible for a Raoul Walsh or a King Hu, a King Vidor or a Francis Ford Coppola—the creation of great popular cinema, or great cinema in a popular vein—is all but lost. It seems to me that the modern attempts to work in this vein, from *Titanic* to *JFK*, have been doomed from the start, by either playing down to the audience with the worst kind of calculation (the Cameron film) or unsuccessfully attempting to create a new form from a collage of "hip" moves (the Stone movie, memorably dubbed "the greatest bad film ever made" by Norman Mailer, who had evidently forgotten his own *Tough Guys Don't Dance*). Of course, any number of critics and fans would counter with the one inevitable name in cinema. Is Steven Spielberg a great artist? From where I sit, he looks like the most stupendous orchestrator of mass action scenes since Cecil B. DeMille (the Normandy landing, the liquidation of the Warsaw ghetto, the revolt on the *Amistad*) and one of the greatest manipulators of shifting viewpoints the medium has ever seen (think of the sniper episode in *Saving Private Ryan* or the moment in *Minority Report* where Samantha Morton reports everything to Tom Cruise five seconds before it happens). He's also terrific at sudden violence (just as Cameron is terrific at death and dying). On the other hand, few filmmakers have ever seemed less interested in the particulars of small-scale human activity. Spielberg's visuals often strike me as indifferently handsome, just as his people seem vague, over-generalized, not quite right in look, posture, attitude, or dress. He knows how to do a few spectacular things very well, but he is one step short of inept at a host of unspectacular items: character, story (he is a director of scenes more than whole movies), interactions between people and the way environments affect those people (unless they happen to be children of divorced parents in suburban California), and modulations within and between scenes. These deficits are supposed to be beside the point. Why? Because they're less easily describable or quantifiable? The fact that Spielberg is regularly offered up as a master seems to me nothing more than an indication of the fact that a vocabulary for describing movies is still less than fully formed. To my eyes, the only truly popular filmmakers we have are the Farrelly brothers, who work in a syntax that is not so different from that of a run-of-the-mill teen comedy (quick bursts of character, full-frontal lighting, music slathered all over the image, adolescent humor) but who make genuinely lyrical films motivated by a real appreciation for something that everyone else seems to have forgotten in their mad rush to stay on top: the working class.

It's remarkable to witness the progress of a filmmaker like James L. Brooks, who becomes deadly and pedantic whenever he's inclined to think popular—as in the highly praised As Good As It Gets, which offers the crudest character typing and the most overwrought notions of insecurity, conveyed through a virtual torrent of words (a superior film in the same vein: Richard LaGravenese's undervalued Living Out Loud). However, whenever Brooks settles down and trusts his instincts, he becomes a more interesting filmmaker, as in the fascinating I'll Do Anything and the triumphant Spanglish. One of the few real wonders of recent years, Spanglish nails the very particular world of the modern upper middle class, with its anxieties about race and aging and failure masked behind a systematic do-goodism and compulsive yessing that verges on the maniacal. Where As Good As It Gets takes place in some impossible New York of the mind (whose mind, I have no idea), the newer film is highly specific about its settings: sprawling L.A. house on tree-lined street, coolly pristine restaurant, tiny maid's apartment, and beachside property. This is also a visually ravishing movie, every scene cast in Auguste Renoir's warm bath of color and light (few recent American movies have been so alive to the beauties of skin tone), and the look is important: it underscores the inviting world of these wealthy, anxious overachievers, eager to realize their own best impulses without considering the viewpoints of others. As in I'll Do Anything, Brooks pushes hard and dares to go off the rails with Téa Leoni, in a performance of high-pitched hysterical intensity that gets close to a Cassavetes exploration. In fact, the film itself is exploratory, risking failure on a regular basis in order to move into some very sophisticated territory: for instance, a scene in which the mother buys her daughter clothes one size too small in order to motivate her to lose weight offers a terrific interplay of emotions—the daughter's embarrassment, the mother's horror that she's been misunderstood once again, the father trying to play both ends against the middle, and the Mexican maid who observes the whole exchange as if she were an explorer who had discovered a lost tribe.

The idea of risk, anathema on the current filmmaking scene, is central to anything worthwhile in movies. Consider Eyes Wide Shut, Kubrick's still-misunderstood swan song, in which a lifetime of reflection on jealousy and power balances in human affairs is played out, never less than daringly, in straight action that is stretched, elongated, sounded for endless depths, and structured in dream logic—the film perfects what the filmmaker began with 2001: A Space Odyssey, the monumental terror and uncertainty around the numbing banality of daily existence, in scenes that regularly court disaster. Consider Claire Denis with L'Intrus, another dream logic narrative, in which only the most tentative connections are established between the wildest extremes, and the viewer is offered a film of pure sensation, reverberant with a lifetime of regret. Consider Arnaud Desplechin with Esther Kahn, in which every scene appears handcrafted, built from the bottom up out of character quirks and actors' haphazard behaviors, and at the center of which sits Summer Phoenix's slate-gray, granite presence—the story of a young Jewish girl's rise to fame in turn-of-the-century London masks the film's real purpose, which is to take a good, tough look at the existential act of acting, as opposed to the glory. The good films in our midst—Rushmore, The Departed, Café Lumière, Zodiac, A Scanner Darkly—are made by people who don't so much transcend their moment as bypass its clichés, its institutionalized inhibitions and prohibitions. They fight their way through the movie, past their own certainties, preconceptions, and tricks, until they arrive in territory that is uncharted, for them and for their audience as well; just as it's the critic's job to scrutinize his/her own certainties and preconceptions and risk entitlement and status in order to go continually deeper into the matter at hand, the movie. Claire Denis once said that a filmmaker, and by extension any artist, must always be fighting against something. It can be the weather, or the producer, or the cast, or the script, or the film itself, or even him or herself. It seems to me that this is a condition of all valuable work. It also leads to a definition of cinema we need, the one we can stick with: the physical evidence that something, anything, has been fought against, surmounted, and overcome, not as an endurance test, but as a movement beyond what is acceptable, to one's self and to the surrounding culture.

I **Directors**

A director I know once told me that it's a mistake to imagine that he and his peers are everything to the movies they make—in other words, that direction (a misunderstood term, to say the least) trumps acting, writing, editing, sound design, and music. He's right, but the general current in film criticism over the last fifty years has happened for a reason—if we now think of *On Dangerous Ground* as "a Nicholas Ray film" as opposed to "an RKO film" or a hard-boiled romantic melodrama, it's not because of critical propaganda. The constant reminders that "film is a collaborative medium" as well as the frantic campaigns for recognition led by the Writers' Guild of America only serve to illustrate the centrality of the director that much more dramatically.

For me, the filmmaker provides a fascinating lens through which to look at a movie or series of movies. A given director's films are, among other things, a series of responses to the immediate filmmaking environment (when the film is working), to "posterity," to film history and personal history, and to the culture around and beyond the film. I suppose these responses are what fascinate me most, and that fascination is reflected in these pages.

Many of these directors emerged within the last ten to fifteen years, or, in the case of Hou and Assayas, made their greatest films during that period. The section begins with Assayas, because the piece has a special meaning for me: it was the first I wrote for *Film Comment* and, to my knowledge, the first on Assayas in English. It also marks the beginning of two long-lasting friendships—with Gavin Smith, now the editor of the magazine, and with Assayas.

Vertiginous speed is a fact of modern existence, and in the films of Olivier Assayas, a young French director whose name you're almost guaranteed not to know, speed is palpable: Assayas is the first filmmaker to give us the poetics of the digital age in all its mean perfection. This former *Cahiers du Cinéma* critic has a rapturously mobile eye, because he makes an event out of every shape and spatial configuration that crosses his camera's field of vision. Yet each move, each color, each visual rush is firmly connected to his characters in particular and quotidian existence in general. He may be expanding an emotion, as in the moment in *Paris s'éveille* when Louise (Judith Godrèche) jumps on the back of her drug dealer's motorcycle and the camera holds on the blur of lights and bridge girders passing overhead to the point of abstraction, a nice metaphor for her psychic muddle. Or he'll weave space and light into a meshlike atmosphere, creating a hypnotically sterile backdrop that throws his characters' unease into relief (*Une Nouvelle Vie*); or, in the spectacular *L'Eau froide* party scene, a mesmerizing interplay of music and image that enhances the nestlike refuge from crushing authority. For Assayas, the manner in which the random events of everyday existence imprint themselves on people is at the center of cinema, and it gives his tightly circumscribed, supertangible world an earned poignance. He never cuts to an establishing shot or a vista except as brief poetic punctuation, and any given space exists only to the extent that it is perceived and inhabited by people: the onscreen reality is always intersubjective.

If Assayas has a signature scene, it's two people in an antagonistic dance, both with something to hide, both perfectly centered in a medium shot and on the move. Neither hates the other, but neither has enough mental time to sort out the knot of emotions in their heads. Scenes always start *in media res*, without any buildup to the immediacy of the emotional material onscreen. Assayas never, ever gives us anything but the most concrete actions, and yet the films have a fairy-tale fluidity and shapelessness. "Reality is always magic," Renoir once said, and for Assayas those might be words to live by.

The slow, steady rhythm Assayas and his actors find in *Une Nouvelle Vie*—his fourth and most daring feature, and the purest expression of his aesthetic—becomes the focus of the film itself, not unlike the inversion of foreground and background in a Velvet Underground mix. In this underrated movie, events are muted and blended together to form an eerie whole, in which small fragments of texture, like the deadly perfect quiet of modern office telephones, are reiterated like musical refrains. The film is so tenderly attuned to the becoming of its characters that it has the odd feel of an early 1970s road movie that is set entirely indoors. Tina (Sophie Aubry) is first seen careening through a supermarket stockroom on a forklift. She's bearing the weight of the world, bickering with her non-functional mother (Nelly Bourgeaud) and her earnest, hotheaded boyfriend (Phillippe Torreton), and we see it in her comportment: she's fiercely self-protective and maintains a wall of silence, yet she's also an open book. In a dissolve of steely perfection, she's transferred as if by magic from the stockroom to the plushly carpeted floor of a strange apartment where she's passed out from a pill overdose, then awakened by a mysterious middle-aged man named Constantin (Bernard Giraudeau).

Thus begins Tina's new life, and a succession of violent ellipses that continually land us in the middle of situations after the connecting events, the content of which we only infer from stray remarks, have come and gone. Assayas purposely shot a film that could only be assembled at three hours and that he was thus forced to sculpt down to two, and the scorched-earth continuity puts a poetic spin on the film's very ordinary events. Each successive episode introduces a new character (or a new wrinkle on an old one) and imbues each with his/her own private aura and density. There's Lise (Godrèche), Tina's half-sister, who lets Tina stay in her dad's apartment after she ODs. She's an odd girl, content yet bereft of illusions or ideals, more refined than Tina but just as guarded. Their fairy-tale twinning will become the heart of the film, as they grapple with two brutish male archetypes. Tina will eventually meet her errant father, Ludovic (Bernard Verley), a cold, terrifying man as hard as granite. And she will soon take up with Constantin, one of Assayas's most haunting creations.

As Constantin, Giraudeau speaks in a soft monotone, whether he's sending a client on his way or placating his wife (Christine Boisson). He's a lawyer through and through, the kind of guy you see by the thousands every day in Paris and New York. But in Assayas's subtractive narrative, which fixes the viewer's attention on the gestural and eschews the social or cultural, placing the characters in a mysterious abstract space (not unlike Egoyan's *Exotica*), Giraudeau's mere presence sends shivers down your spine. By not showing what drives Constantin or what connection he has to Ludovic, Assayas forces us to focus on his nonchalant intrusiveness, his calculated affectlessness, his weariness. As opposed to a lot of modern American cinema, which locates the banality in villainy, Assayas manages the more difficult task of finding the villainousness in bourgeois banality.

In this film, Assayas and D.P. Denis Lenoir work at a uniformly hypnotic level. It's quite close to Bergman and Nykvist's approach (the camera moves in sync with faces and bodies as surrounding space appears to pivot and withdraw), but there's a major difference: instead of Bergman's dreamlike flatness, the faces and bodies in *Une Nouvelle Vie* are as fully defined as in quattrocento painting.

Assayas knew early in life that he wanted to make movies. His father was a screenwriter who worked with many of the hardened pros whose reputations Truffaut worked so hard to demolish when he was still a working critic (Assayas has memories of jokes around the dinner table at the expense of the magazine he would later write for). He studied literature and then painting at the Beaux Arts with the idea that anything would be better preparation for making films than going to film school and still believes he did the right thing.

He made the first of four short films, *Copyright*, in 1979, followed by *Rectangle* (1980) and the "thriller" *Laissé inachevé à Tokyo* (1982), and then *Winston Tong en studio* (1985), a nice portrait of the San Francisco rock legend and the only one he can still bear to watch. He wrote for *Cahiers* throughout the early 1980s, where he was an excellent if unsung critic (Assayas was pegged early as a horror/action specialist because he'd apprenticed on *Superman*, and he wrote extensively on American horror films as well as Hong Kong cinema; he was also one of the first westerners to write about Hou Hsiao-hsien). If he has a mentor in the film business it's André Téchiné, who hired him for his first big screenwriting gig, the fierce 1985 *Rendezvous*; they also collaborated on the subsequent *Scene of the Crime* (1986).

The color blue appears to be central to Assayas's temperament and his poetics. It's especially noticeable in the first three movies, the prints of which were treated with the same silver-retention process Vittorio Storaro often uses in his work. But whereas Storaro hangs $10 million in lights on every set to get his patented burnished glow, Assayas and cinematographer Denis Lenoir allow a lot of color to drain from the image, and they work in some of the darkest hues seen in modern movies. The effect is most dramatic in *Désordre*, which is nearly monochromatic right from its opening crane down from a neon sign glowing in the rain. Dramatically, there's an inner chromaticism to match. *Désordre*, which enjoyed a minor cult when released in 1986, is quite a calling card. It's far more measured and restrained than most first films of the period, but a more idiosyncratic debut is hard to imagine.

Three young people—two men and a woman—break into a music store to steal instruments for their band and get caught in the act by the owner; in a sudden surge of panic, hubris, and pure synaptic frenzy, they murder him. The rest of the film carefully maps their drift away from one another, their band mates (some of whom guess the truth, some of whom have no idea), and their own core personalities. The band—a mid-1980s new wave ensemble that plays CBGB-type gigs in Paris and London—backs away from recognition and dissolves with painful slowness. Everyone ends in either confusion, capitulation, or suicide, and along the way betrayal is the only constant.

Sounds like familiar territory, covered in a thousand ghost stories, but what's pressing down on everyone here is not just guilt over a monstrous act: Assayas blends the guilty and the innocent together so thoroughly that the distinction hardly matters. The murder serves as a maximal metaphor for any leap into the unknown taken by a young adult, followed by a doubling back into the familiar after the shock of recognition. Assayas sees *Désordre* as his most personal film, and it feels that way—not just thematically but in its unusual shape, its strange equalization of every character, the better to follow a just-barely tangible emotional through-line, like an electrician tracing a wire through the wall.

L'Enfant de l'hiver (1989) again works on a relay system; a current of bottomless blue funk seems to pass from Natalia (Marie Matheron), who begins the film on the floor in false labor, to Stéphane (Michel Feller), who leaves Natalia for Sabine (Clotilde de Bayser), an obsession that feels like an evasion. Natalia will later unsuccessfully attempt suicide, before her baby, the winter's child of the title, is born. Sabine is a theatrical set designer obsessed to the point of madness with a delicately narcissistic actor (Jean-Philippe Ecoffey). De Bayser's Sabine is quite a striking creation, the most flamboyantly dramatic character in Assayas's oeuvre. She's a stranger to her own impulses who somehow cannot imagine taking decisive action, and she spends a lot of the movie in uncomfortable solitude. *L'Enfant* is relentlessly austere, and Assayas's control of the emotional tone is so rigid that even small glimpses of the Italian landscape feel heavy-hearted. It is a bit less grounded in quotidian reality than the director's other work, but with its sustained chord of pain and regret it has a bleak grandeur all its own.

Paris s'éveille (*Paris at Dawn*, 1991), Assayas's third and, in France, most popular film, is a decisive turning point. This is the film where he finds a balance between tone and character. Louise (Godrèche) is living with the much older Clément (Jean-Pierre Léaud, truly magnificent in his first real middle-aged performance as a fragile, post–May 1968 adult whose life has

6

gone on longer than he expected it to). They are visited by Adrien (Thomas Langmann), Clément's son, who is on the lam from a shady deal gone bad in Toulouse, where he lives with his mother. Assayas is so specific with the emotional particulars that the "classic situation" of the love triangle seems all but unrecognizable. Once again the feeling of expedience, and emotional avoidance, is overwhelming. Whether they really love one another is open to question, even when they run away together to live in a squat.

Louise is eighteen, and makes her living posing for dirty pictures and occasionally working in her mother's beauty shop. When we first see her she is frantically storming through her apartment looking for the right outfit to wear to an audition for hostess of a TV game show. The audition is a humiliating affair, and Louise gives it her best smile. It's because Godrèche is so photogenic that the scene is as uncomfortable and filled with emptiness as it is. She has the sad smile of someone trying to put her own happiness on the auction block. (Assayas and Lenoir hold on Louise from the POV of the unthinking TV camera throughout most of the scene, pitching it between Warholian fixation and bottomless sadness.) I've heard complaints about Louise—that she's "stupid," that her creator's conception of her as a character is sexist. But this is to miss an essential aspect of Assayas's work: he understands that people often behave idiotically and cruelly, that they are not always in control of their own actions, and that editing out their bad side is an insult. In American cinema, we're used to ambitious characters being identified as complete louts in the moral schema, the better for the intrinsically nice people to congratulate themselves and their discerning viewers. But with Assayas, no one has the last word, and there's no identifiable moral center, except in the director's steadfast concentration on people and the courses they take.

The focus here is not Louise's ambition but her disconnection from that ambition. For Assayas, nothing is gained by scripting something you can show with the camera, so he gives us just enough to underline what is so plainly visible in Godrèche's face, her sunken shoulders, the way she jumps with fright when Adrien catches her taking her works out of a drawer, and her limp body when she passes out on the stairs of her apartment building. This is the only character in any Assayas film who is formally objectified. Several times the camera looks down on Louise from above and slowly revolves: she floats in a subtly abstracted space, passed out in a park (she's been dumped there by her dealer), on the stairs, or lying in bed after having sex with Adrien. These moments are startling and empathic, and they help define her dilemma since she spends so much time objectifying herself. Far from a sexist caricature, Louise is a deadly accurate portrayal of a young woman in search of a helping hand who has no idea how to ask for one from two men who are too self-involved to make the offer.

If Assayas appears to be hooked on young people, I think the reason is more substantial than a mere fixation on adolescence. Each of his films takes place over a long span of time in order to show change, which always comes in the form of capitulation and compromise, as the energies of youth are cruelly channeled onto the assembly line of usefulness. So it's only natural that his most exhilarating film should be about his own days as a teenager in the early 1970s, when the urge to revolt was more of a given than it is today.

L'Eau froide (Cold Water, 1994), shot on Super-16 on a tiny budget, is the best of the wonderful "Tous les garcons et les filles de leur age" series commissioned for French television (the idea was that different directors make films set during the time when they were sixteen). Gilles (Cyprien Fouquet) starts the movie stealing albums from a department store. When he and his girlfriend Christine (Virginie Ledoyen) are about to get nabbed, they make a break for it. He crashes through the window but she gets caught and hauled off to the police station, where she taunts her nerdy interrogator (Jean-Pierre Daroussin) with a tall tale about another cop forcing her to go down on him. Soon she's committed to a mental institution. The film alternates between standoffs with adults and rituals of desecration and defiance; one scene consists of Gilles walking through an empty bus and aimlessly puncturing the seat cushions with a knife.

The poetic turning point of L'Eau froide—a lonely ramble through woods, and a scene so rich in teenage loneliness that it might have been lifted from Kerouac's Maggie Cassidy—is followed by a party in an uninhabited château. The camera goes drifting through a crowd of teenagers in used clothes and tangled hair, each moving with dour purpose, some picked up and followed and some merely glimpsed in passing. Joplin's version of "Me and Bobby McGee" is playing somewhere, and many different energies are swirling across the screen. Dramatically, things keep building and lulling, and the focus veers toward and then away from Gilles and Christine, who has escaped from the institution. The balance between randomness and specificity, an Assayas hallmark, is perfect: the focus continually shifts from the intensely personal minute detail to the carefully observed whole event. The logic of this party scene, poetically, dramatically, and cinematically, is so close to the dynamic of a real party of that era—caught between exhilarations and all-time lows, intense concentration and mental drift, and stud-

8

ded with sudden outbreaks of aggressive behavior within the insular community. Throughout, the needle is yanked off of records like Donovan's "Cosmic Wheels" or Roxy Music's "Virginia Plain" halfway through, only to start the song over again as if it were a protective charm. The mournful cry of "Knockin' On Heaven's Door" begins, and so does the ritual of baking and crumbling hash, filling the pipe, and exhaling luxuriant clouds of blue smoke. Assayas and Lenoir follow the pipe as it passes from hand to hand, and they settle on faces as they are illuminated by the glow of the burning ember. The scene climaxes with a bonfire set to Creedence's "Up Around the Bend," and the camera is brought so close to the flames that the effect is of a frightening taunt to the audience. There's something here of the headlong invention and sensory excitement in pure movement of Renoir's *La Nuit du Carrefour*.

The hard poetry of Assayas's films renders with terrific clarity a world where the struggle against capitalism seems archaic, impossible, yet somehow necessary. I think this may be why some people have a hard time with his work. The generation he's describing has an interesting problem, so different from the teenagers before them. For those who grew up in the aftermath of the 1960s, the struggle is to shrug off skepticism—a tall order.

This generational plight is beautifully embodied in the final scenes of *Paris s'éveille*, which have a singularly plangent sadness. Adrien has skipped the country on a fake passport, and Louise has moved in with Zablonsky, the man who conducted her audition. After a heartbreaking scene in which she goes to visit Clément in their old apartment, which has been completely remodeled and is now close to the white smartness of Zablonsky's place, we see Louise in a TV studio, where she is the new weather girl. "The gloomy gray weather is over, so put away your scarves!" We cut to Louise's face on a television set, and a hand comes into frame to shut it off. It's Agathe (Ounie Lecomte), the most balanced character in the film and the wife of Adrien's friend Victor. She's now working as a waitress in a Chinese restaurant, and Victor is in jail. After she turns off the set, the camera twists and turns with her as she picks up trays and delivers them to tables of smiling customers. There are no lyrical flourishes in these final moments—we're just following this composed, graceful woman dressed in improbable chinoiserie, the uniform of the job that puts money in her pocket. We start to wonder: what will signify the end of this story? What will be the sign that releases us from the merciless rhythm of life and business being transacted? Then Assayas cuts to black, the Chinese song on the soundtrack stops in mid-phrase, and the credits begin over a rolling bassline from a relentless Pixies song.

A couple of decades back, the guitarist Robert Fripp predicted that in the future, if people are going to succeed, if not survive, they will have to become "small, highly intelligent mobile units." Fripp's future is now, and Olivier Assayas fits the description. Here is an artist who works and thinks empirically, carves out his own unique path with tools of his own making, who reckons that the best way to right the wrongs of the world is not to attack them but to give them room to breathe and thus allow them to resonate on the faces of his characters. It's precisely because Assayas imitates no one that he reminds me of another filmmaker from a different age. Faces as reflections of the world also meant a lot to Frank Borzage, and in several of his pre–World War II films the threat of fascism is fully seen and felt in the faces of young lovers. In *The Mortal Storm* (1940), the encroaching terror of Hitler's Germany shadows the youthful faces of Jimmy Stewart and Margaret Sullavan: the world bears down on them just as hard as it does on Adrien and Louise as they say a sadly unresolved goodbye on a dark street. Assayas is, to put it simply, putting his generation on film, just as Kerouac put his own on paper. Ironically, this is a generation that is *so* solitary, it might not even notice.

1996

Where are movies at today? One thing's for sure: we'll never find out from all the critical posturing that's going on. The rousing enthusiasm received by Todd McCarthy's blast at the shared insular elitism of this year's Cannes competition films was breathtaking. Critics were suddenly coming on like the Red Cross, giving aid to the tender-hearted majority. What's up with all this compassion for the common man?

In fairness to McCarthy, his piece was thoughtful and intelligently written and far more durable than most of the diagnostic/prescriptive "think pieces" that have been appearing with laughable regularity for the last five years. The suggestion that world cinema desperately needs (unconsciously wants?) some kind of Hal Wallis/Hunt Stromberg figure to keep out-of-control directorial egos in check is unredeemably nutty. Is it 1942 again? It's as if we're taking our cues from the critic who wondered how Mr. Welles could possibly ask us to care about the Amberson family when our boys were risking their lives overseas.

It seems to me that this particular drum started beating about three years ago with the appearance of Hou Hsiao-hsien's *Goodbye South, Goodbye*. This is the moment when Hou joined the ever-growing number of filmmakers who have supposedly climbed too far out on the limb of aestheticism, showing callous disregard for their paying customers. Not that Hou is lacking for admirers around the world, but in America he has become a marked man before making the transition from cult phenomenon to art house favorite. Others who have received black marks from the ACAFC (Association of Concerned American Film Critics): Sokurov, Tsai, Téchiné, Yang, Gomez, Jarmusch, Assayas, Hartley, Guerman, and Malick. Every one of these filmmakers has been fingered for excessive aestheticism and insufficient populist drive, and in each case the charge has stuck. One imagines a makeshift concentration camp for errant film directors, where the prisoners are herded into a theater every night, exposed to a healthy sampling of Hawks and Hitchcock movies, then treated to a marathon reading of *For Keeps*. Or how about Bill Bennett's *The Book of Virtues*?

Why would any film critic at the end of the century consider a populist litmus test to be a valid tool of the trade, unless they were trying to pitch woo to their readership? When you're an American and your country's film 11

DIRECTORS

industry has dominated the rest of the world since before the dawn of sound, it's easy to imagine a cinema of mass appeal, where the popular and the artistically ambitious merge. Being a non-American filmmaker is tough, since American culture in general and American movies in particular set the standards for *so* much: technology, philosophical outlook, narrative construction, modes of production, and, most importantly of all, the question of how a film should relate to its audience. Compared with a straightforward, viscerally traumatic history lesson like *Saving Private Ryan*, almost anything is going to look minoritarian and elitist. God forbid if your country's history is as messy and complicated as Taiwan's, where national identity is a permanent question mark. Trying to conjure up a form to accommodate such fragmentation and stay true to the odd sensation of losing what there is of your culture to mercenary capitalism is a tall order. So even if Hou *was* an effete aesthete, he would deserve a little extra credit for just trying. But at a time when the cinema is in real danger of succumbing to the digital image, painting Hou Hsiao-hsien as some rare bird who caters to festival directors seems suicidally wrong-headed, a little like turning away a drink of water in the desert because you don't like the tint of the goblet.

Apart from winning the 1996 Best Scene Shot in a Car Wash award, Gao's *Goodbye South, Goodbye* reverie as his car goes down the ramp is magical in so many ways. It certainly beats the corresponding *Crash* and *Sweet Hereafter* scenes in terms of sheer visual beauty. Gao's eyes are caught in the rearview mirror as the pastelled colors from the water and the brushes, followed by the men in straw hats doing the cloth-drying, pass on either side of the static shot. As always with Hou, the setup is decisive, devoted to the moment as visual event, a fairly ravishing play of light, color, and angles. It's also a perfect setting for a film devoted to the feel of time when you're bored and marginalized.

Is there another film with a better sense of just hanging out? It's about how time feels when one is simply *existing*, slogging through life. Hou and his actors catch the state of being itchy and nervously under the gun, under pressure to perform, straighten up, and make a little money. "My theory was that the readers just *thought* they cared about nothing but the action," wrote Raymond Chandler. "The things they remembered, that haunted them, was not, for example, that a man got killed but that in the moment of his death he was trying to pick a paper clip up off the polished surface of a desk and it kept slipping away from him, so that there was a look of strain on his face and his mouth was half open in a kind of tormented grin, and the last thing in the world he thought about was death." In Hou's films, the later ones in

12

particular, the balance between the sense of a story being told and a continuum of life imparted to the camera through such ravishing detail work is not just a happy coincidence, it's the central aesthetic preoccupation.

The hotel room lair of Gao, Flatty, and Pretzel in Goodbye South, Goodbye gets a limited number of compositions that accentuate the boxlike shape of the room—three losers, out of it, spending time together in a cramped box, their boredom itself a numbing opiate. The miscellaneous activity—tossing a ball, angrily tuning out everything else in the room and concentrating on a video game from floor level, trying to talk on the phone and sleep at the same time, a blowup that ends with Flatty climbing out the window, Pretzel sitting on the toilet and not bothering to close the door—is perfect and stretched to just the right length, never quite boiling over into extended improvisations or cute aimlessness. Hou's scenes are never "studies" in mood, nor do they ever get into the kind of poetically tinged sociology that is standard fare in third tier French realism. There's always a balance—every scene is exacting, hitting the right story and character points (here it's the impossibility of Gao's situation, his running out of steam after too much scamming and hustling, Flatty and Pretzel's relative ineptitude, and the strange mix of intimacy and annoyance that colors their nomadic, unmoored life together). But as those points are being made, a physical space and a mode of being register on our senses through depth, color, and hypnotically repeated motion.

Almost every shot Hou has ever filmed has a bewitching arrangement of light and shapes, little corners and crooks of color or darkness into which the eye tunnels and nests. In the three last films the visual/sonic concentration is so great that it induces a form of near-ecstasy. In Good Men, Good Women, Annie Shizuka Inoh sits in front of a mirror and puts on makeup as Jack Kao caresses and fondles her from behind, and little semi-disclosed shadow areas and pools of light surround the tilted mirror, suggesting an array of passages into new dimensions. Almost any given space in Flowers of Shanghai—the dinners, the visits to the chambers of the various flower girls—is multiplaned, jewel-like, entrancing. The ancient Chinese aesthetic concept of liu-pai—allowing what's visible within the frame to open in the mind of the viewer onto the world extending beyond its parameters—is expanded in the new films, where space feels like it could unfurl in any direction.

Jack Kao's Gao in Goodbye South, Goodbye is a leathery but amiable guy in a buzz cut, sunglasses, and loud shirts, with a nice disposition and a friendly, slouching posture, who's watching himself lose control of his own life. Tony Leung's Master Wang in Flowers of Shanghai is prone to melancholy and a delicately formal social manner, wanting to walk away from all the drinking games, the opium pipes, and the beautiful flower girls and spend his life thinking about the world but not looking at it, his head continually cocked aside in a semi-smile. In Hou's work, the question that obsesses the mind of every western filmmaker—"What makes my characters tick?"—has been settled beforehand, and the sense of mystery lies elsewhere. These last three Hou movies are studded with piercing moments in which characters worn down to permanently ruminative states are quietly overcome with the question of how they have arrived at their fate, how they have come to be in this particular place at this particular time under this particular set of circumstances: Gao's little reverie with his girlfriend or his crying episode in the southern hotel over what a fucked-up disappointment he is; the utterly flat, desolate tone of Inoh's crawls to her fax machine to get more pages from her diary in *Good Men, Good Women*; Leung's quiet withdrawal from social interaction during the first, stunning dinner scene in *Flowers*.

Each of these movies is an adventure in form and in tone. *Goodbye South, Goodbye* moves dreamily through time, and "move" is the operative word. Hou reportedly had a tough time figuring out a valid way to deal with contemporary life—this was his first film with a completely contemporary setting since *Daughter of the Nile*—and he settled on movement as the central motif. Gao, Flatty, and Pretzel are only at peace when they're going from one place to another on trains, in cars, on mopeds, from one reverie of failure and regret to the next, from one pipe dream to the next, and one bad situation to the next. Everything devolves the moment that Flatty offends the local gangster chieftains down south by coming to claim his share of family money from his corrupt cousin on the police force. The hard facts of the world dissolve into the floating dreaminess induced by moments of pure motion. Hou cuts to these flights suddenly throughout the film and gets a very graceful, loping form, like a wordless cowboy ballad on the subject of bad luck. The trip up into the mountains on mopeds is a lush, cool, muted idyll. And there's another flight that goes skyward. Flatty (played by Lim Giong, who also composed the score, and gives a very nice performance: lanky, in shapeless bellbottoms, he's like a giant Art Carney) squatting on the roof slowly eating his lunch, looking down as a train stops to pick up passengers and then pulls away. This prompts Hou to cut to the train's viewpoint as it chugs up into the mountains while the view becomes greener and greener. And there are nice little trips down flat rural highways and city thoroughfares, occasionally filtered through the yellow tint of Flatty's mod shades.

The density of Hou's concentration within any given shot is apparently infinite, and there's no such thing as an "insert" or a "cutaway" in his work. Jumps in time or sudden juxtapositions often feel immense. Starting with *The Puppetmaster*, the logic of each film is built around the effects of these breaks and juxtapositions. In interviews, Hou often portrays himself as a chronicler, devoted to preserving the bits and pieces of his culture that are disappearing. True enough, and in a sense it's possible to look at *Good Men, Good Women* as the contrast between a heroic past and an empty, sterile present, at *Goodbye South, Goodbye* as a tour through down-and-out modern Taiwan, and at *Flowers of Shanghai* as an evocation of a disreputable but breathtaking world gone by. But Hou is no documentarian. In Hou, as in Proust, *nothing* is taken for granted, and you get the whole architecture of the world in which the characters live.

This occurs most spectacularly in *Flowers of Shanghai*, which is so cool in its balance between individuals and the network in which they operate, between particular actions and their general context, between the ravishing beauty of what we're watching and the utterly transitory, finite nature of it all. And the repetitions—of dinners eaten over drinking games initiated by overexcited brothel customers ("It's going to be a great night—order some more dishes!"); of pining men hopelessly confused between love and money and addiction and obligation, of jealous courtesans giving their youthful competitors a good talking to—are in place to give you the motoring design of an entire world. By the time you get to the end of the film, the smell of that world, its texture, its pushing/pulling emotional extremes, its vectors of power—the men move to the outskirts of the room while the women tend to hold the center—and the precise placement of every character within it, are all so clear and present that the net effect, again like Proust, is of a luxury hotel removed from its foundations and moved across town.

"It's something new," said the friend with whom I saw *Flowers of Shanghai*. And he's right: there aren't too many other films outside of Dreyer's where every move, every gesture, and every shift in perspective counts. I like Kathleen Murphy's comparison with Henry James in *Film Comment* a few issues back: unlike Dreyer's emptied out images, the images of *Flowers* have a Jamesian feeling for the world of objects and the importance they hold for the characters. As in James, it's not so much a question of value placed on fine objects as much as the fantasies projected onto them.

I've heard that *Flowers of Shanghai* is difficult to follow, that there are too many characters to keep track of. In fact, what there is of the story is very simple, centered around the way that money—the one thing that truly brings 15 men and women together in this world—becomes a bit like the phantom hovering in the room whose presence everyone feels but can't quite describe. Everything that happens in the film—Master Wang's addiction/devotion to love in the abstract, the intrigues between the other flower girls (which suggest warring star actresses at MGM in the 1930s), the constant bargaining, the aborted suicide pact between a young flower girl and her equally young sponsor—is a deepening, a broadening and restatement of the overall world view that informs every square inch of the narrative. We never get beyond these lushly appointed rooms (it's Hou's one and only studio-bound film), but we don't need to—this might be the ultimate example of *liu pai*. As in "The Beast in the Jungle" or "The Jolly Corner," there's the sense of an entire culture bound up in the details.

Hou's characters don't evolve much by western standards, but our *sense* of them does as the parameters of their universe come into ever-sharper focus through the duration of the film. Perhaps the ultimate example of Hou's vertical character development occurs in *Good Men, Good Women*, where you hardly *see* the actress/heroine in the film's modern day sequences—she's usually crawling out from under the sheets to get another faxed page from her stolen diary. The film, which might be profitably described as Hou's *Providence*, operates in three tenses: the heroine's present, her disreputable past as a disco barmaid with a small-time gangster lover (Jack Kao again, one of the finest presences in modern movies), and a film about the Taiwanese dissident Chiang Bi-Yu and her husband Chung Hao-Tung, who were persecuted during the White Terror of the 1950s. These scenes, shot in black and white, are from a movie (called *Good Men, Good Women*) in which she's about to play the lead, as she *imagines* it will be. This may seem too complicated by half, and it must be said that *Good Men* lacks the immediacy of the other two movies. But the tone of each individual scene is so carefully negotiated and modulated that the whole film becomes a fairly breathtaking experience. As opposed to *Flowers of Shanghai*'s ever-deepening perspective from the inside, this film moves from one hallucinatory immersion to another. The connections between the different temporal milieux are surpassingly delicate. Inoh and Kao have a conversation about her pregnancy and impending abortion, and Hou cuts to Chiang Bi-Yu, pregnant, working in a relief camp, a moving transition: as always with Hou, nothing fancy or emphatic, the idea being to let the connection ease into the viewer's consciousness. The net effect is of time, experienced from an ordinary perspective, flowing through the medium of a saddened spirit. When Inoh finally confesses to her mysterious faxer that she has not only set up Kao's Ah-wei for blood money but also that she truly loved him, Hou cuts back to Chiang Bi-yu preparing her husband's body for burial after he's died in the custody of Kuomintang officials. At which point he achieves a remarkable effect by bleeding color into the black and white image. More than just a woman's self-actualization through confession, the moment crystallizes the film's key idea: that the personal past and the historical past are inseparable.

The fact is that no matter how deep an affinity westerners develop for eastern culture, the moment often arrives when the conceptually unfamiliar impedes the flow of pleasure, and the bridge to "universal meaning" must be crossed with intellectual effort. But does that instantly invalidate the experience? We've come to expect a sort of generic "eastern calm" from modern Asian filmmakers, which seems absurd given the convulsive state of modern Asia. Unfortunately for Hou (assuming that he actually cares a whole lot about what westerners think), his early films seem to fill the bill, while his later ones do not. Hou may require a bit of brainwork from the viewer, but does that make him an ivory tower dweller? Isn't there room in cinema for the "semipopular" artist, to use a term coined by the rock critic Bob Christgau? Prompting an artist of this magnitude to make his work more accessible is like asking Karlheinz Stockhausen to write catchier tunes, or asking John Ashbery to appeal to readers of USA Today. It doesn't make any sense. Because right now, it doesn't get much better than Hou Hsiao-hsien.

1999

Family Romance

Simply stated, Wes Anderson is the most original presence in American film comedy since Preston Sturges—not the greatest (Elaine May), deftest (Blake Edwards), or most conceptually brilliant (Albert Brooks in his heyday), but the one who has staked out the most idiosyncratic territory since Sturges. His confidence is as boundless as Sturges's was, and he has a similarly keen ear for gaudy dialogue; a gift for surprise and for topping one joke with a bigger one; a knack for rooting out archetypes hitherto untouched in movies; and a penchant for making films that feel like pageants enacted by a democratically diverse cross-section of humanity. There the similarities end.

Unlike Sturges, Anderson is fixated on failure, hesitation, and depression. He has a very keen sense of class envy. Each of his three films is set within a sheltered, semiexclusive, self-contained universe: upper-middle-class Texas youth with leisure time to spare in *Bottle Rocket*, a boys' boarding school in *Rushmore*, and a family of fallen geniuses in *The Royal Tenenbaums*. Each film is centered on a character who lives one step lower on the economic ladder than his friends and whose aspiration to be part of their exclusive milieu is rooted in a sense of loss and a longing for family. Owen Wilson, Anderson's cowriter and most magical actor, played the role in *Bottle Rocket*, Jason Schwartzman's Max Fisher virtually defined it in *Rushmore*, and Gene Hackman adds a touching dimension of mortality with his threadbare patriarch in *Tenenbaums*. Wilson's wigged out Eli Cash, the overgrown boy who "always wanted to be a Tenenbaum," embodies this poignant strain of upward mobility in just a few scenes, with flamboyantly broad strokes.

Anderson is a fluid, quick-change artist who takes mischievous delight in shifting registers within a given film, but he's also extremely careful to let his characters' emotional dilemmas take root and flower. In one instant, you're watching the most flamboyant expository setup: *Tenenbaums*'s opening index of failure set to "Hey Jude"; the private detective's file on "adopted daughter" Margot Tenenbaum's indiscretions; *Rushmore*'s hilarious checklist of Max's extracurricular activities. Then, almost before you have time to catch your breath, you're into a moment that's as delicately surprising and bursting with life as as early Renoir. *Rushmore* and *The Royal Tenenbaums* are both very fastidious films—the framing is neat and four-square, the action shaped into compact, unitlike scenes (*Bottle Rocket*, a lyrical idyll disguised as a fugitive run from the law, is a looser movie that floats across the screen like a ribbon in the wind). But their formality is emotionally grounded, empathically tied to the depressed characters and their rock-hard defense mechanisms. And the moment captured within each scene is often impossibly fragile, a matter of mood, overcast skies, subtleties of the actors' physiques and postures. For instance, Max and his father (Seymour Cassel) having a talk about life, the son in his school blazer and the father in his dull winter jacket and earmuffs, as they walk through a lower-middle-class neighborhood at the end of an autumn afternoon. It's a little wonder of a scene, with a heartbreaking simplicity. Richie's and Margot's visits to the rooftop of the Tenenbaum mansion have a similarly somber beauty, like illustrations out of a slightly risqué children's book.

Anderson's attunement to his actors as individuals is fairly breathtaking. He fixes on their most private traits and builds their onscreen characters accordingly: Gene Hackman's penchant for bobbing and weaving with his fellow actors, turning the screen into a sports arena; Bill Murray's wistful, sad-sack withdrawal and real-life disenchantment; Gwyneth Paltrow's tendency to singularize her characterizations and narrow things down to a finite set of gestures; Ben Stiller's exaggeratedly physical, high-voltage comic attack. There's a scene in *Rushmore* where Max is talking up his "chapel partner" Dirk Calloway's bombshell mom (Connie Nielsen). Just as he's explaining the values he's trying to impart to his self-appointed charge, Dirk shows up and Mrs. Calloway's attention shifts without so much as a beat. Schwartzman does a perfect rendition of the self-important teenager, making a show of gracefully withdrawing from the company of an adult who doesn't really care either way. His reaction is so perfect (and perfectly gawky) that it appears to have been felt rather than acted. Danny Glover and Anjelica Huston's first kiss in *The Royal Tenenbaums:* he arrives at her excavation site (she's an urban archeologist), decked out in trademark blue blazer and bowtie, backs into the subject at hand, then takes a spectacular pratfall before they both stumble into a highly formal declaration of mutual affection. Other directors would probably break the scene up into cloying, bold-faced details (befitting the post–*Home Alone* era of digital slapstick), but Anderson does it in a minimum of setups and stays on his actors to let the emotion silently build after Huston's Etheline Tenenbaum admits that she hasn't slept with a man for eighteen years. The awkwardness feels real and achingly human.

Anderson is a filmmaker whose work you either "get" or you don't. Some express an honest bafflement at the films, some misinterpret them severely, and some greet them with outright hostility. For those of us who connected directly with his sensibility from the first frame of Bottle Rocket, it seems incomprehensible: how could anyone *not* see the merits of such an exquisite storyteller, such a devastating entertainer, such a deft manipulator of emotions? First of all, there's the sheer velocity of Anderson's storytelling. With each new film, his desire to spell things out for his audience has decreased in inverse proportion to his prodigious inventiveness. From the start, Anderson has given his audience *just* enough to get by. If you blink, you may miss a gesture or a line or a detail that alludes to a crucial aspect of his characters' emotional lives and the core dilemma that they're hiding for fear of being exposed and embarrassed before the world. Max Fisher, more royalist than the king in his ever-present school blazer and games of one-upsmanship with his headmaster (Brian Cox), could easily seem like nothing more than a "creepy kid," as a friend of mine once put it. But that's only if you fail to connect with his profound anger and sadness over his mother's death, alluded to a grand total of two times in the entire movie and ever so briefly at that ("What a coincidence—we both have dead people in our families," he says to Olivia Williams's Miss Cross, in an attempt to be urbanely sympathetic—characters are always using language as a shield in Anderson's films). Otherwise, we're meant to infer it from his outrageously provocative behavior, begging for negative attention (in Bottle Rocket, the emotional dilemma behind Dignan's home invasion drills and seventy-five-year planning is never even alluded to, but felt nonetheless). Anderson never lingers over the causes but hones in on the nuances of the effects and finds a double line of vision in the process: he remains within the obsessive rhythms of his characters' lives but finds a way of laughing at their excesses.

Repetition compulsion is a big item in art these days. It's as if the structural explorations of Warhol's films, Glass's *Music in Twelve Parts* or Reich's *Come Out* or Deleuze's *Difference and Repetition* had worked their way into popular culture and blossomed in the age of chemical personality adjustment. Barely perceptible change within a field of sameness: the perfect form for a depressed age, from Atom Egoyan to Tsai Ming-liang, from Kiarostami's *The Wind Will Carry Us* to Oliveira's *I'm Going Home*, from Roth's *American Pastoral* to DeLillo's *Underworld*, from *Seinfeld* to *Ghost World* to *In the Mood for Love* to trip-hop. Anderson has mastered the form to perfection, making winning, warm movies about angry, dissociated people who never consciously arrive at reconciliation but always stumble into it on their quests to recover what they've lost. Anderson's spectacular showmanship can easily over-

20

shadow the intricate motoring designs behind his work. If you don't recognize the sense of loss that animates Dignan, Max, and the entire Tenenbaum family, then *Bottle Rocket* might seem like another pleasant indie comedy (thus the awful pull-quote in Sony's nonexistent ad campaign: "Reservoir Geeks!"), *Rushmore* an eccentric coming-of-age movie, and *Tenenbaums* a menagerie of eccentrics à la John Irving. And if you can't locate the current of emotion that powers Anderson's collection of boffo effects, knockout one-liners, and over-the-top inventions, his films might seem like a series of endearing mishmashes. His oeuvre provides an object lesson in the degree to which film-viewing habits have been primed by so much TV and blockbusterism, where we've learned to wait for the underlining of emotions before we allow ourselves to intuit them.

What has also made Anderson a tough pill to swallow is his extremely rarefied, almost Brahmin-ish sensibility. His work betrays an overall sense of an artist who's grown up in a polite, quietly repressed environment, accustomed to hiding under the covers with a flashlight and folding his emotions into make-believe, silently cultivating a poetic universe of self-protection. In this homemade, handcrafted world—underscored by Mark Mothersbaugh's magical, precocious scores—there's a strong aroma of sixth-grade shop class, of the ashtray you made for your mom and found in the back of the closet after twenty years. Engraved pocket knives, shirts worn backwards as smocks, old Stones albums, and forgotten board games carry weight and presence as tokens of loss. Given the current vogue for just-plain-folks-ness and the branding of "elitism" as the biggest sin of all, it's no wonder that Anderson gets defamed by man-of-the-people types. At its best, his cinema is built from layer upon layer of self-consciousness, tottering not by mistake but by design, always on the verge of exposing a quiveringly emotional core. It's a highly idiosyncratic way to make a movie, and the fact that Anderson's films veer so close to ridiculousness so often makes them, in my eyes, all the more remarkable.

Is *The Royal Tenenbaums* an inflation or a continuation? It is certainly Anderson's grandest movie, and if it feels like an epic at 108 minutes, it's probably because there's so much territory covered in each briskly paced scene and densely packed Scope shot—visual, geographical, gestural, and emotional. It is also more "invented" than either of its predecessors. The setting is a timeless version of greater New York (as opposed to the timeless version of greater Houston in *Rushmore*), an impossible Manhattan of faded, seedy grandeur, where Holden Caulfield might cross paths with the unlucky hustler of Lou Reed's "Street Hassle." *Tenenbaums* is running over with high-flown comic inventions, such as Owen Wilson's J. Peterman-ish all-star novelist Eli Cash or the outlandish global wanderings of Paltrow's Margot. It's also a little shorter on the kind of detail work that made *Rushmore* so bewitching, like that brief but indelible shot of Sara Tanaka's Margaret Yang at the science fair, delicately craning her neck to look for Max, or the barely glimpsed name "Thayer" printed with early adolescent awkwardness on Max's Latin reinstatement petition. But this is a different film, a little more frantic yet even more melancholy than its predecessor, with a different configuration of characters, one more spectacularly depressed than the last. And it's about a different kind of longing: to "restore" a family that was never that happy in the first place to a glory that never was. It's funny that some critics have gotten tripped up on the fact that none of the Tenenbaum children appear to be part of the same family, because that's pretty much the point. Anderson is tackling a difficult, sad (and sadly familiar) dynamic here: a loving but fundamentally inattentive matriarch, a long-gone father who hides behind layers of guff and nonsense from old western novels ("Look at that old grizzly bear," he says of Glover's beyond-elegant suitor), and three overgrown children with nothing but the memory of their own glory days for company. They've each built their own genius-stricken identity (Stiller's the "preternaturally" talented financial whiz kid, Paltrow's the playwright, and Luke Wilson's the tennis star), in failed efforts to define themselves outside of their unfathomable but inescapable family.

The film proudly wears its inspirations on its sleeve: Welles's *The Magnificent Ambersons*, J. D. Salinger's Glass family stories, the old *New Yorker* of Harold Ross and William Shawn, *From the Mixed-Up Files of Mrs. Basil E. Frankenweiler*, the Velvet Underground, a tinge of F. Scott Fitzgerald, and a dash of Philip Barry. But it speaks in its own quavering voice: at once tender and probing, respectful of New York and its special mixture of grit and glory, but confident enough to mold it into one big, faded magic playhouse, a limitless extension of the Tenenbaum family's private universe. The spectacle of father and children contriving to return home and make amends ("Why are they allowed to do that?" says a childishly disappointed Paltrow, when Etheline tells her that Stiller and family are moving back into the Tenenbaum mansion) deepens with each new viewing. The movie gets funnier (Royal's outlaw excursions with his grandsons, to whom he offers the following condolence for the accidental death of their mother: "I'm sorry for your loss—your mother was a terribly attractive woman"), more moving (Richie and Margot's secret tryst in his tent as they listen to "She Smiled Sweetly" and "Ruby Tuesday" on an old record player, the assorted interac-

22

tions between Huston's Etheline and Glover's Henry, Royal taking Margot out for ice cream over the melancholy strains of Vince Guaraldi's immortal "Charlie Brown Christmas" theme), and more sheerly delightful (Owen Wilson's Eli quietly bugging out on national television). The word epiphany gets thrown around a lot, but it should be reserved for moments like the flight of Richie's falcon over the New York skyline, bearing away the lost glory of the Tenenbaums; or Margot, armored in her fur coat and striped cotton dress, her eyes shrouded in mascara, her hair pushed back with a barrette like a twelve-year-old's, her mouth creased in an adolescent half-smile, approaching Richie to the tune of Nico's evanescent "These Days." Or the moment near the end of the film when Stiller's Chas, a mountain of hyped-up, burning anger in a red tracksuit throughout the movie, suddenly switches emotional gears for a moment of final parting. Truth to tell, I've never seen moments like these in any other movie.

2001

Young and Innocent

One of the finest moments in modern movies is a single shot, a few minutes long. It involves nothing more, or less, than a disheveled man slumped on a couch, as his wife fawns over their toddler son. The action consists of her carrying the boy around a tiny kitchen and in and out of a doorway to a little terrace outside. As the man sits motionless and the mother and child bill and coo to each other, the kettle on the stove comes to a boil. But it doesn't whistle. It makes an unsettling sound that could be a string quartet sustaining one unvarying tone. In fact, the sound is a restatement of the mournful music that's recurred throughout this movie's lengthy duration, spanning a decade in the collective life of a group of performers. They've changed, their country has changed, their ideas of what life is and what it can be have changed, their clothes and the way they talk and the music they sing and dance to has changed, and their sense of what's permissible and what's forbidden has changed. The one thing that has never changed is the strange disharmony between this man and this woman. Now, after all this time, they're still together and still apart. She has a child to keep her company, he has no one. That whistling kettle is a signal: time is still moving forward.

Jia Zhangke is tuned into something very *now*, so up to the minute that his three movies fairly burst with the fullness of their own insight. Like Godard in the 1960s and Altman in the 1970s, Jia gets all of us in general and youth in particular—he knows who we are, he knows what we like, why we like it and, most importantly, how. In the three movies he's made since 1997— *Xiao Wu*, *Platform*, and the new *Unknown Pleasures*—he's focused on young people and their fragile, tender embrace with their own identities. Better than any other filmmaker around, he understands their close and intense relationships to fashion and the way pop culture makes them feel both a part of the world and very far from it at the same time.

Some critics who know Jia's work will laugh at all this "we" stuff. Many people still tend to see eastern films as reports or snapshots from foreign lands before they are anything else. But Jia's films are too good, too exciting, and too uncannily on the money to be denied their rightful status as supreme expressions of the way many of us live: media-addicted, resigned to momentous change and powerless to understand or affect it, preserving a very private sense of hope and rectitude in the hopes that one day everyone will share the spiritual wealth. Jia hasn't had the kind of exposure he deserves (even in China, where it's only possible to see the films on pirated VCDs, if at all). That's a shame and a loss, for him and for us.

It's obvious that Jia, with his long takes, is indebted to Ozu and Hou ("If I were to break up a scene which lasts for six or seven minutes into several cuts, then you lose that sense of deadlock. The deadlock that exists between humans and time, the camera and its subject"). But in terms of the way his films play to their (potential) audiences, the comparisons with 1960s Godard and 1970s Altman are instructive—up to a point. All three are supremely confident artists with talent to burn, gripped by the idea of nailing the here and now yet looking at it all from a serene remove—watching a *Weekend* or a *Nashville* or an *Unknown Pleasures*, you get the sense of an artist who feels like he has it all figured out. All three make movies as environments or organisms, offering a wealth of varied physical detail and behaviors for our delectation, with narratives that feel like a series of linked social, cultural, and rhetorical events. All three have musical aesthetics that don't so much advance with each new film as widen.

With the possible exception of *Unknown Pleasures*, no one will be looking at these films with the kind of nostalgic indulgence they now bring to *Nashville*. Jia might just be wiser than Godard and more thoughtfully analytical than Altman. He's also funnier. Bin Bin and Xiao Ji, *Unknown Pleasures's* two dead-end teenagers who've seen too many movies, plan to walk into a bank and relieve it of its contents by strapping decoy bombs around their waists. "The bomb looks real but you don't," says the one to the other. "The bomb looks phony and so do you," says the other to the one.

Jia is particularly good at romance, the abject terror of revealing yourself to the boy or girl you desire. He's virtually unerring in the way he ties everything together, weaving the halting progression of the romance with the ongoing social documentation, shifting the focus back and forth so effortlessly that personal and political become one. He's very cunning—watching his movies, you have the sense that every couple on earth is shy, stumbling, and filled with Chekhovian anxiety, afraid to give away too much until it's too late, and he traces their emotional developments with the care and delicacy of a nineteenth-century novelist. It may be indicative of a larger cultural shyness—"There are many dramatic moments occurring in our lives, but the Chinese way of managing these moments is to restrain anything dramatic happening. We bury these in our hearts. It's our way of crisis management in human relationships." All the same, there's no denying that staying focused on two insecure people prone to recoil from the slightest shift in routine is a brilliant way of dramatizing large-scale change. For instance, Bin Bin (Zhao Wei-wei) and his straight-laced girl Yuan Yuan (Zhou Qing-feng), sitting in a video parlor: he's slouched, she's sitting upright; his white shirt is wrinkled, hers is starched. She suggests that they not see each other while she's studying for her exams, he meekly agrees, and you know that the end has begun. Which makes the way they hold hands and sing along with the title song ("Our love is strong enough to blind the world . . .") just a minute later, both of them staring at the TV screen, never at each other, all the more poignant. On the other hand, when Bin Bin's more outwardly reckless but equally sensitive pal Xiao Ji promises the gorgeous dancer/singer/call girl Qiao Qiao that he can "soften" her "as fast as instant noodles," you know that the relationship will go nowhere *very* fast.

Unlike Hou, who tells his stories *within* the frame, Jia tends to organize each of his long takes around a single feeling or emotional development, usually articulated with space, light, distance and the continual presence of stray sounds. Like Altman in his prime, his soundtracks are place-specific and excitingly cacophonous. *Xiao Wu* features a nonstop mix of music, ringing cell phones, TV bulletins, and messages announced over the public address system, nicely offsetting the title character's aimless, privately worried wanderings across Fenyang. There's a lovely moment when he's just left the company of Mei Mei (Hao Hongjian), the karaoke "hostess" he's set his sights on. As he stands on a street corner and greets some friends, a radio show emanates from nowhere in particular, climaxing in melodramatic build-up music and a shoot-out climax. It has a triple impact: echoing his romantic anxiety as well as his precarious position in local society (he's a pickpocket and everybody knows it), offsetting the casual rhythms of Fenyang street life, and underscoring the fact that this is an entertainment-obsessed society. The *Platform* and *Unknown Pleasures*'s soundtracks are equally wondrous, the first tracing China's quietly traumatic development from tight socialist collectivity to free-market drifting, the latter film elaborating on *Xiao Wu*'s media-mad present (featuring this priceless announcement from the radio: "Try the lottery and make your leisure time pay!"). Zhang Yang, Jia's sound designer, is obviously a key collaborator, but he seems to be joined at the hip with D.P. Yu Lik-wai, with whom he makes as formidable a team as Claire Denis and Agnès Godard or Hou and Mark Lee Ping-bing. Every shot is carefully thought through and composed, but nothing ever feels fussy or belabored. Jia and Yu favor a few key moves on which they perform endless variations: two or three people sitting or standing in a tight space, with an open window or doorway off to the side, an object or article of clothing to offset the dominant color in the corner of the frame, and a light source that glows bewitchingly through Yu's filters; a long view of a public event or group activity where the distance is never less than electrifying—literally, in the case of the thrilling moment in *Platform* when the Fenyang Cultural Group (later redubbed the Shenzen Electric Breakdance Troupe) takes to an outdoor stage just as the electricity turns on throughout the small town and lights up the purple twilight; or a lonely couple crossing an open space or walking past the walls of deserted buildings in various states of disrepair or construction, from which Yu draws a maximum of texture. Yu and Jia are the first artists to make something genuinely exciting out of DV in *Unknown Pleasures*. DV feels as apt for the film's ultrapresent tense narrative as 16mm does for *Xiao Wu* (whereas 35mm is perfect for the historical pageant of *Platform*), but there's so much mobility, texture, and vibrant darkness in the image that they seem to have located a whole new source of electronically generated beauty.

Jia's most exciting character creation remains Xiao Wu. In part, it's because he's more fully fleshed out than any other single character in the director's work. He's endlessly self-deprecating ("You're a fool," says his sister; "Yes, I am," he answers) and embarrassed by his small-time criminal notoriety, angry that his old friend and partner, now a big-time entrepreneur, refuses to invite him to his wedding, and deeply resentful that he is scorned by everyone around him but that they like his money all the same. The scenes between Xiao Wu and Mei Mei, ensconced in the red glow of the karaoke lounge, sitting in the beauty parlor or wandering across town, are perfect dalliances of shyness, feigned toughness, and boasting, punctuated with little stabs at intimacy. And in Wang Hong-wei, Jia's old film school buddy, Jia has his best natural actor. Jia's performers, many of them nonprofessionals, do variations of shyness, hushed sadness and stoic reserve— even Qiao San, Qiao Qiao's malignant sugar daddy, is a quietly reserved presence. But Wang brings an extra dimension of pathos, with his head and body forever swiveling or twisting with adolescent embarrassment. It's this gesture that makes his final public exposure as a criminal all the more devastating.

Wang is also crucial to the emotional impact of *Platform*. The cinema is filled with sad epics about the passing of time in the *Magnificent Ambersons* mode, but *Platform*, based on the experiences of one-time breakdancer extraordinaire Jia and his sister, captures the actual movement of time's passing—the film conveys the sensation of waking up one morning and realizing that the past has already arrived. Change comes so incrementally that the characters barely notice their own evolution from adolescent naïveté (Zhao Tao's Rui-jan, in her early twenties, asks her friend: "Is it true that if you kiss you get pregnant?") to lifeworn sophistication, as China moves from a centralized economy to a new free-market order. Jia gets a wise, wistful tone, moving gently and inexorably to that droning teakettle ignored by Wang's Min-liang.

Unknown Pleasures is far from a disappointment, but Bin Bin, Xiao Qi, and Qiao Qiao are more conventional creations than Xiao Wu, Min-liang, or Rui-jan: third-hand urban rebels without any cause whatsoever, cloaking their bafflement and disappointment behind flippant tough guy stuff they've gleaned from movies in general and Pulp Fiction in particular, to which Jia and his characters pay a hilarious—and suitably ironic—homage. The central motif of Xiao Wu is circling (around feelings and buried resentments), and in Platform it's the slow surge of time. Here the signature move is back and forth, the frustration of pushing and pulling and getting nowhere—Xiao Qi going up that hill, or getting smacked over and over again by Qiao San's henchman, or Bin Bin going backward and forward with his girlfriend. Not that it feels false. Unknown Pleasures is as true a picture of free-market materialism as we could hope for right now, powered as it is by real-life bewilderment rather than movieish despair. I just wish that it had as beautiful an arc as Xiao Wu or Platform, but then few movies do. On the other hand, it does have a devastating final shot, the last word on the elusive promise of pop music. But my favorite moment is almost a throwaway. As Xiao Qi walks around his apartment, he hears a bomb blast from the textile factory. He lopes over to the window and out of his mouth come words that might be uttered by anyone at any time from just about anywhere around the globe.

"Shit! Are the Americans attacking?"

2002

The collected works of the neat freak Coen brothers Joel and Ethan, the Siegfried and Roy of art cinema, add up to a dizzying, aggressively eye-catching spread: an airless but ingeniously nasty "neo-noir" (Blood Simple); a severely tricked up yet touching Reagan-era comedy of working-class desperation (Raising Arizona); a clever Red Harvest derivative tinged with mechanically absurdist comedy and given an immeasurable lift by a soulful lead actor (Miller's Crossing); a brainy exercise in comic anxiousness that's so perfectly thought out and proportioned as to virtually cancel itself out (Barton Fink); an "epic" American comedy that's as fascinating as it's maddening (The Hudsucker Proxy); a fable of fallen innocence, with their most carefully observed characters, that trips up on its own aesthetic cleanliness (Fargo); a beautiful portrait of underachievement, their warmest and most spontaneous film, again thanks to a smart, intuitive lead actor and a brilliant second banana (The Big Lebowski); and a follow-up epic of all-American absurdism that loses momentum as it builds in invention and finally never quite takes off, but leaves a winning impression all the same (O Brother, Where Art Thou?).

High school seniors and junior college film teachers across America puzzle over the boys' favorite "themes," the fact that they tend to favor heroes who aren't as smart as they think they are, or—most promising of all—discuss the fine points of their "style." The fact that they were the first to ratchet filmmaking up to a new level of streamlined artistry hasn't exactly gone unnoticed, but it also hasn't been discussed in enough depth. The Coen brothers blazed a trail and paved the way for Tarantino, Lars von Trier (who remains a far more cerebral, conceptual filmmaker than his hand-held camera and his interviews indicate), and latter-day Paul Verhoeven, not to mention the parade of lesser artists who've learned from their example and confused the metronomical alternation of perfectly behaved actors in sculpturally lit, symmetrical space with instant cinema. Much more than a new wrinkle in film history, the Coens were the first to achieve (or to want) a complete disjunction between style and subject matter.

They are unparalleled masters of comic irony. There aren't many scenes in modern American cinema as savagely funny as Frances McDormand's meeting with her old classmate in Fargo, more perfectly death-tinged than

Gabriel Byrne's hat monologue in *Miller's Crossing* (not to mention Jon Polito's parting advice to his bored henchman to shave with cold water because "what does metal do when it's cold? It . . . *contracts*"), or more expressive of contemporary unreality than the self-consuming double-talk and nonaction action of *The Big Lebowski*, their best movie. This underappreciated, oddly moving comic gem (set "during the time of the Gulf War") reaches a high point when Jeff Bridges resorts to a George Bush quotation to express his frustration: "This . . . will not . . . *stand, man.*" The film has a perfect sense of people stuck in time, getting nowhere confused with somewhere just so they can give themselves a reason to get out of bed in the morning. Like all their films, *Lebowski* has its needling side, getting laughs from people whose dreams and nightmares are still rooted in the 1960s, but it's no less acute for that. The dialogue exchanges between the spent, exasperated Jeff Bridges and John Goodman's poignant, pseudo-aggressive Vietnam vet represent a peak example of the boys' greatest talent, the creation of distinctive, poetic idioms for their characters. Every Coen character has his/her own voice, and every film has its own unique verbal music. *Miller's Crossing*, for instance, is exciting for the sheer beauty of its language, a thrilling immersion in Hammett-like terseness at a time when everyone else was Chandler-happy.

At a slightly lower level of invention but still mightily impressive is their gallery of motor-mouthed grotesques: the agent and the studio head in *Barton Fink*, Jon Polito's good-hearted mob kingpin and John Turturro's spineless stoolie in *Miller's Crossing*, Harve Presnell's overpowering father-in-law and Buscemi's hapless kidnapper in *Fargo*, and Goodman's cheerful con artist in *O Brother, Where Art Thou?* The Hudsucker Proxy and *O Brother* put the grotesques at the center, and both films are notable for their high-octane, ingeniously skewed evocations of older styles of acting: Tim Robbins' executive is a full-frontal James Stewart–Gary Cooper naïf mixed with a starry-eyed Douglass Montgomery–type male ingénue, while Jennifer Jason Leigh's secretary throws Katharine Hepburn, Ginger Rogers, and Rosalind Russell into a blender and comes out with a performance that's so grotesquely one-dimensional that it's grimly exciting; Clooney's likeable escaped convict is a little bit of Clark Gable and a little bit of George Brent, with a voice courtesy of Johnny Depp's Ed Wood. *Raising Arizona* and *Barton Fink* also have grotesques for heroes, but they feel more rounded than the *Hudsucker/ O Brother* leads (by poignance and inflated self-importance, respectively).

What really makes their oeuvre seem so alarmingly coherent is their monotonous syntax, the sense that any given film has been fed through an image/sound processor with presets for shot-length, centered framing, emotional tone, and visual handsomeness. A friend of mine once observed that watching a Coen brothers film was like driving past a white picket fence (all that I would add is that the fence always looks freshly painted). You can set your watch by their remarkably uniform editing rhythm, which features a percussive yet deadpan one-two combination; probably intended to surprise, it's become as predictable as the rising of the sun. As has the cartoonish play with scale (the enormous space of the *Hudsucker* office sized up against big, beaming Rockwell-ish faces; *Miller's Crossing*'s tinkling ice cubes in the closest close-up vs. the expanse of a cushy dark 1930s interior). As has the deliberately freakish use of actors popping up around the edge of the movie like paper cutouts on sticks. The boys have a genius for turning actors into effects: Goodman and William Forsythe's comic book *Raising Arizona* duo is probably the most extreme instance, where two inventive actors are reduced to CGI's before their time. God knows the brothers have a way with deadpan visual surprise, short-fuse gags that pop like cherry bombs: *Raising Arizona*'s jet-propelled screaming jags, Turturro's agonized bouts with his Wallace Berry wrestling script in *Barton Fink*, that pan to the wood-chipper in *Fargo*. But the attack is always the same, and the short-fuse idea informs the shape and tone of the entire movie. It's as if the on-camera moment couldn't be trusted to stand up on its own and needed regular infusions of cinematic steroids.

No surprise that the boys are so fond of the set piece (most of their scenes feel like set pieces anyway). Albert Finney's machine-gun gig in *Miller's Crossing* is their first big extravaganza, a supposedly ingenious slice of mannerism that plays like a film school short with a $15 million budget, storyboarded within an inch of its life. The *Hudsucker* hula hoop frenzy generates a fair amount of burnished lyricism, suggesting an all-American fantasia that the top-heavy movie around it never quite becomes. *O Brother, Where Art Thou?*, a depression era tall tale about three escaped convicts making their way home through rural Mississippi, is much dreamier and more free-form than the brothers usually allow. It's also a more successful slice of phantasmagoric Americana. The film gets into something quite beautiful with the eerie appearance of baptists clad in white, floating through the woods and down to the river. And its high point is a brilliantly imagined Ku Klux Klan rally musical number, in which the standard imagery (white sheets and hoods, torches, members standing in a circle) is merged with the Nuremberg rally, Busby Berkeley production numbers, and the "Oh-wee-oh" chant from *The Wizard of Oz*. In both cases, the idea is stronger than the execution, which is a little too neat and too hasty (and in the baptismal scene, the sound of the singing voices is bright and studio-clean when it should be unearthly). But the sheer audacity of conception behind the rally in particular is breathtaking. When the red-sheeted leader sings a mournful version of "O Death" and the procession around him threatens to form a swastika, the film gets a purchase on the peculiarly American form of religious delirium that Hawthorne was writing about in "Young Goodman Brown."

The net effect of all the handsome centeredness and machine-tooled rhythmic regularity is a movie whose position toward its own characters is ambiguous and whose priorities are unclear—frustratingly so for cinephiles, excitingly so for fans who aren't so worried about film history. Looked at from the classic cinephilic angle, the brothers' high-velocity, damnably entertaining concoctions feel less than kind to their characters. Do the Coens like the people they create? From the evidence of the films, I'd say yes, in the same way that a hunter likes his trophies. Their directorial stance suggests Albert Dekker in *Dr. Cyclops*, gazing down at his menagerie of shrunken humans with glee (never more so than in the supposedly warm-hearted *Fargo*). Maybe it's less a question of cruelty than of bypassing respect altogether, creating a zoolike enclosure of odd behaviors and eye-catching tics in which all characters are equal. When the movies are really cooking (Byrne's *Miller's Crossing* machinations, William H. Macy's frantic scrambling in *Fargo*, most of *The Big Lebowski*), they generate the strangest sensation: the icy calculation behind the camera vies for attention with the onscreen emotions, and the viewer is thrown into a weird space between identification and lofty superiority. When the films aren't working, the brothers' parody of machine-age efficiency feels stuck somewhere between provocation and limitation. In the end, no matter how much you've been entertained, you're left with the nagging questions: who are the Coen brothers, and where are they coming from? Even Kubrick, the one cinematic idol whose shadow falls over Joel and Ethan's playground (a *Shining*|-*Barton Fink* double bill would be an instructive experience), never hid himself so completely within his work.

The mechanical precision, the sense that the film has remained untouched by human hands, can take its toll on the actors. In theory, Turturro and Buscemi are the model Coen performers. Both supremely self-effacing, they're very good at concentrating their energies, ready, willing, and able to stylize themselves into caricatures at the drop of a hat. They soar in the smaller roles—Turturro' stoolie in *Miller's Crossing* and his hilarious pedophile bowler in *The Big Lebowski*; Buscemi's Chet the Bellboy in *Barton Fink* and his *Lebowski* third banana. But they leave a metallic aftertaste in the larger ones. There's a disconcerting singularity to Turturro's Barton or Buscemi's *Fargo* kidnapper, and both performances have the effect of straight black lines Xeroxed on a white page. Even McDormand's Margie, their most beloved character, is often reduced to a figure in a snowscape, a good actress giving an all-effects performance: misshapen police hat, pregnant waddle, and heavy accent. She's also treated to an instant identification-breaking shot: sitting in a patrol car eating a fast-food lunch with commercial signage looming in the background *Zabriskie Point*–style.

It's actors like Goodman and Macy who really make the films hum, adding an extra layer of realism beneath their technical prowess (they both seem to remember something that most big-time actors forget quickly: what it's like to work for a living). Byrne and Bridges are magical in *Miller's Crossing* and *The Big Lebowski* respectively, because they bend the action to their own ruminative pace. *Lebowski*'s outrageous set-piece dreams work on a poetic level thanks to the wholeness of Bridges's performance: the images of super-clean, orderly rows of chorus girls and bowling pins seem perfect for a disheveled L.A. pothead. But those two films are unusual in the Coens' oeuvre, shaggy detective stories that are actually character studies of tired men whose minds are working overtime, spinning vast intrigues out of thin air, and finally ending up exactly where they started. It's the richest vein in their filmmaking, preferable to their tastes for atomic-powered comedy, mechanical complexity, or nasty shock effects.

O Brother, Where Art Thou? is a semisuccessful attempt to move in a new direction. The brothers have always been very sharp with their pastiches, carefully layering different sources and inspirations into one strangely harmonious single object: *Hudsucker* is a late-1950s, *Executive Suite*–type business intrigue with 1940s production design and 1930s patter, a monolithic never-never land of American movie comedy; *The Big Lebowski* crosses a Philip Marlowe investigative journey with a stoner's disaffection (far more interestingly than *The Long Goodbye*), and gets a convincing portrait of contemporary confusion and anomie. *O Brother*, "based upon *The Odyssey* by Homer," takes its title from the projected film within the film in *Sullivan's Travels* and engages with the Preston Sturges film in an odd way, alternately deepening, broadening, embellishing, and correcting the lesson that Sullivan learns during his chain gang stint. The Coens took great delight in debunking the 1930s enshrinement of the common man in *Barton Fink*, in which John Goodman's salesman taught the author of "Bare Ruined Choirs" a lesson about "the life of the mind." *O Brother*'s Odyssean journey home for three realistically dim bulbs goes down the same road with far less malignant precision (part of the problem with *Barton Fink* was the urgency with which it tore into a fifty-year-old myth) and a far greater sense of fellow-feeling. When the convicts suddenly realize that they've become overnight rural pop sensations—they've recorded a song in a makeshift studio for a blind engineer, to make a little pocket money—the scene is so infectiously warmhearted that it's practically cornball. The Coens have never made a film so eager to embrace mysteries and wonders, and the eagerness is touching even if the success rate is fifty-fifty: they need to loosen the reins a whole lot more before they can pull off the kind of lyrical, balladlike feel they're trying for here. But the odd thing about this film is the way each carefully made, jewel-like aesthetic choice and narrative concoction floats off on its own, like a classy fireworks display on a summer night: Clooney's funny movie-star disconnection from the events around him ("We're in a tight spot!" he keeps repeating in his perfectly clipped 1930s voice, as the barn in which he and his pals are hiding out goes up in flames), an impending flood out of Faulkner's *The Wild Palms*, a Robert Johnson figure who's sold his soul to the devil to play the guitar, a series of impeccably curated and rendered musical interludes, and stops along the way that relate directly to *The Odyssey* (a blind prophet, a cyclops, and sirens by the water). Most interesting of all is *O Brother*'s digitally modified color scheme, which virtually eliminates blues and reds. The result is a lean, hungry image, drained of the hazy lyricism that plagues most Depression-era films, yet very mobile and air-filled.

The disappointment of *O Brother* is in the filmmakers' variable level of inspiration. The two above-mentioned set pieces and the visual design are brilliant, and the most oddly moving sequence in the film puts a new wrinkle on Sturges's original: as the trio sits in a movie theater watching a picture, the projector gives out, a chain gang is shuffled in through the back door, and the movie starts up again after they've taken their seats—a somber reverse of Sullivan's Disney-induced epiphany. But the three leads are less than fully imagined, and many of the grotesques are indifferently conceived: Charles Durning's politician, for instance, simply barks whenever he appears, and Holly Hunter's impatient wife doesn't seem to have been written yet. You can feel the Coens trying to let go here, leaving things purposely loose and disconnected. So why is the filmmaking as airtight as ever?

Why the subterfuge behind so much cleverness and machine-tooled perfection? Is it a defense, a provocation, or a little bit of both? Where does the simultaneous attraction and aversion to the working class originate? Is it personal, or a canny, post-Letterman choice? Why the obsession with tail-consuming circularity (the demonic loop of *Miller's Crossing*, *Barton Fink*'s unconscious cannibalization of his own masterpiece, the buried treasure in *Fargo*, *Hudsucker*'s circles within circles)? Does it reflect genuine or feigned cynicism? Or is it generated by their obsession with neatness? Or did they get too much Foucault in college? One thing's for sure: the answers aren't to be found in their proudly, defiantly impersonal movies.

I know of no other filmmakers whose work is such a puzzle and at the same time so alternately thrilling, annoying, provocative, grating, excitingly unclassifiable, boringly predictable, fresh, and poised to shut down the cinema as we've known and loved it.

2000

A Niche of One's Own

Just as the emotional landscape of the 1950s superimposed itself over the hottest moviemaking of the 1970s, so the 1970s has exacted its revenge by seeping into the pores of the current film scene when no one was paying attention, to the extent that "The Seventies" is now a style of filmmaking, if not a way of life. The first rumbling came twenty years ago, with Gillian Armstrong's *Mrs. Soffel*, a 110-minute genuflection to *McCabe and Mrs. Miller*. Michael Fields and Richard Ford's unjustly forgotten *Bright Angel* and Sean Penn's swoony *Indian Runner* were two early 1990s harbingers, followed by the 1992 bombshell of *Reservoir Dogs*. And 1994 was an obvious landmark, with *Little Odessa* (a film that seemed to have been made by someone who'd locked himself in a room with a tape of *The King of Marvin Gardens* for a month) and, of course, *Pulp Fiction*. The seventies had suddenly become a genre, a dreamscape at once timeless and "realistic." The mid-decade appearance of Linklater's *Dazed and Confused* and Assayas's *Cold Water*, two high-watermarks of Proustian recovery, only cemented the impulse.

On the one hand, you can feel this collective embrace, sometimes defiant and sometimes self-protective, as a withdrawal from so much state-of-the-art handsomeness. It's easy to understand the appeal of analogue filmmaking in a digital world, allowing entry into a forgotten universe of ragged edges, irregular rhythms, and dead-time pauses to observe trees blowing in the night wind, moths banging against a light, and teenagers betraying their awkward beauty. A signature image in all of these films: a character comfortably alone with his or her music. Consider the little interludes at the secret heart of *Breaking the Waves* (it's somebody's private space—perhaps Emily Watson's, perhaps von Trier's, perhaps the viewer's), Bill Macy's rapturous gaze at the bartender accompanied by Supertramp in *Magnolia*, Christina Ricci's lonely King Crimson tap dance in *Buffalo '66*, and Gwyneth Paltrow and Luke Wilson playing the Stones's *Through the Past Darkly* in the pup tent in *The Royal Tenenbaums*. Whether or not the music is sourced or in sympathetic harmony with, say, Pam Grier getting up her nerve in a California shopping mall, it is used to hack out a timeless, solitary space where childlike vulnerability is allowed to flower undisturbed. A key inspiration and starting point: Harvey Keitel's head hitting the pillow in 1973 to the 1963 beat of "Be My Baby."

In the case of Terrence Malick's two 1970s films, which have been key in-spirations, the music in question is the music of speech, a series of discon-nected private observations rendered in an affectless, regionally accented voice. These little philosophical blackouts offer musical accompaniment to scenes structured as a succession of loosely connected moments in time, sug-gesting the sovereignty of God and nature, human time being subsidiary.

Were you inclined to study the brief career of David Gordon Green—three films, each as maddening as it is beguiling, in four years—you would recognize the appeal of Malick's natural world cinema to a young aesthete-type trying to get a foothold in the industry. Back in 2000, the spectacle of this kid from North Carolina aspiring to Malick's condition, that of a so-phisticate with an abiding respect for the primitive, seemed oddly touch-ing. That there was something more than slightly self-conscious about Green's love of out-of-the-way people and places made him that much more lovable. And unlike his hero, he had a keen sense of America as a mul-tiracial nation.

George Washington certainly looked like nothing else when it gently eased its way onto the scene four years ago by way of assorted festivals, critical partisanship, and sympathetic exhibiton. Now it seems reasonable to ask: did the fans complete the movie? Green's debut looks like a near-parody of the once common and now forgotten dream of the "open-ended" film, if not for the simple fact that it is *so* delicate that it has no real drive or end point of its own beyond a desire to cultivate its own considerable charm. Green lucked out in film school, because his long-standing cinematogra-pher, Tim Orr, is a genius with mellow, textured light, and together they've mastered that old Malick frisson: epic framing within the drabbest settings and actions, in harmony with the outsized dreams of the protagonists.

Green's debut almost seems to have been designed to elicit a particular range of critical reactions—"offbeat," "oddly beautiful," "lyrical," "poetic," and so on. I don't mean to imply that Green is an operator. There is not ex-actly a surplus of filmmakers dedicated to getting the feel of small-town American life or giving shape and presence to the inner lives of people with limited cultural horizons. But the willful side of Green's poetry is slightly suspect. One of the many peculiarities of those first two films is the fact that while they are both resolutely working class, little if any work seems to be getting done. Both films are studded with picturesque shots of dilapidated factory buildings and lyrically abstracted montages of machines in opera-tion. Meanwhile, everyone appears to be on a permanent (or is that open-ended?) break from a shift at the local factory, and the subject of work and money rarely if ever comes up in conversation. It's almost forgivable, since the films are all about removing people from their immediate realities and putting their desires and dreams at the forefront. Green is also committed, almost heroically so, to a vision of racial harmony that instantly surpasses the stolid fumbling of most current American cinema. Yet for all the virtues and beauties of *George Washington*, it leaves you with the odd feeling of being, if not exactly sucker-punched, then sweet-talked. Nearly every moment in the film seems to fall somewhere between inspiration, luck, calculation, choice, and intuition, and Green finds all kinds of escape hatches—scenes constructed as stand-alone sketches, stitched together with music suggestive of transcendent otherness or Malick-derived voiceovers ("My friend George, he said that he could read God's mind . . ."). Watching the film now, one has the impression of a real movie buried beneath an overabundance of offhand visual and aural beauty and far too many sophisticated strategies.

All the Real Girls is at once chancier and more maddening. Green and his cowriter (and star) Paul Schneider do a very good job of tracking the fluctuations of male egotism. Schneider's Paul is the nicest guy who ever fucked you over, the sensitive soul who's bedded every girl in town and never managed to call them the next morning. His "redemption" arrives in the form of Zooey Deschanel's Noel, his best friend's sister. Paul does his own private form of penance by refusing to sleep with her as a guarantee of the purity of his love, and then becomes incensed when she loses her virginity to someone else. Deschanel's is a nicely anonymous presence, low on affectation, even when she's delivering Green and Schneider's often-tiring non-sequitur poetry ("Sometimes I like to pretend that I have ten seconds to live"). And while Schneider isn't exactly ready for Shakespeare in the Park, he's similarly unaffected, believably rumpled, forlorn, and frustrated. It's a good, modestly scaled portrait of proud sensitivity. Schneider doesn't carry the movie in any conventional sense (watching him act is a little like listening to a songwriter warble one of his own compositions), but he and his director hit all the right emotional notes. The filmmakers might overplay the fumbling-for-the-right-word bit, but few movies have done better at rendering the dazed sensation of falling in love, followed by the counterpunch of hard-bitten realization. It's the movie around the movie that's the problem. Some of Green's most cherished effects go wrong the second time around—those prized tableau shots of asymmetrically grouped guys sitting in a junkyard/baseball field doing nothing and saying very little, the cultivation of poetic misfits on the outskirts of the plot. As in *George Washington*, there are

38

a slew of lyrical interludes, most of them nice if relatively indistinct and held to the movie around them by the most delicate poetic connective tissue. Some, like that god-awful clown gig in the hospital, are just plain terrible. Even worse is the moment when Uncle Leland and his daughter Feng Shui (bad idea) wander through a field in a haze of lyrically backlit dandelion seeds, one of the worst fixtures of 1960s and 1970s cinema.

The new *Undertow* is less of an advance or a departure than a semi-clever lateral move, a careful sidestep. It's Green's first film with a plot as opposed to a situation or a mood—jailbird Josh Lucas comes to visit estranged brother Dermot Mulroney on his Georgia pig farm, winds up killing him for stealing his girl and their father's affection, then chases his two young nephews across the South in an effort to retrieve the family treasure. Thankfully, Green is forced to abandon his customary structure of loose poetic connections. He's obliged to imagine something beyond the big dreams of small town people and to maintain a measure of tension, even suspense. For the very first time, the many comparisons with southern literature that began with *George Washington* seem applicable. The sense of buried family transgressions and resentments; weak, soft men and impressionable, suffering boys; and ripe evil in a backwoods setting are in tune with Faulkner and Flannery O'Connor, but they sit nicely within the movie, nothing too pronounced. Green is taking a stab at one of the oldest preoccupations in American literature, North or South: the direct contemplation of evil. Whether or not Josh Lucas's grinning golf-pro mug is the right portal to be looking through is open for debate. Lucas is good at unctuous ingratiation, but when he gets angry he looks more like a guy whose flight to Palm Beach has been cancelled than a vengeful ex-con. On the other hand, Jamie Bell energizes *Undertow* and almost single-handedly kicks it up to a higher gear than Green's ever even attempted. Smart young man that he is, Green winds up setting his pace to Bell's sharp, physical acting and angular moves. Where most of the cast, from the little Pica-suffering brother (Devon Alan) to the wayward girl the brothers meet during their travels (Kristen Stewart), is stuck in Green-dale, moving somnabulistically and mouthing the usual non sequiturs, Bell works from an endless store of pent-up energy and quick smarts. Watching Bell and the eternally undervalued Mulroney as his dad locked in a stoical war of nerves—it's a matter of dueling frowns, Mulroney's dark, deep-set eyes vs. Bell's close-set, tensed-up features—is one of the minor joys of 2004 (interesting to remember that Mulroney played a role similar to Bell's in the aforementioned *Bright Angel*). And seeing Bell at work running through the forest, squaring off against his uncle or furiously shoveling pig shit as he curses out his father, you realize the degree to which Green's previous films have tended toward a state of immobility.

Green's saving grace is his love of ordinary people, but his talent/tendency/ shtick lies in his foregrounding of place. The abandoned buildings, junkyards, open untended fields, mountaintops and forests, the tiny bedrooms, kitchens, and schoolrooms are unfailingly vivid, often more so than the characters they house (Green and Orr often make the people themselves into purely pictorial terrain). *Undertow* is a modest enterprise, but it is the first film he's made that's genuinely dynamic. There's a quiet thrill in the sheer variety of terrain crossed (from small farm to forest to dilapidated city to ocean), and the two brothers' *Night of the Hunter* journey is often as magical as Green intends it to be. Yet the new movie remains safely ensconced in Green's privately staked-out territory of natural beauty, with all those associations and assumptions carried over from Malick. It's going to be interesting to see where Green and this generation of American filmmakers go over the next ten years. The whole American indie ethos has contributed to a strangely stunted approach to moviemaking, in which the filmmaker in question wears his or her sensibility like a suit of armor, and appears to make every new movie from the same model. In an odd way, Green's contemplative beauty blends together with Neil LeBute's "unflinching" look at human cruelty, Todd Solondz's attraction to aberrant behavior, and Lisa Cholodenko's schematic psychologizing—four small patches of land endlessly worked and reworked within the vast, cutthroat tenant-farming system that is modern American cinema. Filmmakers have to define themselves right out of the gate to such an extent that their reviews must almost write themselves, and they have to be as talented as Spike Jonze or Wes Anderson, or as gutsy as P. T. Anderson, to rise above it all. This desperate self-definition seems to have started with a bizarre misunderstanding of Jim Jarmusch, a critical overemphasis on his stylistic tics, and an underestimation of his adventurousness. Or perhaps it begins with the layered calculations of the Coens, lazily mistaken for stylishness to this day. The ascendancy of Tarantino has only clinched it. Allowing for vastly different circumstances, the strategy of the self-defined filmmaker is the polar opposite of the old Hollywood idea, in which a cultured easterner like Howard Hawks would make like a cowboy or a John Ford would pretend that he had no use for art—it allowed for greater mobility within the studio system, whereas the current idea seems to guarantee stasis and frustration. In the new, terrifying world of corporate global entertainment, the idea of boxing yourself in has an understandable appeal. Yet it's a shame that more young filmmakers don't take the genuinely independent Richard Linklater as their model. Where Linklater is a free man, obviously unafraid of where he stands from moment to moment and making one wondrous film after another, everybody around him is tagging him or herself to death, almost guaranteeing a state of premature obsolescence.

2004

In the Thick of It

Is there a difference between male and female approaches to filmmaking? To explore the question or to deny it in the name of parity? A quandary, perhaps best left to the talk show circuit or to cinema studies departments. Or some hitherto unforeseen merger between the two—"Welcome back to *Oprah*. Our guest today is Professor Laura Mulvey . . ."

Nonetheless, it is striking to consider that a number of current, otherwise disparate narrative films directed by women operate according to their own stubbornly private rules, logic, timing, and spatial organization. Claire Denis's *L'Intrus*, Ana Poliak's *Parapalos*, and Chantal Akerman's *Demain on déménage* dispense with the need to define themselves right out of the gate, something most if not all male filmmakers find it impossible to not do. Where a Malick, for instance, builds a master narrative (the taking of Guadalcanal) and theme (the duality of man) and then fills it with poetic and intuitive connections and flights, such abstractions form both the actual connective tissue as well as the substance of Denis's brooding meditation on spiritual displacement or Akerman's mother-daughter duet. And where odd shifts in scale or perspective are merely inflections in the work of a Kubrick or an Andrei Tarkovsky, they are embedded deeply within the above films: Denis's dreamy navigations through one sensational vision after another tell the story of her eternally longing hero, while Akerman's maddening (and maddeningly unfunny) comedy has a crazy sense of spatial logic that feels directly connected to the pushing-and-pulling bond at its emotional core. It's not a matter of value judgment as much as differing ideas of control, communication, and order.

Lucrecia Martel's *La Ciénaga* and her new *The Holy Girl* have this sense of privacy in spades, with a value-added quicksilver brilliance. It's hard to think of something, anything, that Martel doesn't do well, either expressively or organizationally. One minute, you're marveling at the acting, then at the precision of the tone, then at the intricacy of the narrative, then at her ability to take almost any space, from the dingiest hotel room to the sunniest patch of woods and create a poetically charged event in fragmented movement and scale, and then at her sense of the frame (no matter where Martel points her camera, one is always keenly aware of what's lingering just beyond). Not to mention her precise use of repetition (of sounds and actions)

or her keen, multilevelled understanding of how all of the various sensual
and emotional components of existence affect one another, leading either
to tragedy (*La Ciénaga*) or some devastatingly comic variation thereof (*The
Holy Girl*). Filmmakers all over the world, good and bad, beat their brains in
trying to achieve what comes so naturally to this director—it's difficult to
name another director her age who manages such a precise balance between
all the various elements of cinema with such ease.

Martel's subject—her only subject?—is family life of the extremely non-
functional variety. It's amazing to see material that has been pummeled into
semiconsciousness by talk show hosts and pop psychologists springing
back to such vivid life in *La Ciénaga* and *The Holy Girl*. You get the sense that
for Martel there is no possibility that any family could behave otherwise,
what with the humidity, the economy, and the unpredictability of children
and their budding libidos, not to mention the human body's tendency to go
slack. In both films, every character tends toward the horizontal, sprawling
across floors, couches, and beds to get away from the heat or to simply pass
the time—meanwhile, sexual exchanges are forever immanent, postponed
until the weather, or the keenness of perception, improves. "I hate this climate," exclaims Graciela Borges's drunken, Indian-hating Mecha in *La Ciénaga* from her bedside command post—she's convalescing after a fall on
some broken glass. One never knows when her dazed son (Juan Cruz Bor-
deu) or histrionically confused adolescent daughter (Sofia Bertolotto) will
come wandering into the room in their underwear or bathing suit and claim
some bed space next to their not-so-beloved mother, who lets them lie there
without a fight. In *The Holy Girl*, Amalia (María Alche) is forever lying down
next to her mother, her best friend, or her uncle, idly caressed or caressing
someone in turn, her imagination locked on the lost, timid doctor (Carlos
Belloso) who has molested her in public and who happens to have turned up
for a medical convention at her family's hotel. There's a remarkable insight
in both movies—that boredom does not stifle the imagination, but excites
it through the byproduct of idle curiosity. Adults and children alike in Martel's films operate almost exclusively at a semiconscious level, the result of
too much time and too little to do, in tired, semistifling environments with
which everyone is so familiar that they could walk through them blind-
folded. The passions excited within both mother and daughter by the ano-
dyne Dr. Jano in *The Holy Girl* are born in a miasma of torpor, lethargy, and
resignation. Similarly, Momi's fierce attachment to the taciturn maid Isabel
(Andrea López) in *La Ciénaga* (in one striking scene, she entraps her with her
leg so that she can't get up from the bed they're sharing to answer Mecha's

call) seems to result from nothing much at all, beyond the fact that they're virtually the only people in the decaying household who can see straight.

Martel's attention is dispersed among so many characters that one is tempted to say that the stars of her films are the settings: the untended house in La Ciénaga and the homely old hotel in The Holy Girl. In fact, the physical surroundings in both films are unfailingly vivid and tangible—Martel is wonderful at getting a sense of decay in the environment, so that you can practically smell the mildew in Mecha's derelict mansion or the staleness of the rooms in the hotel. But living environments make up just one element in the greater constellation of sensations, intuitions, chance meetings, and shared confidences leading to the defining events that wrap up both movies. Both endings have an extra layer of poignancy: one feels that they represent one among thousands of alternative outcomes, so deftly does Martel negotiate between randomness and inevitability. Meanwhile, absolutely everything in her cinema—people, animals, rooms, objects, and mountaintops—is viewed from the same cunning remove. Martel's stance in both films is that of an all-knowing and all-seeing ghost bringing remembered events back to three-dimensional life.

Any Martel scene has its own unique spatial configurations, its own sense of mysterious dislocation. Indeed, certain scenes—the eruption of dancing by Mecha's bedside and the visit to the dam in La Ciénaga and the opening scene of The Holy Girl—are so carefully crafted and tightly organized that they operate like films within the greater films. Martel has a set of strategies to which she keeps returning, perhaps a bit too often for comfort, the most unusual of which is her tendency to break in on her characters as they're absorbed by some offscreen sound or event and show the event only later or not at all—think of Amalia and Dr. Jano joining the crowd to watch what turns out to be a theremin demonstration in a store window or Tali (Mercedes Morán) and her son Luciano (Sebastián Montagna) staring up at the ceiling and locating the source of some undefined sound. The most powerful instance is the opening shot of The Holy Girl, in which the faces of Amalia and her friend Josefina (Julietta Zylberberg) are caught in a state of rapt/hostile absorption as they watch their offscreen teacher singing. Separating the reaction from the action gives a rich sense of the utter weirdness of adolescent girlhood: equal parts tenderness and ferocity, innocence just starting to mingle with experience. Equally arresting is the celebrated visit to the dam in La Ciénaga, where we see the boys standing in the water, tensed with machetes in hand, and suddenly hacking away with abandon, long before we see any actual fish. It may seem corny to slip a vision of savagery into a movie centered around the terrors of family life, but the topography of Martel's films is so richly varied and her sense of human behavior so wide that it's just another element in the greater karmic order.

Part and parcel with such disjunctions is Martel's penchant for breaking up any and all spaces into their component parts and throwing out the center, so that the geography becomes strictly tied to emotions and inter-psychic connections. I'd wager that almost every Martel scene begins with either a close-up, a vista disconnected from any particular point of view (making it everybody's point of view), or a rigidly defined section of a room, in which we are rarely, if ever, completely oriented. And within these Rubik's Cube constructions, Martel builds scenes with one foot in "classical" cinema (everything is dramatically sound and logically sequenced) and the other in a more current (if not modish) sense of the scene as a slice of un-tended reality—everything that happens is connected to time of day, place, and the latest shifts in emotional allegiance. It's the beauty of Martel's cast-ing and her intimacy with her actors that keeps the scenes anchored (not to mention her sharp ear for dialogue). No one is ever simply beautiful or ugly, good or bad, or smart or stupid, but always poised between possibilities, ready to go either way—creatures of fate indeed, but believably so, without the ominous under- and overtones that blight most films dealing with chance and destiny. Morán's Helena in The Holy Girl and Borges's Mecha are Martel's finest character creations: two unstable matriarchs, both more beautiful and more deluded than they realize, both achieving a certain grandeur that is all the more striking for being utterly unconscious.

A friend of mine suggested that Martel seems almost too dauntingly bril-liant for the cinema—perhaps she should be running a government, he sug-gested, or designing the next generation of space probes. It's a kind of com-pliment, but it gets at something troubling in her work. Oddly enough, for someone who displays such remarkable control over the medium, Martel's films feel strangely disconnected from the rest of cinema. It's as if she had settled on filmmaking as the best possible means of rendering all the vari-ous elements of her remembered family life, and one feels that she might turn her back on it the moment it has served her intensely private purposes. Indeed, both movies, so endlessly rich and satisfying, feel like exorcisms, or retaliatory tributes, if such a thing can be imagined, made by someone who remembers every sight, every smell, every small turn in behavior and atti-tude from her adolescence. If anything, La Ciénaga and The Holy Girl feel a little too self-contained and sealed off from the rest of the universe. They could have been made by Amalia or Momi, totemic objects to offer blessings

45

and curses in equal measure. And perhaps that's the weirdest aspect of Martel's cinema—that its point of view is finally that of an adolescent who has acquired the wisdom of a thirty-nine-year-old, or perhaps of a nearly middle-aged woman projecting herself back into girlhood.

I do not want to imply that the two films are interchangeable. *The Holy Girl* is a richer experience than *La Ciénaga*, less resolutely tragic and more open to the possibility of redemption, which laps around the periphery of the film and warms even the most horrifying interactions. Given her love of offscreen mysteries and the *Living Dead* opening of *La Ciénaga*, it's no great surprise that Martel is following up *The Holy Girl* with an excursion into horror. Another house, another set of characters lost in the netherworld of human possibility.

2005

American Movie Classic

for Tom Allen

*"In France, I'm an auteur. In Germany, I'm a film-maker.
In the UK, I'm a horror-director. In the US, I'm a bum."*
—John Carpenter

America doesn't have so many good directors to spare that it can afford to let John Carpenter fall through the cracks. Should that come to pass, and it almost has, he'll have the last laugh: the work will speak for itself. But how did he become so marginalized? The common wisdom is that Carpenter went into a precipitous decline after the glory days of *Assault on Precinct 13* and *Halloween*, but can anyone really back up such a snap assessment? (Is there any other kind of assessment in current film culture?) Examine his oeuvre carefully, and you'll realize that he has one of the most consistent and coherent bodies of work in modern cinema, in which the triumphs—those two early slam dunks, *The Fog, Escape from New York, The Thing, Prince of Darkness, They Live,* and *In the Mouth of Madness*—far outnumber the minor or problematic films. He's never done anything to be ashamed of. He's never made a dishonest film or even a lazy one. Even his Universal-ly ignored remake of *Village of the Damned* is beautifully crafted, with a brilliant opening twenty minutes in the bargain.

I would say that Carpenter's marginalization is due to something less easily identifiable and much sadder, over which he has no control. Whether we like it or not, we attune ourselves to norms and paradigms in filmmaking as they shift like tectonic plates, making unconscious adjustments in our heads about how to watch films and see them in relation to one another. And without knowing it, many of us do something that we often revile in others: we accommodate fashion. And there is no doubt that the fashions in American cinema have shifted far, far away from John Carpenter. He's a ying man in a yang world, who measures his own work according to criteriae of value to which few people still pay attention.

Carpenter stands completely and utterly alone as the last genre film-maker in America. There is no one left who does what he does—not Walter Hill, not David Cronenberg, not Brian De Palma, not Abel Ferrara, not even Wes Craven, all of whom pass through their respective genres with ulterior motives or as specialty acts, treating them as netherworlds to be escaped to or museums ready to be plundered. When we speak of genre films today, we are basically talking about a precedent set in Europe by Jean-Pierre Melville and Sergio Leone, standardized by Hill with *The Driver*, banalized by Lawrence Kasdan with *Body Heat* and made into an art form by Tarantino a little over a decade later. Behold, the "metagenre" film, which rose from the ashes of the genuine article after it was destroyed by the increasingly reductive economic structure of the business. Beyond late-night cable filler, genre exercises are now a matter of either cannily exploiting (Craven) or greedily satisfying (*I Know What You Did Last Summer*) the demands of young audiences. Most of the good genre films of the last twenty years—*Unforgiven, After Dark My Sweet, Near Dark, Blue Steel*—are isolated gestures, just like everything else in American film right now. It's a situation that effectively nullifies the give-and-take with an audience necessary for the survival of any genre. The one thread that everyone follows at the moment, the only common currency, is currency itself. Until the structure of the business changes, all other trends or tendencies will be nothing more than fodder for the Arts and Leisure section. The most recent development—irony—already seems to be on its way out.

So in a moment when isolated gestures are proliferating, why not behave as Carpenter does, remaining content to work in the manner of an Ulmer or a Siodmak, whose artistry was focused on satisfying genre conventions and the demands of narrative, and whose loftier preoccupations were filtered through those conventions? Why not behave as though events like *Independence Day* and *Interview with a Vampire* never happened, as though there were still a vast popular audience tuned to the niceties and subtleties available within genre formulae? Perhaps what makes Carpenter such an unpalatable figure for so many people is the fact that he came out of the same film school generation as Coppola and Scorsese with nary a trace of Europeanism in his work. Carpenter may be the only filmmaker who learned from auteurism, who benefited from it, and who ignored its central tenet of the director–as–central event, divorced from commercial and industrial considerations. There's something moving and yet a little off about his humility, the sense that he truly relishes the image of the artist locked into a system, satisfying its demands and complying with its rules.

Paradoxically, it's these historically obsolete, self-imposed limitations that have allowed Carpenter to stay true to himself. His patient, spatially precise, and exquisitely troubling films have a reclusive air about them, as though they were the work of a man who lived by the heraldic codes or the teachings of Epicurus. While his contemporaries have been endlessly mythicizing old stereotypes and draining them of whatever juice they had left in the process, Carpenter has been able to swim effortlessly from one exciting generic variation to another. He understands that a genre amounts to more than the sum of its iconographic parts and that it can only transcend itself when it sticks rigorously to its own rules, which leaves him unable to do something as outrageously and thrillingly inflated as Miller's Crossing (but then he'll never have a Hudsucker Proxy, either). His recent Vampires is an attempt to beat Rodriguez and Tarantino at their own game, and in the process he cultivates something quite foreign to his sensibility: total mayhem. But even here, Carpenter eschews irony and sticks to his guns by making James Woods's vampire hunter into a valiant crusader who takes evil at face value. On the one hand, Carpenter's films feel like pieces of scrimshaw or model schooners built in bottles—lonely, entrancingly solipsistic enterprises. On the other hand, with the task at hand utterly precise and clear, he is able to communicate with his audience with a clarity that few of his fellow filmmakers can muster. Occasionally, as in They Live or In the Mouth of Madness, he is able to sneak in an act of subversion and speak directly to contemporary affairs. In other words, in the same spirit with which it used to be said of Ulmer or Phil Karlson, John Carpenter is an auteur.

He is also the widescreen master of contemporary cinema. With the exceptions of Dark Star and his terrific TV films (Elvis, Someone Is Watching Me, and two episodes of Body Bags, the trilogy he produced for HBO), everything in his oeuvre from Assault on Precinct 13 to Vampires was shot anamorphically, and the 2.35:1 aspect ratio is a shape that he clearly understands and with which he feels at home. Along with Vincente Minnelli and Elia Kazan in their 1950s melodramas and the Resnais of Last Year at Marienbad, Carpenter is one of the only filmmakers who brings the shape to life, just as the 1.85 aspect ratio becomes a living entity in Spielberg's work and 1.33 does in Murnau and Fritz Lang. The Scope frame is often associated with deserts and windswept vistas, a matter of volume, value, spectacle, and touristic epic sweep. Not to deny David Lean his place in history, but in comparison to Carpenter his "immaculate craftsmanship" is alienated and plodding—Alma-Tadema to Carpenter's Winslow Homer.

One of the glories of Carpenter's oeuvre is watching the thrill that he gets out of adapting the Scope frame to a variety of topographies and climates: the blankest, most desolate urban wasteland at night (Assault on Precinct 13); the tree-lined streets of a small Midwestern town (Halloween); the luminous beachheads and rolling hills of coastal northern California (The Fog, Village of the Damned); the snowscapes of British Columbia and Alaska standing in for Antarctica (The Thing); the inside of a dank, dilapidated church (Prince of

Darkness); the saddest, most pathetic sections of L.A. (*They Live*); the mon-eyed neighborhoods of San Francisco (*Memoirs of An Invisible Man*); and the reddish, sun-parched flatness of the southwest (*Vampires*). *Starman*, the most thematically maddening film Carpenter's ever made, might also be his most sheerly beautiful. Supposedly an act of atonement for his starkly frighten-ing, commercially disastrous remake of *The Thing* and one of his biggest hits, *Starman* feels like a piece of new-aged hokum fifteen years after its release.

Yet *Starman* is also a serenely concentrated road movie, a child's vision of America at night without the Spielberg glow, from the rolling greenery of Wisconsin to spacious western truck stops to the hushed, gorgeous light of Arizona. The revolting plot mechanics are almost redeemed by Carpen-ter's very private sense of decorum, in which the action of any scene is care-fully filtered into the visual tone of the setting and the overall arc and pace of the film: he never spotlights an actor or an object within the frame for any longer than the pace will allow, and one is always left with the impression of a field of interlocking actions rather than prized moves or compositions. Carpenter never attempts the kind of exploratory, digressive moves within a scene that were the hallmark of his hero and alleged role model, Howard Hawks. And the lack of relaxation and breathing room can get a little op-pressive at times, particularly in *Assault on Precinct 13* where the action is preternaturally straightforward and the acting almost nonexistent. But in *Starman* his extreme economy offsets the gooey mid-1980s modishness, and said economy is in turn offset by the charm of Jeff Bridges's precise take on awkwardness and Karen Allen's wide-eyed beauty. And Carpenter doesn't cheat in an area that most directors would have whimsically fudged their way through: when the alien arrives in Allen's house, she is genuinely terri-fied at the possibility that she is face to face with genuine evil.

Starman actually contains one of the most beautiful passages in Carpen-ter's oeuvre. After Allen's Jenny has been shot, the alien carries her away to a mobile home that is being driven west. He works his healing wonders, all acted without a shred of sanctimoniousness by Bridges. And Carpenter cuts with equal measures of discretion and rapture to landscapes of muted, al-most austere beauty as the truck passes through them, and night gives way to morning.

The scene is fairly typical of Carpenter: ingeniously calibrated and rhythmed and nicely textured, with a strange coordination between people and inanimate objects. It's the sweet flipside of the presence of evil on Hal-loween eve in Haddonfield, Illinois, signaled through the sudden appear-ance of a partially hidden figure in the corner of the Scope frame or a slight pan that turns the frame's edge into an unexpected locus of fear. Carpenter's biggest money-maker looks more impressive with each passing year, a perfectly coordinated succession of counterpoints between slow lateral tracking movements, subjective forward moves via the Panaglide, and sudden vertical jolts within the frame (the killer jumping onto the car or lifting up the hunky boyfriend) in which every object and every street corner is perfectly described, the human action serving as punctuation. In fact, so much of Carpenter's cinema is close to a realization of the dream of directors in their dotage like Fuller and Fellini, who dreamed of making films with nothing but objects, devoid of people.

At his most comfortable with deadline structures and severely fixed passages of time (Snake Plissken has twenty-four hours to get out of New York and L.A., Michael Myers has to be found before Halloween night is over, the Starman has to hurry back to Winslow, Arizona, to rendezvous with his fellow aliens, the *Prince of Darkness* team has only a small window of opportunity to keep the devil out of this world), Carpenter has a tendency to turn every space into a grid. *Assault on Precinct 13* might be the most severe action movie ever made. The severity of the design is so extreme that it takes on a real purity, never more so than during the extraordinary shoot-out that climaxes with silenced bullets quietly hitting glass, Venetian blinds, and, most bewitchingly of all, stacks of bureaucratic paper sent flying through the air (there's something deeply satisfying about the "ptt-ptt-ptt" sound the bullets make as they strike). *Assault on Precinct 13* is supposed to be inspired by *Rio Bravo*, to which it bears the same kind of relationship as Mark Di Suvero's sculpture "Van Gogh's Sunflowers" does to the original. Homage mutates into abstraction, and an entirely new object is created in the process. Nothing could be further from Hawks than this perfectly mechanized standoff between a ragtag, makeshift band that assembles under the banner of good and a shadowy, perfectly synchronized, seemingly massive army of pure evil, a sudden threat that materializes out of nowhere and leaves its first and most lasting impression with the sudden shooting of a little girl eating an ice cream cone.

Anyone who's seen the film will never forget this moment. Everything about the scene is clear to the point of transparency: the plot mechanics, the horizon lines of the ghetto at dusk, the one-note acting, the evenness of the pace (and of Carpenter's typically stripped-down synthesizer score), and the quiet burst of the gun with its long silencer held by a languorously extended arm, quickly followed by the sudden bloom of red on the girl's chest and the blank surprise on her face as she crumples to the sidewalk. There's something uniquely disturbing about *Assault*, with its blunt opposition of moves and countermoves. The film has the undiluted force of a terse, savage guitar break. It's an odd starting point (*Dark Star* being a kind of false start, filled as it is with Dan O'Bannon's high school prankishness, but an ingenious film nonetheless), and its punishing concentration appears to originate from something mysterious and troublingly personal. Why create such a blunt instrument? It's easy to see why *Assault* was rejected by American audiences on its first release—Carpenter needed the human ballast of Jamie Lee Curtis, the mature Kurt Russell, or an all-pro ham like Donald Pleasence. *The Thing*, *Prince of Darkness*, and, to a slightly lesser extent, *Vampires* also move in this direction. They share a tone unique in the cinema: hermit-like, unadorned, genuinely terrifying, and genuinely terrified.

It's a fascinating lesson to study Carpenter and his Hawks fixation, his use of groups, "tough women," and task-oriented action, and then to realize how far apart the two artists are. If there's any filmmaker that Carpenter resembles at all, it's Jacques Tourneur. Both are genre filmmakers with an innate sense of visual beauty (which saves even lesser films, like *Anne of the Indies* or *Big Trouble in Little China*), acting is low on the totem pole for both of them, and both are temperamentally fixed on the perfection of tone—in Tourneur's case it's laid over the action while in Carpenter's case it's blended into it. But whereas Tourneur cultivates the supernatural and is preoccupied with the mystery of drives and impulses (Simone Simon's longings in *Cat People*, Robert Mitchum's self-destructive attraction to Jane Greer in *Out of the Past*), Carpenter is one of the few modern artists whose subject is the contemplation of true evil, or to be more precise, the stance that people take when they come face to face with evil. One of the most tiresome contemporary clichés is the banality of evil, the idea that it exists within all of us and can be sparked by random events—thus the serial killer as object of God-like veneration. For Carpenter, evil is horrifying enough coming from outside—his characters never court evil, they simply recognize it, and that is the moment of absolute horror. His films are filled with moments of paralyzing immobility and dry-mouthed terror brought on by the realization that there is something new and awful in the world. This is diametrically opposed to Hawks, where all the energy goes into the beauty of people in action and the conflict is nothing more than a useful MacGuffin (although it's close to Marlowe's encounter with Canino in *The Big Sleep*). In Carpenter, there is a unique mixture of dread and awe, followed by the time taken to sort out the two and muster up self-preservation, which is one of the many reasons why *The Thing* is so vastly different from the Hawks original. Even

Carpenter's admirers had a tough time with the aggressive presence of the Rob Bottin/Albert Whitlock special effects in that film, but what makes those effects resonate is the care given to the varying reactions to the Thing as it undergoes its transformations, and as it becomes clear that it could become anyone at any time (the very un-Hawks-like idea that Carpenter retained from the original story). Even David Clennon's exclamation of "You've gotta be fucking kidding me!" as he sees his former comrade's head sprout insect legs plays less like a one-liner and more like the spontaneous reaction to something hitherto impossible in reality. The Thing now looks like one of Carpenter's best films, easily the winner of the early-1980s mutating carcass competition. And it occupies a special place in his oeuvre for the sensitivity of its ensemble acting, albeit geared in one heavily singularized direction.

The many forms that evil can take, the infinite ways in which it can announce itself, the ease with which it can blend into the rhythms and atmospheres of everyday life—this is Carpenter's focus, and the moral clarity that he brings to that focus is what makes him a great director. Adrienne Barbeau's slow walk down the stairs to her lighthouse radio station, which imparts an odd sensation of reality peeling away its skin, in The Fog; a reanimated zombie standing before a mirror and shivering with a nameless, inarticulate longing for what lies on the other side in Prince of Darkness; the world suddenly turning blue at the will and ease of a demonic novelist in In the Mouth of Madness—these are unique moments in the horror canon, where the balance between legibility and fluidity, between real and unreal, is perfectly achieved and held.

The political side of Carpenter's cinema grows directly out of his sense of evil. The liberal credentials of Assault, They Live, and the two Escape movies have been called into question by some critics, but strict political interpretation is always a losing game when you're dealing with genre filmmaking. For me there's something so powerful about the concrete fact of urban desolation in those films—an expressionist construction in the two Escapes (New York in particular has some of the clean, graphic power of the late silent Lang) and a piercing reality in Assault and They Live. What a shock it was (and still is!) to see Reagan's America confronted head-on in a low-rent sci-fi epic starring Rowdy Roddy Piper. The premise of They Live—that aliens are hiding behind human masks, enslaving America with subliminal messages and can only be detected with special glasses that are being distributed by subversive cells throughout the country—is pretty close to Romero without the excess, a provocative metaphor for a thinly veiled reality. But what really makes the film so affecting is its feeling for the acrid tastes and smells of life on the margins, its boisterous physicality (yes, that is the longest fight scene in movie history between Piper and Keith David, with his terrific slow-burn sneer), its sense of hollow, lapping desperation, and its sad prole poetry. Who else had the cunning, the compassion, the ingenuity, and the efficiency to fashion an ode to the American working class during such a rock-bottom, sickeningly cheerful moment in American history? Similarly, the metaphor for media saturation and paralysis in In the Mouth of Madness (the books of a Stephen King–ish writer named Sutter Cane literally drive people insane) seems a bit straightforward simply taken on its own. But the way that Carpenter delineates the experience of going mad, in which a world seen through long lenses keeps ripping away its cheap surfaces to reveal more cheap surfaces underneath, is a brilliant feat of low-budget engineering and a very disturbing encapsulation of the experience of living amidst so many media and their endless supply of product.

Forget the frequently adolescent sensibility, which finds its outlet in Big Trouble in Little China, Escape from L.A., and Vampires. Forget the occasionally clunky orchestration of parallel events. Forget the variable success of the special effects—for every Starman or The Thing, there's an Escape from L.A. with its computer game landscapes, a Prince of Darkness with its zombies trundling down the street, or an In the Mouth of Madness with its rubber monsters (although in that film the cheesiness of the monsters is part of the subject and is almost overcome by the tautness of the conception). Forget the frequently monotonal characters and acting. Allowances and justifications are constantly being proffered for filmmakers as varied as Fuller, Godard, De Palma, and Malick, their inconsistencies reconstituted as "idiosyncracies" or even strengths. Why not cut some slack to this modest filmmaker who carries a bygone (and perhaps illusory) camaraderie between director and audience in his head? With the exception of his devoted fans, Carpenter is indeed a bum in America, damned for excessive modesty. But if auteurism has taught us any lessons at all, it's that modesty and ambition, prose and poetry, the concrete and the abstract, can walk hand in hand in the least likely places. A paradox: this relic, so self-contained, so respectful of the rules by which his elders were obliged to play, makes films that are often more acutely intelligent than anything his less constrained contemporaries can manage.

Another American solitary, falling out of fashion but carefully guarding his integrity like a dusty old treasure.

We have yet to come to grips with John Cassavetes. To his devoted fan base, he is the most "genuine" and "real" of filmmakers, while to his detractors he is a sloppy, undisciplined improv addict. "Pro" plays easily into the hands of "con": The most spirited defenses betray a queasy, Esalen-era feeling that the films are valued primarily as "experiences" outside of, and therefore superior to, the rest of cinema—the acting class/encounter group synthesis we've all supposedly been hungering for. The hectoring insistence on Cassavetes's absolute emotional authenticity (and hence the relative inauthenticity of everyone else) also provides a sound basis for the common claim that his work is the spring from which far better and more elegant filmmakers have drunk. Meanwhile, the question of what exactly Cassavetes and the cinema mean to each other has gone largely unanswered.

Here and there, we have been afforded a fuller view of his contribution to movies. Sergio Leone, a very different kind of filmmaker, reckoned that Cassavetes was the greatest artist in contemporary American cinema, the only one who had actually invented his own cinematic language. Akira Kurosawa was just as fulsome in his praise. And the French theorist Nicole Brenez has claimed, with some justification, that Cassavetes was one of the greatest editors among filmmakers. This seems a good, logical place to start, because it gets right to the heart of his singular approach to moviemaking. Far from the unbridled love warrior of legend, Cassavetes was the first filmmaker to make people themselves into his mise-en-scène, as his devoted admirer Ray Carney has pointed out. Human events, micro and macro, were the colors of Cassavetes's palette, as light was to Sternberg, as space was to Hitchcock, as time was to Tarkovsky. Far from a smorgasbord of undifferentiated high-key emotions, Cassavetes's cinema is acute on a second-by-second basis: To look away is to risk skipping the equivalent of a sentence, if not an entire paragraph (or stanza). Where Carney goes wrong is in his assertion that Cassavetes's aesthetic is morally superior to almost all others. Cassavetes did indeed create his own particular form of cinematic writing, but in the end it was no less an artificial construction than that of, say, Welles or Kubrick. This is the leap that few critics have thus far been willing to take.

A good critical biography of Cassavetes is a tall order, and I think it's certain that Marshall Fine's *Accidental Genius* will not prove to be the definitive account. Like *Bloody Sam*, the author's 1992 Sam Peckinpah saga, this is what they call a workmanlike job: a chatty, breezily paced book peppered with colorful anecdotes, of which there are plenty to go around. Fine is as careful to not overtax the reader with an excess of facts or interpretation as he is cautious about giving offense to the sensibilities of friends and family (let it be noted that Gena Rowlands, while blessing the project, did not give an interview for this book; let it also be noted that Fine ventures the hitherto taboo suggestion that Cassavetes was not the faithful husband of legend). Fine employs the standard showbiz biography form: childhood, the early years, then movie by movie (genesis, synopsis, thumbnail critique, shooting, editing, critical reception, and box office), with the occasional aside (chapter thirty-seven: "John and Gena"; chapter forty-three: "Approach of the 80s") to break up the steady beat. As a critic, he is attentive and appreciative if not terribly insightful. "His characters' lives didn't describe neatly configured plots," writes Fine. "His films would never be confused with well made plays or conventional Hollywood formulas." This rallying cry was first sounded by the director himself, one of the greatest self-promoters in the history of movies, and it has been echoed so often that it has become a bromide. Cassavetes is indeed sui generis, as Fine claims, but then so is every other great filmmaker. To insist at all costs on his individuality is to sidestep the issue of what actually made him great.

In essence, this is a very un-Cassavetes-like book about Cassavetes. And yet for novices, it's an excellent place to start. "I wanted to write the book that I longed to read about Cassavetes," writes Fine in his introduction, "the one no one had written yet—the one that explained to a mainstream audience why they should know and care about the work of John Cassavetes." This is where the devotees start scoffing. They already know and care, and they've already heard all the stories—the time Cassavetes came home from shooting *Johnny Staccato* to be reminded by Rowlands that they had a newborn baby; the time Cassavetes talked his way out of being mugged and took his would-be attacker out for an ice cream cone; the time he told his young friend Martin Scorsese that *Boxcar Bertha* was "a piece of shit" and ordered him to get right to work on the film that would become *Mean Streets*; the time he threw Pauline Kael's shoes out the window of a taxi. Yet given the legions of young people with access to nothing but HBO, Blockbuster, and the multiplex, Fine's is a worthy goal. His commercial hook—Cassavetes as the man who "invented the American Independent Film"—is a corny, Arts and Leisure-type thesis that doesn't hold water: American independent cinema as we know it today (prepackaged, overly fond of its smallness, eager to be

adored) would have made his subject wretch. On the other hand, if the indie
ethos is the bait that lures nascent filmmakers to Cassavetes, so be it.

Early on, the author acknowledges the indisputable fact that, in the matter
of Cassavetes scholarship, "all roads lead to Ray Carney." He goes on to generously acknowledge Carney's contributions—more generously than the
bowtied B.U. professor himself has ever allowed (Carney's vicious remarks
about Brenez's *Shadows* monograph and Tom Charity's lovely 2001 book,
Lifeworks, being two cases in point). Cassavetes is Carney's raison d'être, his
vocation, and I'm sure he won't stop beating the drum until the filmmaker's
face has replaced Washington's on the dollar bill. He has certainly made
some invaluable discoveries, including alternate cuts of *The Killing of a Chinese Bookie* and *Faces*, and most recently—and prominently—a print of the
long lost ur-*Shadows*, now under lock and key per Rowlands and the Cassavetes estate. Carney has written two books on Cassavetes, numerous
articles, a monograph on *Shadows*, a book each on Dreyer and Frank Capra
(two Cassavetes favorites), has given dozens of interviews in which the
name Cassavetes is invoked with hair-raising regularity, and maintains a
Cassavetes-mad website. He has also compiled an oral history, *Cassavetes on
Cassavetes*, made up of the filmmaker's recorded thoughts and musings in-
terspersed with occasional reflections by associates, not to mention Carney's own polemically tinged interpolations. That book is at once untidy, invaluable, and, given the fact that Cassavetes's every idle pronouncement is
treated as divine truth, maddening.

In this all-consuming devotional context, the very modesty of Fine's
book is a welcome development. To read this deftly engineered narrative of
the director's middle-class childhood in a Greek immigrant family, his evolution into an all-stops-out extrovert, his courtship of Rowlands, his natural (and supposedly accidental) evolution from actor to director, and his creation of a very particular style of moviemaking is a pleasure in itself. What
is lost in depth is gained in brevity and simplicity. Where Carney goes into
great detail about Cassavetes's decision to recut *Husbands* because it was
going down too well ("I'm not here to please the palate of the audience"),
the episode acquires added resonance in Fine's tidier and more neutral account, if only because the author pays heed to alternative viewpoints. Al
Ruban, Cassavetes's sometime producer, favorite cinematographer, occasional bête noire, and all-around closest associate, is the villain of Carney's
book. In Fine, he is a poignant figure, appreciative of his friend's genius
even if he didn't always understand it, and justifiably disturbed by his most
extreme behaviors, such as recutting a movie on which the suits had already

signed off. And if Carney is doubtless better at conveying Cassavetes's commitment to keeping his audience continually off-balance and productively disoriented, thus alive to every fleeting gesture and behavioral nuance, Fine gives us the more fully rounded portrait by simply invoking the terror that such actions struck in the hearts of those who had their friend's best interests at heart. In other words, Fine gives us not just Cassavetes but the bustling world around him as well.

Cassavetes's eleven-work filmography (twelve if you count the negligible but amusing *Big Trouble*, twelve and three-quarters if you add the assorted episodes of *Johnny Staccato* and *The Lloyd Bridges Show*) may be small in number but it is infinitely rich and varied from scene to scene and moment to moment. One could easily devote a whole book to the breakdown in *A Woman Under the Influence*, the girls' night in with Seymour Cassel's stud in *Faces*, or, to name a personal favorite, the duet between Ben Gazarra and the undervalued Zohra Lampert in *Opening Night*—they are among the most formidable passages in cinema. Fine's warm, winningly conventional appreciation only skims the surface, but it does get a purchase on Cassavetes and his restless desire to get into the marrow of daily human endeavor, not to mention the mixture of appreciation and bewilderment—sometimes affectionate, sometimes hostile, and always human—with which Cassavetes was greeted by his friends and his enemies and without which the portrait of any artist remains incomplete.

2005

I am what one might call an "irregular" film critic (my title at Film Comment, "Editor-at-Large," was an invention of Chris Chang, and I suppose it's apt). I have no "berth," so I am not obligated to see most of the crap through which my friends with gigs at newspapers and magazines have to suffer. So more often than not, I'm not focusing on individual films but on filmmakers and groupings of films. Does it change my point of view? For instance, if I were obliged to see and write about the many films now made that are based on video games, would it change my attitude toward the practice of criticism? Probably.

These pieces are all more or less director-based, but intensely focused on one film as opposed to many. Few of them are reviews per se, and most would fall under the heading of "examinations" in the clinical sense. Paul Schrader is fond of saying that the director's job is to keep the baby alive, while the critic's is to dissect the body and find out why the patient lived or died. A grim metaphor, but I suppose he's right.

The word is that *In the Mood for Love*, Wong Kar-wai's latest urban fantasia, the story of two neighbors whose spouses are having an affair, is a departure for the director. For aficionados, it's a welcome return to the contemplative tone of his earlier mood-drenched period piece, *Days of Being Wild*. True enough. *In the Mood for Love* is composed with a more sedate camera than the tactile, handheld point of view of the previous movies, and it shares with *Days of Being Wild* a Viscontian immersion in the ambience and mores of Hong Kong in the early 1960s. But in all other ways, the new movie is entirely consistent with the director's development since *Chungking Express*. Wong's last few films feel like reconnaissance flights over dangerous interpersonal territory, getting off vivid snapshots of emotional stalemates in play. He has perfected a giddy technique, which appears to simultaneously delve into and flit past the repetitive avoidance strategies and game playing of lonely individuals or couples (at times, he seems like a healthier, more sensual Egoyan). Not uncommonly for a modern filmmaker, he has less of an aptitude for emotional gradation and development than for rough-and-ready, lunging portraits of emotion-as-action. His films are made up of moments that seem to have been grabbed out of time, as though he's *almost* always just missed it.

What makes the movies feel like special events, and what makes Wong Kar-wai something close to the Hendrix of cinema, is the way every emotional tone is blended into the swirling color and motion of city life. As a city filmmaker, he's almost peerless. He understands the city as more than just evidence of western infiltration (Edward Yang), as a physical entity that exerts its influence over human affairs (Tsai Ming-liang) or as a romantic repository of dreams (Woody Allen). He sees it, guiltlessly, as the natural state of contemporary men and women, operating at the correct speed, the sedate rhythms of rural life being a thing of the past. And just like Hendrix with his endless bag of tricks, effects segue into one another with matchless fluidity, and the viewer/listener gets a quick trip to heaven. During moments like Tony Leung's fast-motion elevated train ride through the glittering Taipei night at the end of *Happy Together*, questions of representation drop away and film viewing gives way to pure ecstasy. Like Tarantino and Wenders, those other art hero epiphany-builders, Wong is continually going 61 skyward, exploding his exclusive, up-to-date form of cinematic beauty over the narrative like a fireworks display. What makes him a genuinely great director is the fact that his fusion of speed, color, and vision—always linked to desire—dictates both the form and the subject matter of his work.

The fluidity is still there in the supposedly "classical" In the Mood for Love, as is the merging of emotional and physical (meaning urban) space. This time, the director's eye gets quick, brilliant impressions of states of decorum, good manners, politeness, and swallowed feelings, which register fleetingly but vividly. There's a piercing moment early on (one among many) in which Maggie Cheung's Mrs. Su is sitting in her neighbors' crowded room, a beehive of activity, nonchalantly reading the paper. There's a faint smile on her face, meant to signal the appearance of calm. Her carriage is erect, her arched back barely touching the back of the chair. Meanwhile, she's wearing a dress in which it's virtually impossible to be comfortable. In the world of 1962 Hong Kong, which is so overcrowded that people rent out rooms in their apartments to middle-class couples, where the old folks watch the younger ones like hawks with culturally ordained authority, appearances are all-important. The film gets directly at the feeling of always putting up a good front, of being on guard against disappointing people, by isolating small physical events in corridors, tiny rooms, restaurants, offices, and street corners.

This time, the viewer isn't carried along by the gorgeous restlessness of the camera (best exemplified by 1996's Fallen Angels) or the Polaroid-ish visual scheme that reached its peak with Happy Together. In that film, Chris Doyle's cinematography suggested a happier, more modishly color-saturated Robert Frank job (Doyle is one of two cinematographers listed on the credits of In the Mood for Love, and it's debatable how much of his work survived the final cut). But Wong's visual music hasn't disappeared—it's just spikier this time, more rhythmic than melodic. In the Mood for Love moves with elliptical stealth. Very often, the only indication that time has passed is the color of Maggie Cheung's outfit: she wears the same style of Mandarin, or cheong sam, dress throughout the movie, and unless you're paying very close attention, you may not notice that a change from blue to red or green has signaled the passage of days, weeks, sometimes months. The strategy gives every moment an unusual emotional urgency. In the matter of Cheung's Mrs. Su and Tony Leung's Mr. Chow, you start to ask: how much has changed with the passing of time, and how much has stayed the same? How many times will these kind, proper, self-deprecating people displace their longing—for their spouses, for each other, for emotional freedom—with another ritualized walk to the local noodle shop followed by another night alone?

Every Wong movie has its own brand of sumptuousness. This one is more restricted than ever in its locations (it's almost all cramped interiors) and visual focus. In the previous films, part of the thrill was wondering where the camera was going to alight next and the knowledge that a scene was more likely than not to end up in a spatial configuration radically different from the one in which it began. A good portion of *Happy Together* takes place in Yiu-fai's apartment, but Doyle's camera finds so many small wonders that it feels as vast as a rain forest. In *In the Mood for Love*, the camera is pinned down, obliged to repeat the same points of view again and again on semiritualized activities and behaviors, like musical refrains— Leung and Cheung knocking on each other's doors and talking to each other's offscreen spouses, Leung's wife barely glimpsed behind the partition at the hotel where she works, Cheung walking down the steps of the noodle shop and wiping the sweat from her brow with the back of her hand. But even within the locked-down symmetries that comprise the film's form (they replace Wong's customary lachrymose voiceover as a structuring device), every shot remains a quietly ravishing event. Cheung passing her hand over her husband's back as he engages in a mah-jongg grudge match, then sitting on the edge of his chair, in slow-motion: a sad, graceful moment, where the line of her body conveys the sense of a woman playing the dutiful, admiring wife. The palette may be more restrained than in the previous movies (heavy on grays, whites, and beiges, with great swatches of red), but every object glows as ecstatically as ever.

Dramatically, *In the Mood for Love* isn't terribly different from *Happy Together*, which had a similarly fraught, episodic, improvisational shoot. Once again, the structure is theme and variations; once again, the focus is the predicament of a couple. The former film was about two wayward souls wedged between staying together and parting. The new film is about two people who've built their identities on foundations of niceness, who suddenly find themselves stranded and clinging to each other, but who are finally too self-censoring to give in to romance. Where most of *Happy Together* consists of Liu-fai and Ho-ping's dance of devotion and rejection, most of *In the Mood for Love* is given over to Mr. Chow and Mrs. Su's dance of longing and fear, interestingly refracted through an odd dramatic device: each one playacts the role of the other's spouse in order to understand the affair or possibly (intentionally? unwittingly?) re-create its dynamics. Every other character—Li-zhen's philandering boss, Chow's happy-go-lucky friend, the nosy landlady ("Young wives shouldn't stay out so late—people will start to wonder")—is a satellite, and the husband and wife go almost unseen, their offscreen voices used as rhythmic punctuations in a movie that feels less like a narrative than a beautifully drawn out musical improvisation. Call it Wong Kar-wai's "Blue in Green."

Both films lean more heavily on one character than another. *Happy Together* was Leung's picture, but *In the Mood for Love* belongs to Cheung, whose beauty lights up this movie the way the polar star lights up a winter sky. Cheung is one of the few modern actresses who understands her physical beauty as an expressive instrument and who also has the smarts and intuition to take it somewhere substantial. There have been plenty of portraits of repression in movies, but they've rarely been as radiantly filled out as this one. Acting for Wong Kar-wai is a totalizing experience—since there's no script, the actors and the director are creating characters, a dramatic arc, and a new expressive vocabulary all at the same time. Cheung and Wong have found as graceful and supple a through-line for her Su Li-zhen as I can imagine. Even more than for Leung's Chow, with his gelled hair and immaculate bourgeois wardrobe, the clothes make Li-zhen: they dictate the way she moves and the rigid tension with which she displaces her anger and her desire. Cheung understands that the machinery of repression can't reveal itself too readily, but can only be divined through her character's strenuous efforts to keep it up and running (in comparison, Leung plays the Mr. Nice Guy act a little too broadly at times). She understands the inherent sadness of being a "good person." There's a moment late in the film where she's framed in a window, as carefully as Marlene Dietrich was framed in the shadows for her *Shanghai Express* prayer. It's a portrait of beauty at the service of a thankless goal: to draw a veil over a heart that's sacrificed itself to the happiness of others. Cheung's is a genuinely heroic piece of acting, and it puts the vaunted Cannes winner, *Dancer in the Dark's* Björk, to shame.

Where *In the Mood for Love* differs from *Happy Together* is in its decenteredness, its lack of resolution. The further the film moves from the core dilemma in the cramped apartment, the more diffuse it becomes. Chow's move to Singapore feels dramatically vague, as does Li-zhen's phantom visit to his apartment while he's away at work. This is the film's ultimate *almost*, the capper to a series of near-intimate moments in which a shared sense of inner propriety dampens passion, which would be perfect if this was just another movie about two people who don't sleep together. But there are quite a few layers of ambiguity generated between these characters. Are they actually in love with one another? Or are they in love with their projections of idealized images of their spouses onto one another? Or are they just friends who share a need for love and companionship in the abstract? The film touches on every possibility, and when it's at its most powerful it suggests that all these scenarios exist side by side. This delicate, not-so-brief encounter, probably long-forgotten by both Chow and Li-zhen (there's a strong sense that all the action is being recalled—it has something to do with the film's breathless movement forward), deserves to be sifted from the ashes of time in the same way that the story itself was sifted from the myriad possibilities Wong threw on the table during the epic shoot. It's all there, but a little fancy intellectual footwork is required to tie everything together.

Near the end, when we've skipped ahead to the troubled, destabilizing year of 1967, Li-zhen goes back to her old apartment house with a child in tow. A few months later, Chow comes to visit Mrs. Suen, who's left for America. He's told that her old apartment is now occupied by a woman and her son. He thinks nothing of it and leaves. The near-miss is a timeworn, instant heartbreaker, but it feels odd here—if they were to meet again, what would they say to each other? Would they sleep together? Or would they just keep on being polite? As for the coda, where Chow whispers his secrets into the wall of an abandoned temple in Angkor Wat, it doesn't really carry much weight (hilariously, there's a "Tell your secret!" section on the official *In the Mood for Love* website). For some people, the spatial, geographical, and rhythmic change-up is perfect. To these eyes, it feels like a lesser version of *Happy Together*'s final side trip through Taipei, as off-the-mark as its model was on-the-money. In a sense, *In the Mood for Love* tries to duplicate *Happy Together*'s similarly improvised final form: one couple's dynamics are replaced with another's, Hong Kong on the eve of June 1997 becomes Hong Kong on the eve of the cultural revolution and the escalation in Vietnam, the Taipei subway becomes a Cambodian temple, and the falls at Iguazu finds its equivalent in the secret desires locked in Li-zhen's heart, betrayed by her too-eloquent body language and mournful demeanor. But where the geographical displacement of *Happy Together* gave resonance to the whole idea of going home, the idea of leaving doesn't do much for *In the Mood for Love*, which probably would have found a more fitting resolution with a staccato move, a sudden rupture. On the other hand, why complain? This is as intoxicating, as exquisitely nuanced, and as luxuriously sad as movies get.

It's been a while now since Wong Kar-wai first cast his spell of melancholy urban enchantment over America's more adventurous moviegoers. When he broke through with *Chungking Express* in the early 1990s, it was like tuning into a fresh signal on a new frequency: his filmmaking seemed to be driven by a seductive urge to dissolve the viewpoints of director, camera, lonely-hearted hero, and audience into one throbbing, supersensitive entity. Wong made quite a team with his D.P. Chris Doyle. Young directors from all over the world wanted to work with Doyle—plenty of older ones, too. His cinematography had a personality and apparently even a mind of its own. The more love-struck neophytes wanted to *be* Wong Kar-wai, the handsome guy in the colorful sports shirts, always smiling from behind his dark glasses, who made movies on the fly starting with nothing more than an inspiration, like a painter or a sculptor or a choreographer.

Now, in the year 2000, his newness is a thing of the past, the imitators who tried to perfect the slurred motion effect of *Chungking Express* and *Fallen Angels* have come and gone, and he never made the kind of impact we had all hoped he would in the American market: this was one secret cinephiles never wanted to keep. For those who love his films, it's hard to separate them from the legends behind them: the insane financing schemes, the endless shoots, the patient, devoted casts and crews, the hours and hours of material shot and discarded, and the marathon editing sessions as he and his team tried to make the Cannes deadline. It's difficult not to see each movie as the final result of a long, heroic undertaking. And the stories and myths endow them with a certain interactive splendor. Somewhere, there's an alternate universe in which Shirley Kwan's discarded *Happy Together* character exists and where Maggie Cheung and Tony Leung make love with abandon. I'm sure these moments and characters are just as fully achieved as their corollaries in the finished films. This is an artist who's generous to a fault, compiling a stock of grace notes and delivering the final products, and the sagas of their creation, like gifts to his audience.

Many thanks to Vivian Huang for her help.

2000

Calling *Beau Travail*'s images of bare-chested legionnaires training under the African sun "homoerotic" is a little like calling an Eric Rohmer film "talky"—okay, but then what? Could it be that Claire Denis went all the way to Djibouti with a crew of beautiful men just so she could forge a chain of images to get off on? And why this chain of images, so carefully balanced between the rough and the voluptuous, fixed exclusively on activity within the cloistered enclave of the Foreign Legion and set against the terrifying expanses of the North African desert? About an hour into *Beau Travail*, sympathetic viewers might feel like they're being treated to some new form of serene cinematic space travel.

At this moment, when divining homosexual overtones in a Hollywood classic still qualifies as a major insight, it may seem perverse to downplay the now-standard sexual angle, particularly when the film is as consumed with skin, muscle, and vanity as this one. But here's a question: is "homoerotic" really an adequate word to describe the current of emotion that runs between the legionnaires in *Beau Travail*?

There's no doubt that the mythic coupling of Man and Woman, a New Wave staple, is alive and well in Garrel/Carax/Doillon. But one of the many felicities of post–New Wave (and post–May 1968) French movies is the beginning of a cinema without a strict sexual orientation. In a sense, it all begins with Jean Eustache, whose films delved into the dark, roiling anxiety of heterosexual coupling. Chantal Akerman is another obvious pioneer, nullifying both the shock value of lesbianism and the sacred centrality of heterosexuality, so that you're focused on nothing but pure desire. And in André Téchiné's nervously energetic movies, sexual orientation is purely a roll of the dice, just another manifestation of basic human vitality. It's not just a question of destroying sexual categories: it's also an unmooring of old dramatic structures, allowing for a vision of people that's less fixed, more fluid. With sexual orientation thrown out as an organizing principle, desire came come anytime, anywhere, in any form.

In Denis's rapturously materialist cinema, absolutely everything is imparted through the spectacle of human beings in motion. She's been moving toward this superfluidity since 1994's *I Can't Sleep*, which shuttles deftly between a collection of characters loosely affiliated by a central trauma (like 67

Téchiné's *Thieves*). In her subsequent film, the emotionally dark but visually light Marseille fantasia *Nénette et Boni*, Denis and her comrade in arms, D.P. Agnès Godard, achieved a magical buoyancy—even the air in that film feels charmed. But with *Beau Travail*, Denis and Godard push the tension between psychic and physical space to an intoxicating high.

With her new film, Denis is revisiting the concerns of her earlier *No Fear, No Die*, where she settled into the relatively unexplored terrain of male friendship. In most movies, it's the site of competition, resentment, escape, posturing, displacement, the settling of emotional debts, and, oh yeah, repressed homosexual desire: in other words, *anything* but men enjoying one another's company. French cinema has always been the exception, from Jouvet and Gabin in *The Lower Depths* to Amalric and Cluzet in *Late August, Early September*, but in *No Fear* Denis really hunkered down and looked at the unspoken rituals of male companionship, the quiet beauty of two men (Isaach de Bankolé and Alex Descas, two terrific actors and real-life friends) completely secure in one another's company. At the end of this somber but excitingly mobile film, the camera suddenly rests to observe an extraordinarily tender event: De Bankolé's Dah carefully washing the lifeless body of Descas's Jocelyn.

Denis's films are always leaping into surprising disjunctions, sudden breaks from one sensual event into another one of a completely different shape and texture. Jumping from scene to scene has become a standard move in modern cinema, but Denis keeps her imagemaking attuned to her characters and grounded in the beauty of natural forms. Formal excitement and emotional specifics are in perfect alignment: the first never misshapes the second, and the second never curtails the first. And Denis really knows how to get one image harmonizing with another (the harmony is always thrillingly modern, near-atonal). In *Beau Travail*, she manages—miraculously—to (more or less) tell the tale of Herman Melville's *Billy Budd* through fugitive gestures, asides, and the mundane chores and punishing workouts of foreign legionnaires under the hard light of the desert sun. The scenes—or is it image chains? or instants snatched from time?—that seem to have critics all hot and bothered are, in fact, relatively few. They involve bare-chested legionnaires doing stylized versions of training exercises, choreographed by Bernardo Montet and set to the "O heave away, heave!" choral section of Benjamin Britten's opera. No doubt these beefcake displays would rate a nine from habitués of Chippendale's, but are they really indications that Denis has caught a bad case of penis envy and turned into a Riefenstahl adept?

In fact, there's an overlooked comic aspect sewn into the lining of the training scenes, an exceptionally wry humor to this spectacle of human need hiding beneath the cloak of ritual. When Michel Subor's Commander Bruno Forestier (a reprise of his character in Godard's *Le Petit soldat*) sits back, cigarette in hand, and observes his men training for some mythical conflict, you'd have to be doing some mighty fancy reading-in to imagine that he's undressing his men with his eyes. Subor, in a pure-behavior performance that surpasses the idea of performing, effortlessly conveys an exclusively male feeling of womblike warmth, refuge, and comfort after a violent recoil from . . . not so much women (the legionnaires all spend their weekend nights in town cavorting with the local prostitutes) as much as *interaction* with women, the painful effort of reaching out to the world at large, a retreat from self-revelation.

In other words, this is the universe of men silently faced towards one another and away from life, the universe of Neil Young's "A Man Needs a Maid" (another Young song, "Driveby," unexpectedly turns up on the soundtrack during a mountain trek). It's somewhere between touching, pathetic, and wholly mysterious, this state of communal solitude. We've seen it before in movies, of course, but by setting it in the strange world of the Foreign Legion, where you and your brother-in-arms are forever training intensively for nothing in particular and where you must always keep your creases ironed to express an "internal elegance," as Forestier puts it, Denis leaves this male posturing as comically yet touchingly exposed as Scorsese did in *Raging Bull*. And here, it is broken down to a few primal elements, elongated and magnified—acres of flesh, sky, sun, mountains, and desert.

"Why didn't I pay more attention to the beauty of the world, of women?" muses Denis Lavant's Galoup/Claggart, after he's been ejected from the legion for baiting Grégoire Colin's gloriously beautiful and virtuous Sentain/ Billy and sending him on a march to nowhere with a faulty compass (in one of the film's most beautiful images, the compass is later found encrusted with salt crystals). Anyone who knows Lavant solely through his three films with Leos Carax will be shocked by his stark, forbidding presence here. The boyishness has vanished, and the muscular rigidity has become slightly terrifying. But where Carax was always honing in on the warmth behind Denis's pockmarked ugliness, Denis locates the force. The beauty of Lavant and Subor is *hard* male beauty—aged, marked, worn down, weathered— upended by the *prettiness* and innate virtue of Sentain, who's only barely glimpsed by the camera.

Ultimately it's not his story. It's the story of men who believe they've stumbled onto another world all their own, a world where there's no need

69

for emotion and where everything is comfortingly ritualized. When the disgraced Galoup finally celebrates this world, now lost, he's alone, in the corner of a club in Marseille, dressed in black—we might be in his head, at the moment he's putting a bullet in his brain. And in these final moments, Denis and Lavant give us a miracle. Galoup breaks into a swaggering, ecstatic dance to "The Rhythm of the Night," the memory of every beloved training maneuver in one furious surge of physical power. The pathos is in the enclosed solitude of the shot (he's touchingly pinned into the corner of the frame, against a mirror, as a row of disco lights flash at his feet) coupled with the slow build-up to an uncontrollable release. It makes for that rarity of rarities in modern cinema: an epiphany.

2000

Godard has a key move that he's been working and refining since the late 1960s, which is to thrust an image before us and then weave an assortment of inquiries and stray bits of information around it, thus getting it to pulse with associations. In the first half of *In Praise of Love*, we get the Bois de Boulogne, the old communist trade union headquarters, a rail yard at night, a multiplex as it's closing, and an ugly stretch of superhighway in exquisitely somber black and white. As we confront these places, Godard builds up a nice sense of awestruck immobility in the face of time and history. His insufferable, thirty-ish protagonist Edgar (it's hard to say how much of the insufferability is by accident or design) and the men who are financing his "ode to love . . . in the documentary tradition," know the tangled history behind every vista and every building in Paris, with which Godard and his camera are having a melancholy reunion. The words set the images vibrating with an unusually refined sense of regret.

And when Godard films people in this movie (here, he tends to concentrate on the bodies of men and the faces of women), the vibration becomes a throb. Edgar rehearses a young woman with red hair, Eglantine to some faceless Perceval. When she's onscreen, she's alive in a way that few people ever are in movies. Part of Godard's genius as a filmmaker lies in the fact that he can harness such moments, where women are caught within the frame—in one spine-tingling instant, you can actually feel her heart jump. On the one hand they're trapped like birds in a cage, while on the other hand they're free from the decorous restraints of acting. Every scene with this exquisite woman makes up for every dead loss of a scene with Edgar the human paperweight lamenting the loss of cultural memory or soulfully thumbing through a book with blank pages.

The bracing shift to painterly digital video (DV) color in the film's second half, which takes place two years earlier on the Brittany coast, packs a sensual/existential wallop—an altogether different form of beauty and perception. A friend of mine, a painter, thought the color in this section smudgy, but I found Godard's impressionist seaside images rapturously beautiful: the movie of your dreams as you're listening to *La Mer*. The scenes with the Bayards, a married couple of one-time resistance fighters, are quite unlike anything else Godard's ever done. They're old people with troubled pasts, trying to reconcile who they've been with who they are. Godard catches this tension in their stillness, where you feel the struggle between mental resolution and physical fragility. Here is where his film's most powerful idea really blooms—there is only youth and old age but no such thing as adulthood, whether in love, art, or an enterprise like the resistance. I confess that I don't know if this idea comes from Brasillach, Blanchot, or any of the other writers Godard "credits" in a list at the end of the film, with his usual Olympian disdain for specifics.

Beauty and eloquence aside, there's something disconcerting about *In Praise of Love*. It has to do with this Olympian thing, which crept into Godard's work with *Hélas pour moi* and formally proclaimed itself with *JLG/JLG*. Jonathan Rosenbaum observed that in that film, Godard imagined himself as Goethe. At this point, he seems to be imagining himself as Goethe, Homer, Shakespeare, Chateaubriand, Montaigne, and Heidegger rolled into one. Godard has always played cat and mouse games with his own personality, not unlike Bob Dylan. But where Dylan is now at ease with his mastery and his massive influence, Godard comes on like the grand spirit of western civilization itself—it won't be long before he writes himself into the Bible. A lot of the positions in the film seem to have been deposited into their structurally appropriate Godardian slots without too much consideration. The much-discussed anti-Americanism is less annoying than the desultory manner with which it's expressed. It's as if Godard had an assistant lurking over his shoulder—"Sir, we need some material to fill in the space between the blue boat and the man silhouetted against the window." "Okay, throw in another Spielberg joke." More troubling is the way the business about the rounding up of French Jews in 1942 and the resistance seems to have been dropped into the movie from a great height. On one level, *Eloge de l'amour* is a movie by an old man who bitterly resents the fact that the trains no longer run on time.

As Wallace Stevens said, the probing of the philosopher is deliberate; the probing of the poet is fortuitous. At this point, Godard is a poet who comes on with a philosopher's deliberation, but only when he's working in film. His mind and body now seem more attuned to the associative speed afforded by video, where he's free to concentrate on his one true subject: cinema. When he's making an actual film, he's too slowed down by the technical laboriousness and the lack of total control. He made his *Time Out of Mind* ten years ago with *Nouvelle Vague*, but his *"Love and Theft"* will be on video.

2002

According to a majority of critics from around the world, Abbas Kiarostami is the greatest filmmaker of the 1990s. So for those among us still unexposed to his formidable talent, *The Wind Will Carry Us* is a perfectly good, if fairly heady, place to start. The idea of a grand thematic summation in mid-career might seem a little off-putting, but this is, after all, a filmmaker of real genius. Kiarostami has the keenest sense of visual/sound combinations imaginable, nudging a documentary image of a Kurdish mountain village, surrounded by lush wheat fields, into poetically mapped correlation with the mental makeup of a TV producer who's thinking in urgently digital city time. Kiarostami's soundtracks might be low-tech, but they're as elaborately patterned and arranged as anything from Oliver Stone or Ridley Scott and just as thrilling as Bresson's similarly homemade jobs (they're far less contrapuntal and more slyly sifted into the action). You have to look and listen closely before you notice the fact that you're hearing an extraordinarily artful sonic collage—that the careful modulation of birdsong, clucking hens, barking dogs, and wind blowing through the grass has been delicately and painstakingly ordered and placed to give the natural world a maximum of bewitching, mysterious presence; or that the tough, self-assured woman (a Kiarostami constant) quietly dispensing information about village customs to the hero as he shaves across the courtyard sounds as if she's in the next room.

Kiarostami manages to get multiple levels humming here. Reduced to its bare bones, the situation of *Wind* is very simple. A TV producer named Behzad arrives in a remote mountain village with his crew, where a friend from Teheran has tipped him off that a secret ceremony of self-mutilation will occur following the imminent death of a hundred-year-old woman. And they wait, for two weeks, as the crew grows restless and Behzad's family grows irritated that he's not back in Teheran to mourn the death of his own relative.

So the action consists of Behzad in his holding pattern among the villagers and their ravishing golden-toned landscape. He's waited on by his friend Hashemi's eleven-year-old nephew Farzad, with whom he half-heartedly tries to work up a friendship. And he's constantly plagued by calls on his cell phone. Whenever it rings, he drops everything, makes a mad dash through the village (looking like he was drawn by Chuck Jones), hops in his car ("Whoever it is, stay on the line! I'm going to higher ground!"), and takes the same route up to a nearby mountaintop graveyard, where a guy named Jossef is digging a hole to install something to do with "telecommunications" that may or may not be connected to the impending shoot.

The manner in which this information is parceled out—piecemeal, sometimes out of order—is odd to the point of perversity. Behzad introduces himself and his team as "engineers," and you only figure out that he's there to film something, as well as exactly *what* he's there to film, from stray bits of information, asides. Not only do you never see any equipment, you never actually see the crew. At all. You only hear their voices, off in another room or just out of camera range. You never see Jossef, either—you hear his singing, his shoveling, and you see the bone of a human leg that he's dug up flying in the air for Behzad to catch. Kiarostami isolates his hero, as both a figure in a landscape and as a mass of human urgency, wearing out his mammoth brain in a futile effort to make time speed up. Like the Dardenne brothers with *Rosetta*, another recent film that isolates and stays fixed on its protagonist, Kiarostami is trying to establish a sense of moral or metaphysical blindness—in this case born out of a counterfeit modern urban consciousness.

So what we get in *The Wind Will Carry Us*, quite unlike *Taste of Cherry*, is the spiritual passage of someone who doesn't fully comprehend the fact that he's undergoing a spiritual passage until the last minute, after he's permanently alienated Farzad by suddenly blowing up at him, after his crew has deserted him, and after the earth has caved in on Jossef. The insistence of the landscape, both visually (this is without a doubt Kiarostami's most sheerly beautiful film) and aurally, and of the slow speed of lives attuned to nature, finally forces Behzad to "give way," just like the dirt around poor Jossef. It makes very fine poetic sense to spend so much time isolating the long, lanky hero, to leave so much unseen or just out of sight (like the face of Jossef's beloved as she milks a cow in the darkness while Behzad recites the Forough Farrokhzad poem that gives the film its title—the center of the movie). This is the drama of a very plausible urban everyman coming in from outside, dicing up his surroundings, sorting them into a mental grid (the violence of this internal action is imparted through the actor's sharp features and fiercely concentrated stare), and staying locked on an exotic event that had better happen within his narrow time frame.

It's also a magnificent portrait of a place, which is delivered to the viewer via Kiarostami's characteristic repetitions and well-traveled, zigzagging pathways. Some people might be inclined to regard *The Wind Will Carry Us* as a summation, because it contains elements of every other Kiarostami movie. Or as a companion piece to *Taste of Cherry*, offering a ringingly affirmative answer to the grand rhetorical question that the earlier movie left impressively unanswered: to live, or to die? But it does pose a troubling question: is Kiarostami's aesthetic becoming as narrowly defined as Antonioni's was by the mid-1960s, or as Wenders' was by the early 1980s? Because as thrilling as the movie is, it also feels a little too cozily self-contained, comfortably resting on its downy array of sophisticated strategies and eye-filling landscapes.

2000

The alleged "indie" movement, always primed to make "heartfelt gems" rather than masterpieces, now seems to be on its last legs. It's odd to remember that Jim Jarmusch and Rick Linklater, its two most noteworthy originators, are unapologetically artistic types. Of the two, Linklater has always been the more unassuming. Not unlike one of his charming, intelligent, loquacious characters, he wears his artistry lightly. If Jarmusch is the poet of American bitterness, then Linklater is the poet of American freedom, his characters comfortably operating as solitary units or within supportive enclaves of artists and eccentrics, free from alienation and happily giving voice to their theories, obsessions, and impressions.

It's not an uncommon occurrence in film criticism to get the artist mixed up with his/her subjects—just as Scorsese is often confused with his De Niro/Pesci characters, Linklater will probably always be thought of as a charming slacker. In fact, he's a supremely attentive artist, dedicated to the little things: the mood in a coffee shop or a 7-Eleven or the precise manner in which time passes on a long train ride. He also possesses an acute understanding of the endless searching that lies at the heart of every well-examined life. It's easy to miss the undercurrent of tension in Linklater's work, perhaps because it's a form of everyday tension that haunts us all at one time or another, consciously or unconsciously: whether to seize the moment, clarify it, or just live it.

Like a lot of other filmmakers around the globe, Linklater has gone digital, with not one but two new projects. *Tape* is a nervy little chamber piece made on a shoestring for IFC's InDigent project, which sponsors digital moviemaking on B budgets. Based on a funny, perceptive play by Stephen Belber, *Tape*'s action unfolds in real time in one Michigan motel room. On paper, it looks like your average who's-got-the-upper-hand, table-turning three-hander. But Linklater and his cast (Ethan Hawke, Uma Thurman, and the perennially callow Robert Sean Leonard, in his finest role as a pompously self-regarding "nice guy") are unapologetic about the apparent modesty of the enterprise. They bite into the action with gusto and glee, and the geography of the room is cunningly worked for endless spatial inventions and variations. Linklater and his actors keep re-invigorating the action, while the mobile camera executes terse, surprising, and often funny moves up, down, and around the tight little space. It's a modestly scaled but invigorating piece of work.

Where *Tape* is a minor triumph, *Waking Life* might be the most remarkable thing Linklater's ever done. The film is a flowering of dreamlike encounters contained within a series of dreams that become increasingly extended and disturbingly cryptic as the film goes on, just like a night of real REM sleep. They are dreamed by one of Linklater's relaxed, quietly self-questioning heroes, played by *Dazed and Confused*'s Wiley Wiggins. Part of the excitement of *Waking Life* is that it seems to be thinking itself through as it goes along—in other words, not merely a "smart" movie but a movie with a brain of its own. Sometimes it feels like the brain belongs to Wiggins, but his point of view keeps thinning out, expanding and dissolving into the events and landscapes he encounters. Thus the scary question at the heart of *Waking Life*: in the end, how important is the distinction between the world and our perception of it?

There's a novel aspect to *Waking Life* that will doubtlessly overshadow its complexity and subtlety. The film was shot on DV, cut, and then animated by thirty different artists (including Wiggins) under the supervision of Bob Sabiston, who designed the proprietary software animation program used on the project. The look of *Waking Life* has been likened to rotoscoping, but it feels more solid, less amorphous, and yet it moves with greater fluidity. Every shape has real beauty and presence, with objects on multiple planes gently floating and swaying against one another.

The movie opens with a young boy pondering the message "Dream is destiny" written in a girl's cootie catcher (she's played by Linklater's daughter). Later, he gazes up at a shooting star, his enormous eyes hovering away from his small face, then wanders over to a car, and holds fast to the door handle as he closes his eyes and dreamily floats off his feet. He wakes up as a young man, sitting on a train with his head propped against the window (a signature Linklater image). From there, we move through a string of visions and encounters that includes a chamber group rehearsing the stark, properly dizzying tango score for the film itself, a scientist breathlessly elaborating a new paradigm shift in human evolution, a man trumpeting a metaphysical wake-up call over a loudspeaker as he cruises the streets of Austin, and a monkey showing a film collage in a packed basement lecture hall. Each new scene is animated by a different artist, and while the world feels different from moment to moment (and style to style), it also remains eerily the same. Linklater articulates something very delicate here—the way that life seems to keep turning over another page, forever promising that it's bringing us one step closer to ultimate reality.

As all these ideas, inspirations, and pronouncements segue into one another, each one of them reckoned definitive by the person articulating them,

Wiggins keeps trying to wake up (often to dismembered, floating digital numbers on his clock). A subtle form of anxiety starts to build—how much can one consciousness handle? Like previous Linklater movies (*Slacker*, the Proustian *Dazed and Confused*, *Before Sunrise*, even the lovably wayward *The Newton Boys*, the only one of the director's films lacking a time-sensitive structure), *Waking Life* takes a deceptively simple path. On the surface, it may feel repetitive and hopelessly collegiate, a gaggle of eccentrics with big theories about the nature of existence mixing with sociopathic malcontents and inner-journeying slackers. But it's the resounding certainty behind the statements more than their actual content that counts, the poignancy of so much searching, of banking on this or that theory or notion or idea that promises to Explain It All. Meanwhile, time keeps flowing, and Wiggins keeps waking up to another dream. As *Waking Life* moves into its final section, it becomes less playful, more troubling, and more mysterious: the nature of time seems to be urgently imparting itself, through dreaming, to this befuddled young man. When Wiggins follows a suggestion from a character played by Linklater himself to "just . . . wake up," the numbers on the clock are still discombobulated. He winds up back at the house where he began, and the presence of the material world itself suddenly becomes moving—the house seems ineffably sad, like the early-twentieth-century houses that Linda Manz sneaks past in the final moments of *Days of Heaven*, a movie by another phenomenologically-minded Texan. Just as he did with the slow track down an endless road that closed *Dazed and Confused*, the declaration of faith at the end of *Before Sunrise*, or *Slacker*'s final images suspended between chaos and order, Linklater ends *Waking Life* with an image nicely pitched between transcendence and terror.

It's a film that might leave you giddy with its multiplicity of viewpoints and its beautiful freedom. What touches me most about *Waking Life*, and about Linklater's work in general, is its devotion to a particular strain of American experience—the act of talking one's way to nirvana. We're a nation of statement-makers and opinion-holders, but unlike our European cousins we tend to speak in a voice that carries the ring of hesitation, doubt, and humility. Linklater has a feel for that voice, which encompasses mystics, scholars, and sociopaths. He sets it against just the right banal backdrops, in just the right relaxed key. If Tarkovsky had been born in the heartland and raised on Superman and fundamentalism rather than Pasternak and the Orthodox Church, he would have made a movie like *Waking Life*.

2001

The "wunderkind" concept may be what keeps blood pumping through the veins of film critics, but it hasn't exactly done wonders for young directors. Paul Thomas Anderson's *Magnolia* is a maddening, deeply pretentious, impassioned, guileless, sprawling, severely miscalculated movie, as chancy as *Boogie Nights* was safe, as unsettled as that film was smugly content. Over his third movie's three-hours-plus running time, Anderson piles the works on top of the works, over and over again, and crowns every layer with a cherry. About an hour and a half in, following one of the longest passages of sustained musical accompaniment in movie history (by Aimee Mann), the movie achieves a veritable ecstasy of cross-cutting, and its shortcomings become as thought-provoking as its assets. Before it finally burns out its store of self-manufactured fuel and floats off into the ether, *Magnolia* has become a swirling, barely controlled fantasia of juxtaposed emotional predicaments. Far from a great movie but much more impressive than 90 percent of what's now occupying multiplex screens, the movie has no sense of propriety whatsoever. It's the work of a young man who has paradoxically allowed his titanic ego to run amok in the name of the cursed, the maladroit, and the just plain unlucky, pumping up their doubts, fears, and panicky episodes of self-loathing until they assume the form of an epic. It's also the first Anderson film to go beyond the level of wish fulfillment. Unlike *Hard Eight* and *Boogie Nights*, there's more going on here than the spectacle of a youngster projecting himself into a movie-ish netherworld. Of course, it's that, too. No one who's familiar with Altman's phantasmagorical roundelays or Alan Rudolph's lugubrious but soulful (Altman-produced) debut *Welcome to L.A.*, will miss the connection. But *Magnolia* manages its own poetry of desperate, morbid loneliness.

Relentlessly, mercurially, at times haphazardly, at times profitably, *Magnolia* splinters its attention among twelve almost-characters in six tenuously connected high-strung situations during a twenty-four-hour period in the San Fernando Valley. I use the word "almost" because by the time the movie comes to a halt, it's clear that Anderson has never figured out who these people are or exactly what he wants them to do beyond taking part in a cool cinematic tapestry, which poses a big, abstract question: what's it like to be alive and unlucky in urban America on the eve of a new millennium? For 79 anyone who recalls the multiple melodramatic turnabouts of *Boogie Nights*, it will come as no shock that Anderson either abandons his humanoid creations altogether or gives them a standard-issue Emotional Breakthrough. Earl Partridge (Jason Robards), an old, wizened media mogul, is (very believably) wasting away from cancer. He is fretted over by his neurotic young wife Linda (Julianne Moore) and watched round the clock by his live-in nurse Phil Parma (Phillip Seymour Hoffman). After a deliriously muttered entreaty from Earl, Phil goes to a great deal of time and effort to track down his estranged son Frank (Tom Cruise), a nationally renowned motivational speaker who gives training seminars in how to get laid ("Respect . . . the *cock!*"). Jimmy Gator (Phillip Baker Hall), a game show host, is also dying of cancer. He comes apart on live national television at the same moment that his boy genius contestant Stanley (Jeremy Blackman) chooses to buckle down and quit submitting to one more minute of pressure in his already pressurized life. Thus choosing a path of emotional health never taken by Donnie Smith (William H. Macy), the forty-ish failure who introduces himself to strangers as "Quiz Kid Donnie Smith" and whose main claim to fame since his glory days on Jimmy's show is that he's been struck by lightning and lived to tell the tale. There's another estranged child, Jimmy's daughter Claudia (Melora Walters, Don Cheadle's porn partner in *Boogie Nights*). She holes up in her apartment binging on coke and cranking her music up to eleven, which brings Officer Jim Kurring (John C. Reilly) to her door. Who is left to complete this "complex tapestry of human frailty and universal chaos," to quote the eye-popping press kit? The ever-earthy Melinda Dillon as Jimmy's wife, Michael Bowen as Stanley's spineless failed-actor father, Emmanuel Johnson as a little street rapper, Luis Guzman, Felicity Huffman, Altman-ites Michael Murphy and Henry Gibson, Alfred Molina, Eileen Ryan, and Ricky Jay, who doubles as the narrator of the film's arresting, hyperkinetic prologue of loosely linked believe-it-or-nots.

Anderson knows how to create an exciting surface texture—his understanding of the way movies feel is matched by his fuzziness about their infrastructures. So as long as he's in the early stage of his narrative, joyfully throwing down possible scenarios, pathways, and connections between people and events, he's on safe ground. What Anderson basically does in *Magnolia* is use his license as hot-shit filmmaker of the moment to indefinitely prolong his "first act," as Syd Field would say. In other words, the setup is the movie. The air starts to get pretty thin after a while—a filmmaker can postpone the moment of character definition for only so long. To be fair, Anderson does manage to keep his twelve balls spinning in the air for most of his lengthy running time—confidently for the film's first half, frantically throughout its second, and then a plague of frogs comes raining down from the sky. Literally.

But there's a lot of excitement, and even suspense, in that first hour and a half. Anderson withholds vast amounts of information about his characters and keeps them as mysterious as he can for as long as he can while he slowly links them together through their doubts and terrors and through his actors' least wholesome attributes: Macy's rubbery skittishness, Moore's glacial sublimations, Cruise's ugly slickness, Walters's blanketing bathos, Blackman's compliant repression, Hall's suggestion of physical and mental decomposition, Reilly's near-pathological humility, Hoffman's repressive nice-guy veneer. Like *Welcome to L.A.*, *Magnolia* immerses itself in a peculiarly Californian brand of middle-class self-pity, in order to illuminate the individual souls from which it's emanating. But unlike Rudolph's characters, Anderson's creatures aren't given to speechifying. Nor are they mobile. *Magnolia* shuttles between a series of confined, static situations: Phil's death watch over Earl, Frank enduring a painful investigative interview, Donnie sitting on a barstool trying to explain himself and his impossible love for the hunky bartender, Officer Jim making nice with Claudia, the game show nightmare. Only Linda puts in extensive travel time, but she has a series of concrete goals to accomplish: consult with Earl's doctor, attempt to change his will so that she will get nothing, and fill his and her various prescriptions. Once these core dilemmas have climaxed, the film shifts to another set of confined cell-like dramas. What gives with all this immobility in a movie set in a land where cars reign supreme? Sometimes it seems intentional, and sometimes it seems like the last-ditch strategy of an overwhelmed novice.

One could make the argument that this is, after all, a movie about emotional paralysis. But Anderson has no interest in anything as mundane as a regular old form/content match-up. In a very real sense, *Magnolia* is the work of a director who is trying to sort out his feelings about cinema, himself, and the moment in which he lives, which become so hopelessly tangled that he ends up leaving his characters and his audience out in the cold. He doesn't even take the time to confirm the significance of his title—only eagle-eyed viewers will spot the street sign for Magnolia, which is where the frog torrent begins. And he never really links those raining frogs to the rest of the movie, except in the most general sense imaginable—there's no moral, psychological, or thematic resonance to one of the most whacked out episodes in recent American cinema. But then this is a movie that's at its best precisely when it's at its most careless and self-indulgent, luxuriating in its ability to cultivate mysteries and suggest endless possibilities before, behind, and beyond every action and every encounter.

It's as ravenous for time as 2001 was for space. Anderson stretches, slows, reconfigures, and often stops time altogether and recognizes no structural limitations. Sometimes the different cells of action run parallel to one another; sometimes they run sequentially. And all kinds of unsettling characterological red herrings are thrown out at the viewer. Jim seems like a decent guy who prays to the crucifix hanging over his bed, but he's also one of those "nice, quiet" types who turn out to be serial killers. Linda suggests a modern, ice-cold variant of the gold digger, and everything she's doing may be an act. Most disturbingly of all, when Phil calls the grocery store and orders porno mags, you really have to wonder what he's going to do with them (especially if you remember Hoffman's character in *Happiness*)—jerk off over Earl's dying body? The postponement of knowledge and the undefined synchronicity of the cross-cutting, unified by Mann's semibombastic music and a nicely placid, settled camera eye, erects a very odd aesthetic space. What *really* unites these people? It could be anything, but it could just as easily be nothing at all. You need lots of room to develop the terror of entropy and lots of chutzpah as well, and Anderson has plenty of both.

When Hoffman finally explains his purpose (he's purchased the porno mags so he can track down Frank), when Jim turns out to be a genuinely decent guy after all, and when Jimmy and Stanley simultaneously renounce the pressures that are killing them, it's genuinely cathartic. It seems that Anderson has been ratcheting up the anxiety in order to show us how large it looms in people's lives, in turn revealing how quickly it disappears in the face of genuine kindness, courage, and honesty. Too bad the epiphany comes at the halfway mark, after which the dread starts building up again to far lesser effect.

When all is said and done, as in the first two movies, the most lasting source of sustenance here is the acting. Macy's Donnie Smith is the gaudiest ornament on the tree, a terminally unstable neurotic child-man short-circuited between superiority and longing, and he gets some good, Mametish dialogue duels with a Quentin Crispesque Henry Gibson. There's a creepy feeling of simultaneity between Cruise's perceived narcissism as an actor and his character. There's nothing terribly original about Frank, but Cruise's terminal narcissism for once finds the right fit: this foul-mouthed king of male sexual actualization feeds off the actor's self regard and in turn gives Cruise a charge he never gets from his more bankable projects. Hall and

Reilly have always been Anderson's aces in the hole, and his devotion to them is by far the most touching thing about the first two movies (actually, Anderson has a real feeling for second bananas in general: he should think about filming the life of Bud Abbott). Once again, Hall carries the aura of a lost 1960s TV icon who never existed: a weary, tired angel of regret in a trench coat, a squarish haircut, with a clipped, croaking voice. While Jimmy may not be as rich a character as *Hard Eight*'s Sidney, he's also less of a *noir* wish fulfillment, and the pain that he's feeling is more genuine. Reilly is pegged with a stale idea—the decent cop overwhelmed by the moral chaos of the world—but he's never been better. His behavior as he watches his flashier fellow officers soak up the media attention at a crime scene or as he uselessly assumes the moral high ground with a street-educated kid are extraordinarily subtle: he makes a little show of how dutifully he withdraws, as though his good will and faith in God will win him points in heaven. Reilly, Hall, Macy, and Hoffman, as well as the lesser actors like Cruise, Moore, and Walters, get something in *Magnolia* that Anderson has never given his beloved actors before: time to stretch out.

Magnolia is finally a big, self-important, overreaching, but fundamentally sweet movie that fancies itself a major achievement by a young director who's probably read one too many Don DeLillo novels. Fortunately, there's still plenty of time for Anderson to understand that in order to transcend the stale dramatic formulas that are killing Hollywood, you have to actually understand them.

2000

"You've got history to burn here," says a real estate developer in John Sayles's *Sunshine State*. The image is literalized at the beginning of the film, when a replica of a pirate ship with the too-clean look of a manufactured symbol is set ablaze by an impassive teenage firebug named Terrell (Alexander Lewis). Sayles is very incisive here on the way history is used as a tool to boost commerce. And he begins with this placid orphaned boy, himself a victim of an economic downturn in his community, fighting fire with fire. The phony pirate ship, a marketing tool that represents a romantically enhanced past, symbolizes everything that has made his own life so miserable.

History is everywhere in *Sunshine State*, but it has no solidity, no reliability, and it comes with no guarantees of stability. Everyone in the film is believably oppressed by the floating rootlessness of capitalism as a way of life. They're obliged to live beneath a bland aura of hope amidst an endless cycle of exhaustion and renewal, gleeful forgetting and soulful remembering, disintegration and preservation. You can feel it in the way Francine Pickney (Mary Steenbergen) carries herself as she chairs a dispirited five-day non-event called Buccaneer Days, intended to generate civic pride in the malled, consumerized town of Delrona Beach, Florida. Or in the quiet guardedness of Eunice Stokes (Mary Alice), Terrell's great aunt and caretaker and an inhabitant of neighboring Lincoln Beach. A proud African-American stronghold during the Jim Crow era, Lincoln Beach is now an impoverished community fighting off the twin assaults of predatory buyouts and eminent domain. Delrona has the economy but no connective tissue, whereas Lincoln is nothing but connective tissue, aging with its inhabitants to a papery thinness.

Sayles will probably always be a little too rhetorical as a filmmaker, and you can always feel his characters' origins on the printed page. But in this film, just as in *City of Hope*—his first stab at a multicharacter portrait of a community in a state of spiritual emergency, the richest vein in his work—his customary stolidity and the way that his characters seem to start all over again with each new scene are all but dwarfed by the breadth of his thinking and the pointedness of his attack. What is he attacking in *Sunshine State*? Namely, a very, very bad American idea, which is the equation of capitalism with reality. For anyone who still has the memory of that idiotic moment in

Godard's *In Praise of Love* when someone observes that "Americans have no past of their own so they buy the pasts of others," Sayles has a stinging comeback. He knows the way things work here on a region-by-region basis, down to the smallest details. And he counters all the hazy generalizing about American life, whether it's done by William Safire, Thomas L. Friedman, Michael Moore, or Jean-Luc Godard, with patiently observed and formulated specifics—always the most effective political tool. It's not that we lack a past, but that we use it so thoughtlessly, forever mining it and melting it down to a malleable substance—the process known as "Disneyfication."

In *Lone Star*, a group of friends agree to forget the past in order to build a workable future. "Forget the Alamo," is the last line of that movie, and it's offered as a radical break with rancid tradition. But *Lone Star* was about a different place with a different problem. In *Sunshine State*, racism has been folded into rampant, unbridled capitalism, just another step on the march of progress. There's a very good exchange early in the film—the first of many—in which "Hurricane" Desiree (Angela Bassett), returning home for the first time in fifteen years after a notorious departure and with a brand new northern husband (James McDaniel) in tow, pulls into a local restaurant to use the bathroom before an anxious reunion with Eunice, her mother. Her husband waits for her in the lobby, with visions of Bull Connor and the KKK galloping through his head. But he gets nothing more than a polite nod from the owner Marly Temple (Edie Falco) as she heads out the door to attack the real enemy, a landscape artist employed by real estate developers (Timothy Hutton) who's mentally reconfiguring an already overdeveloped beachfront. At this stage of the game, we're all in it together, trying to hold on to our pasts and at the same time trying not to let them weigh too heavily on the burdensome present.

As *Sunshine State* proceeds, the throughline between slavery, Jim Crow, and New South economics comes into clearer focus, and the film becomes the fictional counterpart of Stephanie Black's agitprop *Life + Debt*. Lincoln Beach is a community built on the solidarity of resistance to institutionalized racism that has lost all its economic muscle in the era of political reform, leaving its inhabitants to spend most of their time trying to stay afloat and not get sucked into the free market undertow. Most of the historical background information about the community is spoken by Dr. Lloyd (Bill Cobbs), its weary yet stoic self-appointed leader and the only man with the energy or inclination to fight off yet another tag-team effort by Exley Plantations Inc. and the Delrona Beach city council to appropriate yet another stretch of Lincoln for luxury housing. Dr. Lloyd is one of a number of characters who deliver historical soliloquies to semi-interested listeners or, in the case of Ralph Waite's blind patriarch or the Shakespearean chorus of golf-playing tycoons led by Alan King, to thin air. Again, while the rhetoric gets mighty lofty and the ideas often overshadow the action, the accuracy of Sayles's social observation and the way he grounds it in daily experience tips the balance in his favor.

For instance, Terrell is a mite too self-contained, more of a figure than a character. The way he shadows Desiree's situation (she's left her hometown as a shamed pregnant teenager, miscarried, and left unable to have children) is too neat by far. But the idea of a lost child floating in a tradition-free zone, with people all around him trying to invent "support systems," is very powerful. Sayles will never be a great director, but he understands the value of mise-en-scène, and there are great beauties in Sunshine State (for instance, the dissolve from an overcast sky to a blue one that marks the film's first passage from the strictly poetic space inhabited by King and his golf buddies to the real-life space of the action proper). But the best moments, the zingers that go straight to the heart of the matter, are spoken. "He's good with a saw and a hammer," says Desiree's husband, who's been asked to assume the role of male authority in Terrell's life. "If this were 1925, he'd have a future." Later, in what has to be the saddest moment in an already very sad movie, Desiree and her mother are having a last, tense heart-to-heart. Eunice, once a terrific cook, is reheating some Popeye's chicken in the microwave. Opportunity has come knocking in the form of Flash Phillips (Tom Wright), the former college all-star running back once known as the Florida Flash, who is buying up property to "revitalize" the community. Desiree tells her mother that if she sells the house after Eunice is gone, she'll make sure Terrell gets some of the money. "Money isn't what Terrell needs," says Eunice. It's an eloquent complaint and a hidden plea, not to Desiree but to time itself, to turn back and re-form the bonds that once held everyone together.

In a way, the central characters played by Bassett and Falco, who cross paths only once, are the least compelling in the film. Both Desiree and Marly are far too saddled down with complications and emotional baggage (perhaps Sayles's biggest shortcoming as a filmmaker is his temperamental inability to let his actors breathe the backstory into their characters—he always feels driven to construct personal dilemmas that underscore the overarching social dilemma). But the actresses find ingenious ways of working with their cumbersome narrative enhancements. Bassett and Falco are both overflowing with life—they're strongly, almost harrowingly physical presences (with real, lived-in physiques) who can ring some juice out of the dryest scenes. In a way, they seem a little too grounded to play such troubled, flighty characters, but they also give the film a real punch that it would have lacked if, say, Jennifer Jason Leigh and Halle Berry had played the roles. Falco in particular has a heartbreaking moment when she admits to her dad (Waite) that she can't run the family business any longer and needs to sell out. But it's the second-tier characters and the actors who play them who really charge the action. Wright's Florida Flash is perfect, a huckster trading on his former glory: every time he receives a compliment, you can see the faintest tinge of embarrassment and self-loathing color his smiling face, and you really get a sense of the effort behind his "self-confidence." Jane Alexander has a role that fits her like a glove—a hammy community theater matron and earth mother–type who's mounting a play based on *As I Lay Dying*. But the best character in the film, and the best performance, belongs to the indomitable Steenburgen, who, along with Sissy Spacek, is one of American cinema's greatest natural resources (her *In the Bedroom* is long overdue). "People don't understand how hard it is to invent a tradition," she says, and you can see her coming undone trying to accomplish this ridiculous task in the film's finest moment: Sayles simply rests the camera on Steenburgen's face during an onstage portion of the ahistorical historical celebration, working up a smile whenever she's on mike, only to let it dissolve into delicately shaded disappointment when she's off.

These are the things that Sayles does better than anyone else in American cinema—the tawdry inventions of city governments trying to jazz up their economies, the strange unreality of leisure developments and their fabricated "natural beauty," and the sadly transitory lives of the guys who operate the heavy machinery for the developers and go from place to place stripping landscapes of their individuality. For anyone who grew up in a failing American small town, *Sunshine State* will carry the ring of truth. The finest thing about the film is its slow, enervated, humidity-induced pace of life. It's the rhythm of the American South, at least as I've encountered it, and every realization, every conflict, every melancholy reflection, and every expression of anger, resentment, or love is set to that rhythm. Most filmmakers set their pace according to more abstract notions, but Sayles knows that climate is crucial. It gives *Sunshine State* a depth that none of his previous work, not even *City of Hope* or *Lone Star*, has had. It also puts the film in a class with Satyajit Ray's *The Chess Players*, where historical tragedy unfolds at a similarly leisurely trot. Only at the end of *Sunshine State*, history gets its revenge. As it always will.

Some American Comedies

Celebrity, Woody Allen's 368th film in thirty-five years, is his pocket-sized re-make of *La Dolce Vita*, just as *Stardust Memories* was his pocket-sized *8 1/2*, *An-other Woman* his pocket-sized *Wild Strawberries* (or maybe *Deconstructing Harry* was the pocket-size and *Another Woman* the discount knockoff), *A Midsummer Night's Sex Comedy* (his worst title) his Xeroxed *Smiles of a Summer Night*, and *Hannah and Her Sisters* his paint-by-numbers *Three Sisters*. I know that at this point in his career I am supposed to be cherishing Allen, respecting his in-tegrity as an artist and realizing that he is, after all, a national treasure. The world would certainly be a poorer place without him, but the level of self-satisfaction running through his work and the fact that he settles on filmic elements the way one might plan a birthday party or an outing in the coun-try (or, in Allen's case, an outing across the street), is unusually high for such a "major artist." David Thomson once accused Rohmer of moral com-placency, and while the point is debatable, it's certain that Rohmer would never dream of sending up such a pretentious skyrocket of cultural distress as *Celebrity*.

Nor would he ever make a film with such a polite relationship between the camera and its subjects. *Celebrity* was photographed by Sven Nykvist, an infrequent collaborator of Allen's (Woody recently terminated his long-term relationships with cinematographer Carlo di Palma and editor Sandy Morse—this is her last Allen film). In this loosely knit, God's-eye-view of the "modern fascination with celebrity," Nykvist makes every pore in every face come alive, only to have his director embalm said faces in a deliberately shallow, glaring, black-and-white image that appears to have been lit by flash-bulbs popping behind a layer of Plexiglas. This is one of those Allen films where the director takes a set of one-note elements and shoves them into a storyline rooted in questionable clichés, in this case about celebrity worship (the soullessness of fame and the lust for it, the callousness that accompa-nies fame once you've acquired it). *Celebrity*, which maintains a punishing pace, has a deceptively loose-knit structure that moves from one lengthy scene to the next as it illustrates its central point, with the alternately de-scendant and ascendant journeys of a former husband and wife on the ladder of fame as its structuring device. Each scene swarms with semi-believable activity, and the film's strangely benumbed tone is set by its central performance. In the best of all possible worlds, Kenneth Branagh's performance as a frantically ambitious journalist would defy description. Unfortunately, it can be described as a hair-raisingly accurate Woody Allen imitation.

Plenty of other actors have fallen into Allen's vocal rhythms, hunched gesturing, and impulsive, darting lateral movements. His practice of writing flat dialogue and then having his actors step on one another's lines has brought everyone from Michael Caine to Edward Norton into his nebbishy orbit, but Branagh's performance soars beyond any previous Woodspawn and touches down in the pathological. I've heard varying explanations of why this occurred: (a) Woody Allen didn't like it but somehow tolerated it (unlikely), (b) it just came naturally to Branagh because there is no other way to play Allen's dialogue (perhaps), and (c) Allen and Branagh were both hit on the head with bricks and made the decision once they regained consciousness. In fact, someone once told me a story about John Cusack's experience on *Bullets Over Broadway* that explains everything. Cusack was trying out a variety of approaches to his character, none of which pleased Allen, until he started to play the role like . . . Woody Allen. At which point, Allen exclaimed, "Perfect! That's it! You've got it!" Given the fact that Branagh's face is starting to widen into Albert Finney–ish beefiness and since American accents have always had the curious effect of thinning out his acting, the choice is a provocative one. Like so much else in this quizzical little white elephant of a movie, it is nothing but provocative.

Judy Davis puts some tension into the film with her trademark brittleness, Joe Mantegna manages to inject a little warmth, and the final twenty minutes of *Celebrity* get very close to the tone of pure melancholic misanthropy Allen has been cultivating for years but never quite pulled off. Yet compared to the bracing self-observation of *Husbands and Wives* and the delight of *Manhattan Murder Mystery*, *Celebrity* is paltry stuff. Further self-observation will most likely be feigned rather than actual, as in last year's *Deconstructing Harry*.

Allen's influence has been enormous. The tradition of comic films composed of skits organized around a single mood or attitude, or around one person and his relationship to the world, is his creation. Moreover, between Allen and *Saturday Night Live*, the sketch structure has all but overtaken comic filmmaking. One need only consider Todd Solondz's new and already extravagantly praised *Happiness* to see Allen's influence in full flower. Actually, Solondz began his career with a film that he would apparently like to forget but into which he seems to have put a lot of himself. In *Fear, Anxiety* and *Depression*, the director himself played the starring role of a nebbishy young writer, insensitive to the needs of others, and neurotically fixated on his own artistic dilemmas. Luckily for the moviegoing audience, the film was met with indifference and another young auteur was forced to rethink his aesthetic approach. Which led to a furnace blast of adolescent humiliation called *Welcome to the Dollhouse*. In that film, Solondz had the novel and quite-arresting idea of making his onscreen alter ego a thirteen-year old girl played by Heather Matarazzo. Somehow, by taking the humiliation and cruelty that he seemed to know so well, setting it in the placid, overengineered world of suburban New Jersey in which he grew up, and imaginatively projecting said humiliation and cruelty onto a female adolescent, Solondz created a uniquely haunting spectacle of middle-class cruelty.

In *Happiness*, a succession of scenes of variable quality each follows the same plan: a dominant tone of "happiness," meaning the fragile, illusory feeling of limitless gentility in TV sitcoms and pop songs, is "undercut" by the suppressed desires and emotions lurking beneath the surface. This already felt old to me in *Blue Velvet*, but *Blue Velvet* was by a great filmmaker. Imagine a graduate film class in which the students are shown the sequence near the beginning of Lynch's movie in which a healthy suburban lawn is revealed to be teeming with bug life. Imagine that the students are given the task of making their own film based on said sequence. And finally, imagine that a nerdy kid at the back of the class with lots of comic promise but little visual talent turns in a 135-minute-long opus called *Happiness*. Some sequences are very funny, some that are meant to be funny are not, some that are not meant to be very funny are merely quizzical, and some are skillfully engineered but still merely quizzical.

The action is centered on three sisters, from whom the rest of the characters appear to grow like branches on a tree of misery: parents, next-door neighbors, husbands and kids, and suitors. In truth, there is just one story. The husband of the most contented of the sisters, a quiet and eminently reasonable psychiatrist played by Dylan Baker, is a pedophile. We watch him as he listens inattentively to one of his patients, and then we become privy to his fantasy of walking into a park and spraying bullets from an automatic at the passers-by (he zeroes in on a gay couple). We see him furiously masturbating in the back of his car to the image of a male teen pop idol, counseling his son through his adolescent anxiety about ejaculation, drugging his entire family and his son's friend with sleeping pills (he rapes the friend offscreen), and hopping in his car to rape another boy (also offscreen). After he is found out, his son asks him what he did to his friends. "I fucked them."

"Would you ever fuck me?" asks the son, tears rolling down his cheeks. "No," says the father, now crying too, "I'd jerk off instead." More tears.

Other episodes: a phone sex interlude climaxing with a load of cum decorating a wall, the suicide of a spurned lover, unfeeling sex between two middle-aged specimens, a confession of murder and dismemberment, extra helpings of disgust with men, hidden insecurity, hidden envy, and—you guessed it—self-loathing. In other words, every currently hot American media obsession rolled into one film, a slow comedy of discomfort artfully pitched between ambiguity and arrogant craftiness. *Happiness* is a morally indecisive film that "dares" its audience to react any which way. Solondz shifts gears from laughter to horror and then back again throughout the entire film. This is supposed to be impressive, but why? Why cook up such a deliberately cold, conceptually pretty meal of repression and superiority masked as kindness? It's revelatory that the character and actress in whom Solondz seems most interested (Joy, played by Jane Adams) is never really given her full due, that another character (the mother, played by Louise Lasser, of *Mary Hartman* fame and former wife of Woody Allen) is thrown into the mix and subsequently dropped, and that the character of the pedophile, the one with the most sensational problem, is followed so attentively. Beyond Solondz's naked desire to cement himself as an auteur/personality lies the curious fact that, for a movie whose time is so taken up with allegedly daring subject matter, *Happiness* feels so ordinary. The boring American obsession with serial killers, the banality of evil, the horrors lurking beneath the surface of life, are of a piece with the idea of America as a land of plenty, of endless variety and mystery, so endless, in fact, that even our collective unconscious is teeming with the most dramatic uprisings, the dankest evils, the most grotesque behaviors, the most deadening banality. As always, we're number one! In fact, it's not at all difficult to imagine the supposedly transgressive *Happiness* ending with its characters gathering around a kitchen table and singing "God Bless America," as in the similarly provocative but slightly less pretentious *Deer Hunter*.

The Farrelly brothers' *There's Something About Mary* is like an antidote to Solondz's film. *Mary* has no pretensions whatsoever but a far more nuanced sense of what it is to be a loser (not to mention a much funnier cum gag). The severity of the filmmaking in *Happiness* represents a strenuous effort to postpone moral reckoning, while the cultivated sloppiness of *There's Something About Mary* signals a winning eagerness to involve its viewers in an infectious, liberating round of taboo breaking. Where Solondz posits an imaginary viewer who will regard the pitiful lives of his characters with the proper amount of disdainful sympathy (or sympathetic disdain), Bobby and Peter Farrelly's affectionate humor is directed at everyone and finally insults no one because it imagines its audience in the broadest possible terms. Everyone on every side of *Mary*—audience, characters, filmmakers—is equally vulgar, while *Happiness* is conceived according to some kind of tortured hierarchy.

The aristocracy of aesthetic and moral knowledge implied in *Happiness* is an object of scorn in John Waters's *Pecker*. More than one person has noted that Waters has been superseded and outdone in the last few years by the Farrelly brothers, his heterosexual disciples and inheritors, and they may well be the superior filmmakers. *Pecker* is a very modest film, but it has a terrific affection for the people of Waters's eternal Baltimore. A sweet kid named Pecker (Edward Furlong) who spends his life photographing the inhabitants of his home town is suddenly "discovered" by a Soho art dealer (Lili Taylor) and automatically taken for an ironist ("He's like a humane Diane Arbus"). In the film's final scene, after Pecker has renounced the art world and decided to devote himself to his home town by opening a club with his ill-gotten gains, there's an infectious scene in which the art world snobs and the Baltimore locals dance away their differences, and someone makes a toast to "the end of irony." It's an offhandedly moving moment, particularly if experienced in such close proximity to *Happiness*. Irony will never die, thank God, but the form of ironic distance peculiar to this moment, pioneered by Woody Allen, updated by Jerry Seinfeld, and ratcheted up to delirious levels by Todd Solondz, already feels old, decrepit, and as gruesomely unhealthy as a Charles Dickens orphanage.

1998

The question of violence and its representation in movies is a kind of ideo-logical parade float, so big that it obscures everything else in sight, towed down the boulevard every so often for no apparent purpose. Even the most elevated and morally engaged responses, like Jacques Rivette's famous con-demnation of an innocuous pan across the electrified fence in Pontecorvo's *Kapo*, amount to all-or-nothing propositions. One wrong move, and your film has been disqualified from serious consideration on moral grounds. Questions of what can and cannot be represented in the cinema are eternally relevant, but they almost always lead those asking the questions down a blind alley, not to mention a stunted form of critical thinking. When I was young, the complaint that a film or filmmaker had "glorified violence" was often heard, as was the similar, if not identical, complaint that the violence in a given film was "violence for violence' sake" (a mouthful, thus not heard quite as often). Similarly, one became used to such condemnations as "psycho-logical," "sentimental," "sexist," "racist," "manipulative," or that old chest-nut, "fascist." Such words were, and occasionally still are, carelessly thrown into the stew and just as carelessly ingested as a kind of low-calorie substi-tute for actual thought. Cinema studies students, born-again Christians, and aspiring politicians employ them with equal abandon.

I don't mean to imply that racism or sexism or even fascism have never existed in the cinema or that filmmakers have never exploited the emotions of their customers. What I'm getting at is the way that moviegoers on all sides of the political divide fall so easily into the role of moral watchdog, no matter what their political affiliation. There are the Michael Medveds of this world, and there are the Jean-Marie Straubs. And if Straub gets the benefit of the doubt because (a) he's a great artist and (b) he doesn't have a silly moustache, I think he's just as tone-deaf to the intricacies of moviewatching, and thus moviemaking—when the movie is made by someone other than himself and his wife, that is.

If we are exposed to, say, *Mystic River*, and if we "fall" for it, then we will emerge that much more debased and unenlightened, deeper in the haze of moral relativism. Meanwhile, our time would have been better spent watch-ing *Au Hasard, Balthazar* (the Straub imperative), or *Seabiscuit* (the Medved im-perative). The reactionary European leftist and the reactionary North American conservative share the same core belief: that the road to perdition is paved with morally unaccountable movies, which offer an imperfect, unfinished, or skewed (consciously or not) vision of the world. Moreover, there's another more insidious idea buried within such judgment-based criticism: that it is not "we" who will be debased by the likes of *Mystic River*, since we have our intellects to protect us; rather, it is "they," the viewers, on whose behalf such watchdogging is undertaken, but who are actually being condescended to, since it's implied that they can't watch and judge for themselves.

Let us say goodbye to Mr. Medved and M. Straub (and to Armond White, in whose criticism these two extremes are improbably united), and have a chat with M. Godard. Some years ago, perhaps ten, Godard did a television broadcast in which he addressed the topic of filming war. He offered us newsreel footage, and, in contrast, a few sequences from *Full Metal Jacket*—war as filmed by a great director. Anyone familiar with Godard and his recent preoccupations will correctly guess that Kubrick came out on the losing end. It's been years since I've seen the program, and I don't recall all the particulars of Godard's argument as clearly as I'd like. If I remember correctly, it all boils down to this assertion: that the proximity Kubrick offers us with his slow motion and squibs and reconstruction of Hue in a deserted London gasworks can only be a false proximity. From there, a hop, skip, and a jump to Deleuze's false consciousness.

The idea being that the creation and placement of every image, and the corresponding act of receiving those images, is a moment of truth. Ideally, every image must exist at a proper moral distance from its viewer without promising a form of communion or revelation that can never be. Noble? Perhaps. Not to mention untenable, since it presupposes a moral hierarchy, a pyramid construction with Bresson or Rouch lonely at the top and Michael Winner and J. Lee Thompson crawling around the bottom. And on some level, it also presupposes that, since it promises what it can never deliver, *Full Metal Jacket* is a cheat, an impressive but fundamentally worthless object. That some of us may find some worth in the film—that we might apprehend its fiction in a spirit of curiosity rather than unqualified awe, that we might imagine it in conversation with all the other films we've seen and books we've read and thoughts we'd formulated about war, never enters into the dialogue.

And now on to Cronenberg. Whose new film, *A History of Violence*, is indeed "a movie that could drive you crazy," as Jim Hoberman put it in his *Voice* appreciation—Straub, Medved, Godard, my mother, whoever. It looks and even behaves like a fairly satisfying revenge melodrama, featuring that old western standard, the retired gunslinger who breaks his promise to himself and avenges himself against past demons who have returned to plague him and his loved ones. It even features two quick, remarkable special effects shots that wouldn't be out of place in, say, *Van Helsing*, not to mention an early Cronenberg movie: anatomically detailed close-ups of two faces, one half blown off and the other smashed in so far that it resembles a Francis Bacon painting. If someone were to approach me in outrage and inform me that Cronenberg had "glorified" violence, I'm not so sure that I could find reasonable grounds on which to disagree. Come to think of it, I'm not at all sure that he even "condemns" or "critiques" violence." Most damningly of all, he not only refuses to deny the satisfaction of violence, but actually makes such satisfaction a focal point. It's as if Cronenberg were saying, "See how much this movie looks like other movies you know, and how much it doesn't, and then see where the difference leads." Cronenberg is not showing us an excess of violence in order to appreciate its essential ridiculousness (De Palma's *Scarface*) or rubbing our noses in its spectacle as proof of how desensitized we've become (*Irreversible*, *Funny Games*). These all seem to me losing or at best ineffectual strategies, variations of that old standby: shock value—always heavily dependent on the surrounding context, of which the shock element quickly (if not instantly) becomes a constituent part. Rather, he is telling us, quite reasonably, that violence is an all-too-human response, and that we would do better to understand it as such rather than waste our time condemning it or denying its satisfactions. Clint Eastwood is probably the only other modern filmmaker who has gone as deeply into the question of violence as such, and to his clarity and seriousness of purpose we can now add Cronenberg's. Watching *A History of Violence* is, for me at least, like stepping out into the sunshine after a month of rain, and seeing the world from a fresh perspective. As in Eastwood's films, this clarity is forceful and moving in and of itself.

I was surprised when I realized that many of my friends in Cannes were underwhelmed by the movie, which I take to be one of Cronenberg's greatest. On second viewing, *A History of Violence* seemed that much greater, but I began to understand the divergent reactions. If one dismantles Cronenberg's construction, almost an automatic operation in film criticism, it does indeed look suspect: the heavy dose of Americana in the opening section, accentuated by Howard Shore's surging score; the high school bully who drives the hero's intelligent, sensitive son to strike back; the wife who takes her husband out for the night so that they can "be teenagers together"; the comedy around the film's violence and its fallout; the hero returning to hearth and home.

Let's look at these components one by one. The Americana is indeed laid on thick in the film's opening half-hour. There are crane shots of sprawling vistas and vast corn fields straight out of Delmer Daves at his crane-happiest; placid exchanges and hearty bonhomie among the contented townsfolk (one character takes his leave with the exclamation "See you in church"); the standard iconographical rundown familiar from countless films and TV shows, in both its pure version and its ironic mirror image—the town diner (run by Viggo Mortensen's hero, Tom Stall, aka Crazy Joey Cusack), the high school, the baseball field, the sprawling backyard garlanded by brilliantly colored autumn leaves, the family at the dinner table, and so on. Some people I talked to found this objectionable on its own or perhaps a little tired after *Twin Peaks*, *American Beauty*, et al. The assumption being that everyone who does Americana is playing the same game, i.e., rolling out the Norman Rockwell surface in order to expose the tensions and savagery lurking beneath. But is this really what Cronenberg is up to? First of all, the aforementioned items are not dwelled on as much as ticked off. In fact, the all-American atmosphere doesn't even begin to resonate the way it does in *The Dead Zone*. I would say that Cronenberg is more concerned with showing us a "happy family" that happens to live in North America and then filling in the details accordingly.

Then there's the high school bully, a ubiquitous presence in American movies, from *Christine* to *A Christmas Story* to *Spider-Man*. Cronenberg gives us the standard locker room confrontations: Tom/Joey's son Jack (Aston Holmes) placates and publicly deflates his opponent the first time, then reaches the end of his tether and beats the shit out of him. In between these two contretemps, we also get the bully spotting the wimp outside on a Saturday night as he cruises Main Street in his car. At which point he almost runs afoul of two genuinely menacing guys, then drives off in the other direction. A hierarchy of violence is established, and the bully is nowhere near the top.

Then there's Maria Bello's blond-haired, blue-eyed wife Edie, who begins the film in a state of serenity and who slowly realizes that her husband is not who she thought he was. We know this scenario from countless films—*Suspicion*, *The Stranger*, *Conspirator*, *True Lies*. The difference lies in the behavioral particulars. The exchanges between Bello and Mortensen, with and without the kids around, are the heart of the movie, and they are remarkably subtle. There are two sex scenes, one before Joey Cusack has been unmasked, the other after the fact. The adoring wife of eighteen years kidnapping her husband for the night and concocting a naughty-teenager scenario to liven up their marriage is another old standby, and here we have all the usual ingredients: the wife coming on like another woman ("No wives here, mister") in a cheerleader's uniform ("Shh—my parents are in the next room"), the husband exclaiming in wonder at his spouse's transformation, and his surprise when she goes down on him. Two elements give this scene its strange undertone. First of all, there is something studied in Mortensen's reactions, as if he'd practiced them in his head. Every move, every gee-wiz exclamation, is letter perfect but betrayed by the slightest lack of spontaneity—a constant in the performance that becomes increasingly relevant as the film goes along, and this scene is where it becomes noticeable for the first time. After she goes down on him, he reciprocates, and she curls into the sixty-nine position. Apart from the fact that this configuration is rarely employed in American movies, there's a kind of instinctive animal quality to her movements that trumps the sense of intimacy: it's as she were burrowing into him. A striking visual detail: Bello straddling her leg around Mortensen's neck, less titillating than arresting, and borderline disturbing.

This move is repeated during the second, far more brutal sexual encounter on the stairs. Bello now realizes that Tom and Joey are one in the same, and she avoids him. He grabs her; she pulls away. He slaps her down. She runs up the stairs. He grabs her again, she hits him, and he gets on top of her. We think we're going to see a rape—violent Joey Cusack coming back in full fury. Instead, they do what many couples do when things become too complicated to even formulate, let alone put into words: they have sex. It is neither good sex nor bad sex. It is reciprocally aggressive and reciprocally passionate, and at its peak moment, she curls her leg around him just as she does in the earlier scene. After they've both come, she pushes him away and heads upstairs. What seems like a decisive moment or a turning point is instead a strange kind of déjà-vu for the Bello character, a prolongation of her love for Tom but also an acknowledgement of Joey, a rejection and an embrace at the same time. This after she's confronted the town sheriff head-on and instinctively proclaimed her husband to be Tom Stall Family Man, long after she knows better, and just before she wanders out of the bedroom in her robe, which opens as she walks toward Tom. Another aggressive vision, this time casually so, not a come on but a kind of fascinating animal provocation: I'm your wife, you've fucked me over, and you're going to look at me! What director has ever been better at finding the animal in the human, within the confines of ordinary gestures and behavior? The final, striking detail, that almost anyone else would have left out: a glimpse of the bruises left on Bello's back from the stairway encounter.

Then there's the comedy. *A History of Violence* is comic throughout—dryly so. So dry, in fact, that it's possible to experience the film in a number of ways: as a pale Coen brothers retread (in which the comedy is drawn from a heightened, tightly ordered vision of everyday life, in which almost everyone is seen as a grotesque) or as an ever-so-slightly skewed variation of the light humor that now seems to be the exclusive property of cable TV juggernauts like *Six Feet Under* or *The Sopranos*, in which the assorted elements of a "typical" household, every sociological element locked firmly in place and on display, is thrown into relief by one discordant element—a paterfamilias who happens to be a mob kingpin or a family-run funeral home (the strategy probably originated with the *Godfather* films). One could just as easily experience *A History of Violence* as a straight drama—Cronenberg's comic sensibility is *so* subtle that for some, even among the admiring, it may not even register as such. At this point I'm obliged to bring up what has already become a Cannes legend. About a third of the way through the press screening, during a moment when many of us were laughing with rather than at the film—the scene in which Edie questions Tom/Joey about the particulars of his twenty-year deception ("And what about our *name?* Oh, Jesus . . .")—a certain European film critic screamed at the top of his lungs: "Can't you fucking piece-of-shit critics start taking this fucking movie *seriously?*" I bring up this incident not to shame my friend, who is already embarrassed enough as it is, but to point out the intricacy of Cronenberg's conception and execution. Simply put, it plays funny *and* it plays serious—your choice. Cronenberg sticks very close to the standard narrative of the retired gunslinger, and he actually changes very little. But given his own predilections (a biological, as opposed to a sociological, psychological, or metaphysical vision of existence), I suspect that he finds the narrative itself inherently absurd. In other words, the comedy is built in rather than applied from without, which is why I can't find fault with my European friend's outraged reaction. The strength of *A History of Violence* lies in its lucid understanding of its hero's core delusion: that he has successfully made himself over into a completely different human being. It's enough to make you laugh. Or cry. Or both.

The Coen brothers comparison, which more than one critic suggested, doesn't hold water. Nowhere in the film are we forced to contemplate the grotesquerie of everyday life: there's nothing here on the order of George Clooney's dental work in *Intolerable Cruelty*, Tim Robbins's smiling boisterousness in *The Hudsucker Proxy*, or John Turturro's self-righteous intensity in *Barton Fink*. Every grotesque element—the disfigured face of Ed Harris's Carl Fogaty, the two more severely disfigured faces of Tom/Joey's first victims, the outrageousness of William Hurt in a goatee as Joey's gangster brother Richie—is directly related to the theme of violence. As self-sufficient spectacles of grotesquerie, they don't amount to much—Harris's face is a nice makeup job (his left eye has been taken out with barbed wire years before by Crazy Joey) but it doesn't carry much of a charge on its own. Nor do the two victim's faces, since they are held for only brief intervals, just long enough to leave a mental impression. As for Hurt, his acting (stylized and carefully modulated braggadocio) is less about grotesquerie than animal power-gaming, luring his brother into his lair and getting him settled in before he can do away with him.

The sociologically correct comedy of suburban despair is also a million miles from Cronenberg's movie. First of all, the details of the household, the high school, the Philadelphia bar, etc., are pretty bare bones, emptied of eye-catching tell-all details except for the bare necessities, just enough to give the action credence. Every space becomes a kind of arena or cage, every interaction a contest for dominion. Moreover, Tom/Joey is not a figure of suburban pathos like Joey Soprano or David Fisher. There is pathos here, but of the most rarefied variety. Tom/Joey's pathos is that of a man who realizes that the irrational, the instinctive, and the altogether unfathomable constitute a far greater portion of his being than the comprehensible, the rational, and the malleable.

As for the violence itself, almost all of it perpetrated by Mortensen's Tom/Joey, there is not a single moment in which Joey appears triumphant, nor is there a moment when he succumbs to sorrow over his forced return from retirement—two standard scenes in the retired gunslinger subgenre. Rather, and this is the film's subtlest point, he's *embarrassed*—by his ridiculous efficiency at killing people (the scenes are fast, brutal, and carefully detailed) and by the fact that he's been found out. His instincts go into effect on cue, and then the embarrassment begins. Not middle-class embarrassment, but the embarrassment of a man whose fundamental conception of himself is dismantled by circumstance and reassembled in a crazy pattern he can't make sense of. Mortensen's collaboration with Cronenberg is a wonder—it's difficult for me to imagine many actors who would be receptive to such an unusual conception, let alone able to put it into such vivid relief.

Tom/Joey's embarrassment is mirrored by Edie's (Bello's is an almost equally impressive performance) and then Jack's, and it's what gives the ending its power. Once again, we're confronted with another cliché: the flawed but noble hero warmly welcomed back into the family circle. But there are no smiles or hugs, just a rote return to the old domestic pattern: the little girl, largely oblivious, sets dad's place at the table; the teenage son gets him some food. It's touching but crazy. Cronenberg ends with a final shot of Tom/Joey, aware that he is being studied by his family, his face betraying the slightest trace of Joey's atavism. It's one of Cronenberg's greatest question marks. The last line of the underrated *eXistenZ*, capping an equally penetrating image of irresolution, wouldn't be out of place here: "Is this still the game?"

A History of Violence presents us with a vision close to Buñuel's, in which sanity and normalcy are not pure states but compromises with madness and where everyone finds themselves trapped and dizzily looking for the escape hatch—meanwhile, the unacknowledged front door remains wide open. As in Buñuel, the internal consistency is as extraordinary as the lack of outward signals of abnormalcy or aberrance is potentially disconcerting. One might place Cronenberg's film in the company of such Buñuels as *Wuthering Heights* or *Los Olvidados*, which, based on their plot outlines and basic imagery, can be (and have been) easily dropped into ready-made categories: romantic melodrama and social conscience. Yet unlike the upper-middle-class phantoms who populate Buñuel's later films, Cronenberg's people actually have a grasp of the absurdity of their own positions and an awareness of their inability to disentangle the threads of circumstance. Which brings his greatest films, including *A History of Violence*, close to genuine tragedy.

2005

The New World may be the ultimate Terrence Malick film by virtue of its title alone. In Malick's cinema, the world is *always* new, from scene to scene, moment to moment, breath to breath. For this filmmaker, every shot is an establishing shot or perhaps a *re*-establishing shot—an inauguration of a brand new moment in time and space, the preceding moment buried and consecrated with the cut. Discontinuity and ellipsis are at the heart of Malick's aesthetic, and disorientation is the norm. Any given transition in The New World might signify weeks or months or even years or perhaps a minute or a second. It hardly matters, because Malick is interested in time only to the extent that it allows his films to perpetually crash-land in a primordial vision of Life On Earth. A lock and key, an open book, a flash of lightning, a candle, a girl's face—Malick jumps onto everything and startles us (and never lulls us: he is not exactly the becalmed sensibility of legend) into *looking* before placing, comparing, evaluating, or any of the other (largely unconscious) tasks we bring to moviegoing. Malick is the only working narrative filmmaker who devotes entire movies to the wonder of presence. His kind of revelatory vision of the world is far from unprecedented—it's there in the late silent work of Vidor, Epstein, and Murnau, and later in Godard, Bresson, Straub/Huillet, Roeg, and, ever so preciously, early Wenders. But it is usually just one component of the larger grammar. Only in Malick does the actual sensation of looking at (and through) the material world occupy the center of the movie itself, physically, thematically, and emotionally.

The flow from person to man-made object to nature and back again is the regular rhythm of Malick's editing, and the contrast between the finite human drama and the endless drama of light, air, earth, water, and sky is never less than palpable. In The New World, during a violent battle between the Algonquins and the settlers, Malick suddenly cuts to a shot of the sky. This quixotic move is neither punctuation nor editorialization but a way of simply getting us back into Mother Nature's groove. It's a nice moment, though more willful and less resonant than the little scene in The Thin Red Line in which the clouds part and sunlight spills over the tall grasses in which two G.I.s have just been shot down. Malick, as one can easily divine from watching his movies, is a connoisseur of the accidental, and he must have wept for joy when he arrived at this stunner, as quietly shocking as the child's coffin bumping against the post in Renoir's *The River.*

Malick lives comfortably within the chaos of the natural world, and he is not just ready but eager to turn away from the demands of plot toward the wind in the trees and the rush of water over ancient stones. Dramatically speaking, the most resonant moments in *The New World* are the ones that run parallel to the filmmaker's lust for first things. When the colonists arrive, we get a few glimpses of the natives on shore; then, in a thrilling reversal of popular American history, we shift to the awestruck wonder of the Algonquins at the English ships on the horizon. Not long after, the film spends a lot of time—too much, perhaps—on John Smith (Colin Farrell) and his woodland idyll, but the accumulation of time in the forest is exactly what sets us up for that initial, shocking vision of the English fort: the doors open to civilization at its most wretchedly utilitarian, the pitifully functional wooden structure as inimical to the landscape around it as a Burger King or a Price Chopper. The first sight of Pocahontas (Q'Orianka Kilcher) in western dress packs just as much of a punch, but her steadfastly serene face also boomerangs back the film's transcendental idea: this supremely graceful girl can't help sending her natural beauty back to the culture that's hijacked her.

In a sense, Malick's severely elliptical cinema of metaphysical disorientation began not with his heralded debut but with *Days of Heaven*, the first but not the last time that his actors came away from the premiere scratching their heads and wondering what had happened to their performances, let alone their dialogue. As the filmmaker enjoys his second wind, and as he has moved from twosomes and threesomes on the plains to an army of semi-characters tramping through swamps, rivers, and forests (and from emotional dissociation to prayerful meditation in the voiceover), his growing urge to dissolve human drama into the forces of surrounding nature has started to bewilder even sympathetic viewers. Jonathan Rosenbaum, for instance, finds that all the reveries and reflective monologues and transcendental passages in *The New World* "can be defended, even celebrated, but I couldn't find my bearings." Understandably so. I'm more inclined to defend and celebrate than to denigrate, but Rosenbaum has a point.

Malick is a formidable artist, but he has more than a few truly eccentric if not disturbing traits. Chief among them is his willingness to cut corners with human affairs, matched by his steadfast refusal to do so in matters of landscape and light. Which is why *The New World* imparts such a strong sense of first encounters—between mankind and nature, man and woman, native and conqueror—and such a fuzzy sense of the results of those encounters.

Many of the dramatic particulars of Malick's historical romance—the power struggles amongst the settlers, the harshness of their first winter and the approach of starvation (why couldn't they hunt?), the destruction of the Algonquin village—tend to dissolve in the natural light and fresh air. All of which is Malick's prerogative. To understand the real oddness of this film, though, one must bring up the dreaded subject of acting.

Malick is a director who seems to love actors, and appears to work in a low-key variant of the behavioral register we identify with Ashby, Grosbard, Altman (think "seventies"). On close examination, he becomes something else entirely—a director interested in the representation of emotions but little if at all in the quality of the representation. In a sense, he's like one of those parents who smile at everything their children do, but turn to jelly when things get difficult. We all know that Malick is fond of filming actors when they're not acting, and these are some of his finest moments—they give form to something impossible to mimic, namely contemplation in action. On the other hand, he's also fond of filming actors when they're doing a whole lot of acting. Malick's last two movies are acting free-for-alls, leaving behind both the dramatic specificity of *Badlands* and the severe fragmentation of performance in *Days of Heaven.* There is a rough equivalence in these movies between generalized acting and generalized behavior and between diegesis and exegesis, which must make for an exceptionally odd performing environment. Given the discontinuous presentation, actors often commit the cardinal error of "playing" emotions, and they have to be as resourceful and intuitive as Nick Nolte or Sean Penn or Christian Bale, or as instinctually savvy as Q'Orianka Kilcher (where on earth did they find her?), to hack out a viable character. In many ways, they have to make their own movie. Nolte's Colonel Tall in *The Thin Red Line* is a towering creation, Melvillean in stature and depth, and he seems to be in a completely different film from Dash Mihok's fireplug grunt (1940s Hollywood), Jim Caviezel's beautiful dreamer (like Zachary Scott in Renoir's *The Southerner*) or Ben Chaplin's cuckolded husband (early-1980s L.A. soft-core).

Similarly, Kilcher's serene vitality in *The New World*, which Malick wisely allows to spill over and give almost every scene she's in a rainbow wash (her invocation of Mother Earth may get a little annoying after the ninetieth repetition, but it maintains its charm), is a world away from everyone else in the movie, not least her Algonquin brothers and sisters. I appreciate the fact that any representation of the Algonquins has to be largely made up, and I also appreciate the efforts of the actors to create an ensemble "physical vocabulary." The final result bears no small resemblance to a performance by an especially earnest and hardworking theater group. Again, there's nothing inherently wrongheaded about the idea, but I think it's a mistake for Malick to film it as if he were a documentarian who had journeyed back in time, which winds up diluting the impact of both the actors *and* the sense of character. By the same token, the "colonists" amount to a thirty-headed monster of uncorked behavior, sometimes taking the form of two jabbering children and at other times bearing a remarkable resemblance to David Thewlis. The fort itself is far more impressive than the emotional babel within, which suggests a bad weekend at the Esalen Institute. Fittingly, Colin Farrell suggests a group therapist who's thrown up his hands in exasperation and retreated to his cabin to freak out alone.

I don't begrudge Malick the use of big name stars to bankroll his movies. I can believe that he actually wanted to turn John Smith into a moony, "soulful" poetic rebel without a cause, a biker who's lost his bike (with tattoos, no less), and create a classic teen romance out of his relationship with Pocahontas (as Amy Taubin put it so well, it's the story of "a girl who starts off with the bad boyfriend and winds up with the good boyfriend"). It's even possible that he encouraged Farrell to maintain his knitted brow anxiety throughout the entire movie, thus giving himself a *tabula rasa* on which he could write with the voiceover. What I can't believe is that he wasn't thinking that the *very* twentieth-century side of Farrell's "characterization" might play at the box office, especially since he's cavorting in the grass with one of the most beautiful young women to cross the screen in years. Anachronism and a kind of softening around the edges to fit the demands of the day have always been present in Malick, from turning Starkweather and Fugate into a younger version of Beatty and Dunaway to Richard Gere's very 1970s swagger in the middle of 1916 to Farrell's hazy, disengaged, very un-seventeenth-century Smith. To put it simply, this strikes me as neither a historical nor an aesthetic choice but a commercial one, albeit a commercial choice that might have made a snug fit with history and aesthetics—which is not the case. Farrell's acting is *so* unfocused that there's an extreme dissonance between the (Irish-accented!) voiceover (Smith's dreams of a free and just society, his wanderlust, his ambition) and the willowy, aimless sad sack onscreen. Meanwhile, it's impossible to not notice the fact that the film gains a lift the moment a good, quietly concentrated actor (Bale) enters. Whereas Kilcher is a highly entertaining perpetual motion machine in the scenes

with Farrell (she might be trying to wake up her coactor), she takes on more mystery and depth in her scenes with Bale, which are alive with eloquent silences, incremental advances and retreats, and a very moving dignity that seems like a joint creation of the two actors.

One might ask: what are acting and character to Malick, and what is Malick to acting and character? My answer would be: a lot, just as they are to everyone, from Godard to Nancy Meyers. Putting this key area of narrative filmmaking on the bottom rung of the totem pole, perhaps one level above music, is a big problem in film criticism, a hangover from the earliest days of auteurism, when the primacy of the director was the (necessary) rallying cry. I think that Malick has always given himself quite a bit of leeway when it comes to his characters and the actors who play them—artfully fudging the issue of Kit's mental disorder in *Badlands* in order to maintain the film's delicately haunting tone, allowing Ben Chaplin and Miranda Otto to "do" love in *The Thin Red Line* (some of the worst scenes ever shot by a major director), and giving Farrell plenty of rope to hang himself. To be fair, his laissez-faire approach creates moments of great beauty. As hazily undifferentiated as the scenes with the Algonquins and the settlers are, they do create the unusual impression of wandering through a garden of humanity: one becomes attuned to the infinite variety of shapes in the human form in a way that I don't think any other filmmaker has managed or even attempted. However, the downside is impossible to ignore: that the behavior on display is not real but acted, sometimes well and sometimes not so well, and that the actors often bear an uncomfortable resemblance to animals "performing" in their cages, i.e., their "frames."

And yet, I wouldn't trade a frame of it for most of contemporary cinema. The final passage, in which Pocahontas's spirit is transported via montage (and Wagner) back to Virginia and the forest, is Malick's most stirring. It is *the* great metaphysical return—the redemptive death in *Ride the High Country*, the ditch-digging climax of *Our Daily Bread*, and the final avowal of love in *Pickpocket* all rolled into one, not to mention a passionate rebuke to Fitzgerald's cautionary *Gatsby* ending. *The New World* is the most amorphous of Malick's films, far more so than *The Thin Red Line*, another grand choral work made from the perspective of Emerson's Over-Soul. Some see an elegy to an Edenic paradise wiped out by the forces of civilization. Others see the chronicle of a young girl's transformation. A smattering of teenagers might just see a swooning romance in which love reigns triumphant. Still others (like me) see a game attempt at a transcendentalist visual symphony, in which everything under the sun, from the natural to the man-made, from love to warfare, is viewed from the same benign distance, a distance that Malick has been cultivating throughout his career, if not his life. I reserve the right to complain about the dodges and hidden compromises he makes with actors and character, but I have to admit that I'm hard-pressed to think of another living filmmaker so alive to the possibility of revelation in reality.

2006

III "Think Pieces"

These pieces are broader in scope, or at least different: they attempt to look at ideas and developments outside of the immediate "ecology" of the films in question (that term comes from the great Elaine May, and I'm borrowing it proudly). Some of the pieces were suggested by editors and some represent nothing more than my own responses to changes as they were in process. I suppose it's worth noting that the piece on documentary/fiction hybrids was almost two years in the making and stretched thousands of words in many different directions before it reached its final form.

The term "think piece" is an odd one (thus the quotation marks). The implication is that we're doing something else the rest of the time. Like what? Reacting? Judging, in the same fashion that one might judge a beauty contest ("I give Malick an 8 for execution and a 7.5 for presentation")? Yarn spinning? Which is to say that these pieces are neither more nor less thoughtful about than any of the others in the book. They just represent a few attempts to track the shifting of a tectonic plate or two.

The Summer of Our Discontent

Summer 1996 was good sport for movie lovers, who get a lot of mileage out of trashing the season's blockbusters: we enjoy doing it amongst ourselves, but we get a special charge out of throwing wet blankets of intellectual expertise on the enthusiasms of the unenlightened ("You liked that?"). The complaints are so uniform and constant that they've now become a litany: there are no characters, there's no story, there's no reality, there's no movie, etc. Every film has its own priceless brand of cheesiness that is jawed over endlessly. My preferred target this summer was the scene in *Mission: Impossible* where computer whiz Ving Rhames successfully jams Vanessa Redgrave's modem (from about four feet away), which the sharper members of the audience just might have gleaned from the message on his laptop: JAMMING SIGNAL BEING SENT. And I'll always cherish the memory of President Bill Pullman ("During the Gulf War we knew what we stood for . . ."). Pullman, on his most confident day, looks like he might possibly make a good Junior Vice-President of Customer Relations at the Knoxville, Tennessee, Wal-Mart.

After awhile, though, the fun wears away. Faulting *Independence Day*, the cinematic equivalent of a Barcalounger, for its deficiencies as a movie is like sitting around a dinner table and "solving the world's problems." Like most avoidance techniques, the feeling is momentarily energizing and ultimately unrewarding. So what are we avoiding? There have been reams of copy devoted to the idea that *Independence Day* is a failed piece of sci-fi and that *Mission: Impossible* is a failed thriller, which are in turn based on the dubious proposition that everyone in Hollywood has suddenly lost their marbles and forgotten how to tell "coherent" stories or how to make "real" movies. (Based on my limited experience of Hollywood and Hollywood types, my impression is that it's a town filled not with fools but with intelligent people who think it is a good idea to conduct themselves as fools, in order to put themselves in closer touch with the viewing public.) To deal with what *Independence Day* is as opposed to what it isn't is a sobering and difficult prospect for film lovers, because it falls so far outside of what we would define as cinema. The central fact of such an enterprise is more frightening than mere failure: it does precisely what it sets out to do and on its own narrowly defined terms, it's a raving success. Those terms are set by corporations and accepted by paying customers who are so humbled, bored, or bewildered by a pounding, torrential media culture that there's little if any opportunity to establish terms of their own or see themselves as anything but lowly consumers. This is where the current I-Know-It's-A-Piece-Of-Crap-But-I-Liked-It-Anyway school of critical thought originated: consumer fatigue.

ID4 (which sounds like exactly what it is: a nickname cooked up by a marketing department) and its ilk expend enormous amounts of time and energy on submerging any trace of individuality, not unlike a health-and-fitness nut trying to rid his or her body of impurities. One could argue that this has always been the goal of Hollywood, but in fact Hollywood built itself into an empire by harnessing individuality even as it pampered away its rough edges and milked it dry. With the summer 1996 blockbusters, however, we have "evolved" to a new stage in which each actor/technician/writer/director is flattened out and smoothed down to a Formica-like nothingness (the only escapee: the wily Vanessa Redgrave in *Mission: Impossible*)—the strategy being to make the film as easily recognizable and uncomplicated as a Happy Meal. If you want to take *Independence Day* seriously, good. If you want to laugh at it, great. If you want to take a nap, cool. It's Democratic. It's Republican. It's "sophisticated," providing ample opportunities for anyone interested in spotting "cinematic references." It's "stupid," and functions as its own built-in MST 3000. It's global. It's isolationist. It even throws in Pat Buchanan's campaign slogan for good measure. And unlike the government-penned love songs sung by the washerwoman in 1984, it signals the fact that it's a counterfeit on a regular basis.

Which is why the old critical tactic of marking cultural flashpoints or divining metaphors for widespread cultural fears doesn't wash with such a perfect, easily adaptable object. The most striking aspect of ID4 is the strangely disembodied manner in which it finally meets its audience: it's close to the poignant effect William Gibson gets in *Neuromancer* when the dead character "preserved" in a computer chip glitches and repeats a sentence. There's an unavoidable freakishness to all the calculation involved in this simulation of a movie, a subtle but marked stuttering effect, as if the storytelling had skipped a microstep ahead of the army of people supposedly controlling it. I had the odd feeling when I saw both *Independence Day* and *Mission: Impossible* that a lot of audience members didn't really like them but worked up a reasonable state of excitement anyway. One guy in front of me kept getting up and walking out, then coming back and cheering. Why? A sense of obligation? Memories of better films? The desire to participate in an event?

It's as if a contract had been written between the suppliers and the demanders of America, prohibiting reality in movies: to break the contract would upset the precarious balance that currently exists. Reality in American cinema has virtually disappeared from the screen and shifted to the unhealthy relationship between the film and a viewing public now erotically familiar with images, for whom each new movie is a matter of ticking off variations on rock-solid formulas. The complete lack of a human center in ID4 is the double negative high sign to the audience that their part of the contract is being respected: if we give you our money, you'll do us the service of not representing our existences—the ones you keep telling us are so ordinary—onscreen. In fact, the only onscreen reality in *Independence Day* is kinetic, geological, technical, and coloristic. Aside from that, it's strippers living in middle-class neighborhoods, old Jewish guys dispensing wisdom to the joint chiefs of staff, and a perfectly controlled presentation of action/character/typage that is as inhumanly clean as a sine wave.

All of which sounds deeply depressing, as though the long-prophesied death of cinema was upon us at last. "So, finally, in entertainment we see ourselves, the audience, clamoring for a repeal of the laws of dramaturgy and a reversion to entertainment as pure titillation," writes David Mamet in a recent doomsaying essay. The common wisdom is that commercial culture has nudged the dormant masses over the edge, and that there's no going back. It's as if the aggressive reporter riding down French art cinema in Olivier Assayas's giddy, frightening *Irma Vep* ("It is only to please yourself, not for the public. But now it's over, it's finished . . . I *hope*") was a true prophet warning us to start counting the hours.

I'm not totally unsympathetic to Mamet's dour formulation, but the unavoidable reality of corporate capitalism is that, given its speed and efficiency, you must adapt to it as you reject it. It is so pervasive and reaches into so many corners of existence that you have to respect its integrity as a force, as something that exists within reality rather than something outside of it, at the same time that you're trying to get beneath its structure. Whenever people start warning that the end is near, I know that the beginning is close at hand. Who really believes that the idea of art is so flimsy that it can be squashed like a bug under the heel of commerce? In the twentieth century, we've seen the blossoming of an artistic movement followed by its absorption by big business followed by despair followed by a new movement that builds off the then-current reality, again and again. The problem with doomsday/death-of-cinema thinking is that it ignores the fact that a lot of good art is cooked up over the heat of business. It's as if there was no world outside of the cinema and nothing for it to build from but its own happy conditions.

But are ID4 and M:I really so isolated from the cinema we know and love? Think of the identical aesthetic/business strategies of *Independence Day* and *Fargo*, an art film that is just as canny as the blockbuster about allowing the viewer to take it any way he or she wants. It's just that in the case of the Coen brothers' movie, the target audience is smaller and (supposedly) has more refined tastes. In the blockbusters the action is so disconnected from reality that it's impossible to imagine anyone doing anything offscreen, but there's an echo of that tendency in many American films, even the good ones. There are some good, stinging contemporary moments in *Heat* (most of them in long shot or thanks to Diane Venora, Val Kilmer, or Ashley Judd), but the film mostly feels like mythmaking, L.A. crossed with Melville's already mythic Paris.

Nobody's Fool films bedraggled, economically devastated small-town America on the outskirts of its story, but when the characters start interacting it becomes a nice, mellow variation on the early 1930s, complete with friendly card games between enemies in the back of the bar. The same odd, post-modern timelessness figures prominently in Lars von Trier's *Breaking the Waves*, with its curious amalgamation of saintly/retarded naïf heroine, Dreyeresque townsfolk, 1970s music, and 1950s melodrama. Von Trier makes something moving out of his bizarre pop object, which has next to nothing to do with "questions of faith," "the power of love," or martyrdom, but which transmits itself on an intersubjective wavelength, at least for people of a certain generation: with its heady visual scheme (shot in handheld Panavision, transferred to video for color correction, then back to film), it feels as if it's happening in the head of someone who grew up watching movies on TV and listening to the poignantly acerbic strains of 1970s British rock late at night. As a near-perfect embodiment of the abstract feelings produced by all that moviewatching and record-listening, *Breaking the Waves* partakes of what *Independence Day* so ruthlessly exploits.

On a more complex level, the insistence on a decentered approach to the very idea of character, on a coreless, floating vision of identity, is common to both blockbusters and a lot of current serious work. The "people" who parade through ID4 are deliberately flimsy, almost ghostlike—which is oddly congruent with a nonconsumerist movie like André Téchiné's remarkable new *Thieves*, in which the director's Hitchcockian, almost strident clarity is employed to highlight the lives of people for whom control is momentary, fleeting, and always shattered by impulse. The denial of a solid foundation on which character can be built is also to be found in Atom Egoyan's eerily weightless films, and in the ecstatic kaleidoscopic swirls of

Wong Kar-wai. Perhaps it's fair to say that what ID4 embodies, these films are trying to represent, but the squarishly American blockbuster and the tough, serious films of Wong, Egoyan, Assayas, Edward Yang, and Hou Hsiao-hsien all meet their audiences on the same playing field. They share the same unconscious. They find common ground in the reality of speed and omnipresent forces moving people out of control. They are all creatures of corporate capitalism, but whereas ID4 is its creation, the other filmmakers have either built their work from its leavings or quietly manufactured materials of their own devising in its shadow.

The reality of blockbuster movies is a decidedly alienating affair, and an unpleasant historical development for film lovers who would prefer to retreat into the comfort of ahistorical essentialism: "Leave the masses to their tawdry entertainments—we know what real cinema is." As someone who's been watching movies steadily since I was eight, I know how tempting it is to escape to the kingdom of abstract movie appreciation, to give up the ghost and spend your days studying videotapes of *Wagon Master* and *His Girl Friday*. And here's what's especially galling about blockbuster cinema: we film lovers pride ourselves on the fact that we've traditionally been so democratic in our embrace of mass culture, and these films have put us in the unfortunate position of looking as reactionary as John Simon, which does no one any good at all. I hated every second of *Independence Day*, but I can't fault the people who enjoyed it, or consider them "dupes of the system." They're responding to their own desire for a shared response, and if they're not as picky as I am about the event that they choose to respond to, then so be it.

The fact is that, beneath all the layers of irony, corporate safety measures, commercial alienation, and coats of protective shellac that formed the event that was *Independence Day*, there's still the beating heart of its audience.

1996

Digital Cinema

It has been suggested, as it often is in America when such things happen, that pervasive media violence was the culprit behind the Hitler's birthday shootings in Littleton, Colorado. In the numbing week after the shootings, the question was asked, endlessly: how did this happen? Of course it was asked in that rhetorical fashion that we all know from the American news media, with its perpetual tone of solemn moral urgency. The motivation behind all this questioning feels transparent, a purely reflexive procedure. At times like this, the country gives itself over to a sickening nonstop busyness, and what people supposedly want to hear and see is voiced, visualized, articulated, and rearticulated again and again and again. Anyone who wants to know why Littleton happened should simply look at the monstrous barrage of activity that went into motion once the shootings were underway. A human act was immediately transformed into an "event," an *image* of action rather than an action, ready for "analysis."

The small details are boundlessly sad. One of the boys' houses was searched and the sawed-off barrel of a shotgun was found lying on his dresser. His father recalled that about a month before the incident he had noticed that his son's behavior seemed troubled, and "made a mental note of it." A gun store owner later claimed that he had seen the boys and their friends snooping around his shop a few months before, and commented, unforgettably, "You know how kids are when they walk into a gun shop. They want everything—it's like a candy store." The boys allegedly asked one of their victims if she believed in God and shot her after she answered in the affirmative, which elevated her to instant posthumous media stardom.

And frequently, in many of the "think pieces" after the shootings, one would see footage or stills of Marilyn Manson, the German metal band Rammstein, the video game *Doom* (which the boys played obsessively—again, allegedly), and from the new film *The Matrix*. Over and over, one was treated to a still or a clip from the climactic scene in which Keanu Reeves and Carrie-Anne Mason shoot up the marble foyer of an office building. They are dressed in floor-length black coats to hide the arsenals strapped to their bodies, which came to seem in the wave of Littleton like an eerie evocation of the terrifying image of the Trenchcoat Mafia members on their rampage. Each time the clip or the still was shown, we were told that this particular film opened only a week before the shootings, and therefore could not have inspired the killers. And the clips and stills kept appearing all the same.

The Matrix is a largely digital experience, and it makes a nice companion piece to The Phantom Menace, which, as Jim Hoberman put it, is "an animated film based on photographic elements." In the narrative of The Matrix, the world of the late twentieth century is merely a virtual veil pulled over the eyes of humans who have been harvested by a race of extraterrestrial machines and employed as batteries. In reality, it's the late twenty-first century and true existence is motionless, vegetablelike. There is a small group of rebels who know the truth, and they're led by Morpheus (Laurence Fishburne), who recruits Reeves' Neo in the belief that he is The Chosen One, the supreme being able to resist all the virtual violence of the agent-machines and lead the world to freedom. According to the logic of the narrative, the only actual human activity consists of a group of people in a tiny spacecraft jacking into computers through ports in the backs of their heads. There's an interesting moment when Morpheus "takes" Neo into a martial arts training program, and explains to him that he is now experiencing a "mental image" of his "digital self."

I find it increasingly difficult to speak about films like Lucas's or this sleekly outfitted concoction by a shrewd pair of brothers named Wachowski—how much can one say about films designed as high-end consumer objects? But as I watched the sequence where Reeves and Moss storm the office building, I was chilled to the bone. Digital technology in the cinema has led to digital thinking, which has in turn led the cinema in an increasingly experiential direction: in order for the experience to function smoothly, just the right amount of reality is required. Too little makes the experience too light and too much makes it too burdensome. The Matrix makes use of practically every religious myth known to mankind (as does the Star Wars series, never more crassly than at the moment when Anakin Skywalker's mother announces that her son was immaculately conceived) and also avails itself of many modern philosophies, movements, and slogans: "Free your mind and your body will follow," Deleuze and Guattari's false consciousness, even a little Carlos Castaneda. Apparently, there's a dash of Baudrillard thrown into the stew, which I was unable to detect but which has thrilled art students across the country.

The resemblance to what we've all imagined the Littleton shootings to have been is indeed striking, and what with all the unbridled associative thinking in the air, the search for parallels has taken on its own special thrill and become infectious if not addictive. Two beautiful yet sexless figures in long black coats and dark glasses walk into a room and coolly start shooting everyone in sight—those left alive are hunted down and mercilessly eliminated, as in a video game. The quiet with which the sound engineer imbues the scene gives the foyer a cryptlike poetic overlay (one of the constant press clichés: whatever room Klebold and Harris walked into became an "instant coffin"). On the other hand, and here we flip from one metaphor to another with digital precision, the destruction and crumbling of the marble and concrete evokes the quick, sudden destruction of a seemingly "solid, permanent" institution, such as a school. And in a detail that has escaped mention in any account of the film I've ever come across, the sequence is scored to techno music, in which the sounds of the shells being dropped and pump action guns being reloaded are incorporated as rhythmic punctuation. Here we switch from metaphor to an accidentally chilling idea of the way the boys might have imagined themselves, according to press accounts: superhuman, supremely masterful, and operating in perfect sync with an internal rhythm that only they understood. If you've been primed with enough Littleton media coverage, these images, as handsomely dark-toned (everything is blue, black, gray, or pale flesh-colored) and sleekly choreographed (a perfect, harmonious progression of lateral movements at a dreamily sloweddown speed) as anything in modern movies, might just give you the sickening sensation of donning a pair of virtual reality goggles and getting a peek into the interior worlds of Eric Harris and Dylan Klebold—as dry as the desert and as cold as the Arctic circle.

What a strange feeling to suddenly realize that one is engaged in the sport of looking for intimations of a lonely, pitiful act in a digitized Hollywood blockbuster. After the fact. Fittingly for an age that is enamored of digital reproduction, every happening, gathering, or piece of consumer detritus is converted into a "cultural object" or "phenomenon," and studied as if it were the Rosetta stone, containing information that might unlock our darkest secrets and liberate us. The machine-built mythology of *The Matrix* actually feels quite apt under the circumstances: you have to remind yourself, over and over again, that behind each among the billions of disconnected images lies an accompanying human action—a choice. We're all business in America, which is why we make films that try to, and often succeed at, erasing every trace of their origins. Which is also why we have pockets of individual artists but no art, at least not as a force on the cultural horizon that equals business or religion. If there is one current film that has any relevance to what happened in Littleton, it's *eXistenZ*, in many ways the exact opposite of *The Matrix*. Cronenberg's is a film of action rather than images, specifically the action of seeking and experiencing sensorial/aesthetic/ experiential pleasure. And it's barely even a memory at the box office and for critics as well, a small handcrafted rowboat running in the wake of the Lucas and Wachowski ocean liners.

The Matrix and The Phantom Menace are pure products of engineering— mental and digital. It's not difficult to picture Lucas emitting a little sigh of pleasure once he figured out a way to keep his pesky human action from gumming up his sleek design. Perhaps the ultimate in the filmmaker's bloodless strategizing is his use of Pernilla August as the mother of Anakin Skywalker, who, as everyone knows, will grow up to be Darth Vader. As I was watching the film, I knew that I was looking at a familiar face, but I couldn't quite place it. And once I got over the shock of realizing that the face belonged to one of the most soulful actresses in the medium, I realized that my failure to recognize her wasn't attributable to mere physical exhaustion. August is shorn of all individuality, given an American accent (which sounded to me like it had either been dubbed or digitally altered) and kept almost motionless, a frozen image of motherhood. But it's difficult to remember any given action performed by a human in either film that breaks from the overall scheme of stylized functionalization. Most of the memorable movement is generated by a computer—the pod race in the Lucas film, a miracle of whizzing motion and booming sound; the bullets fired in The Matrix that seem to be pushing through water, leaving pretty spirals in their wake. Digital imagery needs some kind of aesthetic grounding if it's going to resonate, as in Starship Troopers; the two ingenious Pixar films, Toy Story and A Bug's Life; and Cameron's Terminator 2. Whereas Lucas and the Wachowskis operate in the naïve belief that digital imagery is self-effacing, an instant, perfect replacement for reality (there's a comical misalliance between the size of the image and the thinness of the texture), and an efficient way of streamlining the film experience so that the pesky bugs dropped into the image by tired, old analog reality can be quietly stamped out.

What is a young viewer to make of the sequence in The Matrix where Reeves and Moss hover outside a skyscraper window in a state-of-the-art military helicopter and fire round after round of high-caliber ammunition from an enormous machine gun? Forget their expressionless faces or the fact that both the helicopter and the gun seem to have been designed specifically for the film or the fact that after thousands of rounds, no one inside, least of all their fearless leader who is tied to a chair in the center of the room, suffers even a scratch. The main, very expensive event of the scene is the shell casings raining from the helicopter in luxurious slow motion with an accompanying tinkling sound, not unlike a set of Marin County wind chimes. In their previous film *Bound*, the Wachowskis had already revealed themselves to be shrewdly exploitive types, who had built their "neo-noir" out of decorative bits of window dressing reminiscent of the curlicued rhythms and echo effects of trip-hop: the more violent the detail, the more rarefied the kick. In this sequence, which doubles the mortuarial cool of the shoot-up scene, the fetishism becomes even more freakish than the film-makers seem to realize. One can only imagine the horror that Bazin might feel if he were allowed to come back to life for one day and shown this film, in which the camera is only one of many tools employed to make something that is to his conception of cinema as a mall is to a log cabin.

1999

Midway through *Massoud l'Afghan*, Christophe de Ponfilly's thoughtful meditation on the "Lion of the Panjshir," a pair of obtuse Russian TV journalists comes to interview the great warrior. An oddly comic interlude in an otherwise mournful documentary that now plays like an eerie foreshadowing of Massoud's assassination by suicide bombers posing as an Algerian TV crew three days before September 11.

"What's your favorite weapon?" asks one of the journalists. Massoud's priceless answer: "The Kalashnikov, of course." Then, "What's your favorite movie?" This, asked of a man who has been at war for over twenty years and seen his entire country, from north to south, from east to west, ground into dust. Always the courteous host, he answers, "Unfortunately, I'm very far from cinema."

People just can't stop talking about movies, even with the one-time leader of the Mujaheddin (what if he'd said *The Silence of the Lambs?*). Everywhere you go, you can feel a collective sigh of relief whenever the topic of conversation shifts to film, and I'm not just talking about cliquish discussions among cinephiles. Movies and the movie business make for a dependable, orderly stand-in for undependable, disorderly reality—easier to talk about, less of a bother to puzzle out.

Yet since September 11, slowly but surely, our attention has been drawn to another Ground Zero. Many among us have been trying to piece together the reality of Afghanistan, which we previously had the luxury of viewing in a fragmented state from a haphazard angle—when we bothered to at all, that is. "Are you like me?" a friend queried in an e-mail. "Do you feel you're becoming an expert on Afghan internal affairs?" There's now a mad urge to purge ourselves of our carefree, pre–September 11 ignorance. This nervous quest for instant historical expertise has already been the subject of a *New Yorker* cartoon (exasperated wife to defensive husband: "Two 'Charlie Roses' doesn't make you a middle east scholar") and an article in *The Onion* with a headline that says it all: "Area Man Acts Like He's Been Interested in Afghanistan All Along."

In the tiny, roiling world of international film culture, any movie even tangentially related to Afghanistan now rivets the attention. There's *Baran*, soon to be released by Miramax (I have a feeling they'll do a better job with this one than they did with *Through the Olive Trees*), and the upcoming *Delbaran*, both of which take place on the Afghan/Iranian border. There's the sensationalist BBC "investigative report" *Beneath the Veil* ("We were in trouble . . . *big* trouble" . . . fade to black). In France there's Ponfilly's film, shot in 1997 and rereleased in 2001,which incorporates footage from many of the seven previous films Ponfilly has made about Massoud since the early 1980s. There's Alberto Vendemmiati's and Fabrizio Lazzaretti's stunning documentary *Jung (War): In the Land of the Mujaheddin*. And, most intriguingly, there's Makhmalbaf's *Kandahar*. Although its now famous image of artificial limbs floating down from the sky has drawn quite a bit of attention, Makhmalbaf's typically blunt movie was written off when it premiered in Cannes. Now it's become the center of attention. It was picked up in America before September 11 by a small distributor who, the film's aesthetic and moral worth aside, must be feeling like the cat who suddenly realizes he's already eaten the canary.

That shot of the airborne prosthetics in *Kandahar* is a real lightning rod. It's doubtful that artificial limbs have ever been dropped into the desert individually by helicopter. But what was once a "striking" image, thanks to Makhmalbaf's usual primary-color frontality and hard rhythmic/didactic attack, now seems powerfully and metaphorically apt. There's a young man in *Jung*, lying in his hospital bed in Charikar, who no doubt speaks for Afghanistan's countless landmine victims (eighty-eight per month in the year 2000 alone) when he utters the words: "My life is over." So the image of a mass of people on crutches hobbling through the desert to grab their new limbs stands in fairly well for a multitude, conveys a sense of genuine desperation, and achieves an appropriate overlay of hushed outrage thanks to Makhmalbaf's percussive sensibility.

In *Jung*, the sheer volume of land mine victims throughout the film, lying on stretchers or operating tables, having their wounds inspected or bandaged or operated on, is staggering. I don't exactly disagree with Stuart Klawans's comment in *The Nation* that the form of the film is "jury-rigged," but then what on-the-spot documentary isn't? *Jung* partakes of certain devices that are fairly common in documentary now—synth washes on the soundtrack, shifts to black and white, and skipped frames to keep things moving. But the filmmakers amass a mind-boggling wealth of detail— human, geographical, and ethnographic—as they follow the progress of Dr. Gino Strada and Nurse Kate Rowlands, two stoic, bullheaded westerners laboring to set up an efficient medical facility to deal with the endless stream of casualties, civilian and otherwise. The form that Vendemmiati, Lazarretti, and their brilliant editor Giuseppe Pettito have jury-rigged is finally a fairly beautiful and compelling one, because *Jung* has the feel if not the look of a long, unfurling tapestry.

Jung and *Kandahar* share the same intention, which is to alert the world at large to the horror of life in Afghanistan. If anything, Makhmalbaf's fiction is more didactic than Vendemmiati and Lazarretti's documentary. *Kandahar* is structured as a journey, and on each stop there's an encounter that is emblematic of the then-current state of affairs in Afghanistan. The mere fact that Nafas, the film's heroine, is so consistently held up, slowed down, or discouraged from going any further on her mission to save her mutilated sister from committing suicide is emblematic of a "backward" country, already bombed into the Stone Age. Both films make sad little poems out of women hidden beneath their brightly colored burkhas, speaking through slotted mouthpieces. It's one of those features of life before the downfall of the Taliban that John Sifton, in a *Times* piece ("Temporal Vertigo," September 30, 2001), referred to as oddly "cinematic," particularly when glimpsed against the backdrop of a country that exists in a time "in which reality [is] just more real, a time without images and ideas and representations, only actual events."

Both films foreground this sense of a land out of time, all but abandoned by modernity. *Jung* features a protracted and touching episode of a man whose face is half-eaten away because his melanoma has gone untreated but who is too proud to let his wife work so that his family can eat; *Kandahar* is a pageant of desperation, from Khak, the boy who is sent away from the *madrasa* to fend for himself, to the family held up at knifepoint by a Taliban thief. Both films feature interesting cross-cultural haggles—*Jung* has a moment in which Strada tells two Northern Alliance soldiers who have convalesced in his hospital to fuck off after they refuse to give blood, another where he watches in amazement as a recovered soldier chooses to go back to war; *Kandahar* has the stubborn man who insists that his wife's artificial limbs are too big. Both films make the nomadic refugee population an important background presence, and the visuals in both are suffused with the starkness of the Afghan landscape—*Kandahar* is more of a road (meaning, in this case, "desert") movie, whereas *Jung* is filled with images of destroyed cities and villages, overturned tanks and burned out cars (*Massoud l'Afghan* also has a quick, pointed series of before-and-after-bombing shots of Kabul). Finally, both films are grounded in the POVs of outsiders without overt political affiliations, on single-minded, entirely human missions that try their patience and fortitude in what appears to us an alien landscape, permanently at war.

121

In the case of *Kandahar*, there are two western outsiders, and it's obvious once you hear their flat line readings that Makhmalbaf isn't exactly trying to take the English-language market by storm. Most people consider the scenes with Nafas and Tabib Sahid to be major failings (despite an added frisson: Sahid is played by Hassan Tantai, aka David Belfield, who is wanted for murder in the United States). On the contrary, I would say that these no-frills briefings on the particulars of a devastated country, in awkwardly spoken English, are quite bracing: *Kandahar* has the stark simplicity of Godard before he went metaphysical, but none of the intellectual opacity. It's possible that Makhmalbaf's film is not completely "successful," but what would constitute success given the task he's set for himself, which is to ignite the consciousness of his viewers—his western viewers in particular—with a lesson barely disguised as a folkloric fictional journey?

The political chaos in Afghanistan is in the air, so to speak, in both movies, in the general confusion, the desperation, the every-man-for-himself quality of life. Sahib makes a passing reference to changing sides from the Pashtuns to the Tajiks (the Taliban and the Northern Alliance) before devoting himself to God. And at the beginning of *Jung*, veteran war journalist Ettore Mo makes a sweeping generalization: "They will always need war to live." Apart from the brief encounters with Massoud and Rabbani near the beginning of *Jung* when Strada is getting permission to set up the hospital, you don't get much information on the subject of Afghan political affairs. It's more present in Ponfilly's film about his old friend and hero. *Massoud l'Afghan* is different in every way from *Jung* and *Kandahar*: meditative and self-reflexive, elegiac (the film was shot four years before Massoud's assassination, but Ponfilly speculates on his impending death), and filled with the lush beauty of the Panjshir valley. Massoud was a western media favorite, because of his glorious past fighting the Soviets and his last stand isolation in the Panjshir, and because he was far more photogenic than his opposite numbers in the contentious factions that make up the Northern Alliance, some of whom were in turn more politically adept and effective as leaders. Handsome like Che Guevara, ruminative like Dylan, he seemed to be forever smiling to himself, his eyes alluringly downcast. At one point, Ponfilly leaves in disgust after Massoud has backed himself into a political corner but later rejoins him for another offensive against the Taliban. He catches the loftiness of this charismatic man, so possessed by the impossible dream of uniting and pacifying his fractious country with one godly sweep that he has no patience with the nuts and bolts drudgery of politics.

122   It would be impossible for anyone to make a film that captures the com-

plexity of Afghan history or the conditions that gave rise to an entity as single-minded and systematically vicious as the Taliban. The very modesty of *Kandahar, Massoud l'Afghan,* and *Jung* is fitting given the extremity of the situation in this country of "actual events." The details are laid out by Strada at the beginning of *Jung,* the finest and fiercest of these films: twenty years of war, 1,500,000 dead and counting, 4,000,000 refugees, "total destruction," and "total neglect by the international community." Until recently, of course. But I wouldn't want to take any bets on how long *that* will last.

2001

Walking the Line

It would be impossible to tick off all the various documentary/fiction hybrids floating around right now, combining and recombining at an alarming rate. There is the endless parade of DV faux-documentaries and diaries like *Zero Day*. There are films like Alejo Hernan Taube's *Una de dos*, in which the "protagonist" is a political crisis (the Argentinian economic meltdown), and the human drama is dispersed among multiple characters. There are one-off dead ends like *Ten* and *American Splendor*. There is the now-musty phenomenon of Reality TV. There is the onslaught of recent "documentaries," from *Bowling for Columbine* to *Capturing the Friedmans*, with 100 percent–guaranteed dramatic knockout subjects. There are movies that stretch narrative like a skin over the form of ongoing reality (Michael Haneke's *Time of the Wolf*, Apichatpong Weerasethakul's magical films). And, most interesting of all, there are movies that make an event out of exploiting the gray area between documentary and fiction, like Michael Winterbottom's *In This World* or Hany Abu-Assad's *Nazareth 2000* and *Ford Transit*. The degree to which fiction and documentary are having their way with each other is enough to send both movie buffs and Flaherty seminarians through the roof.

Not that it's anything new. All good fiction aspires to the condition of documentary and vice versa, and thus it has ever been. Any documentary filmmaker worth the name, from the Lumières to Fred Wiseman, sees the poetry, the metaphors, and the narrative contained in the material they catch/search for/cultivate, just as any respectable fiction filmmaker moves away from artifice and toward simplicity. Renoir put it all very simply: "Reality is always magic." Yet, despite the fact that such commingling has been present since the birth of the medium, there is a strikingly singular aspect to the current wave of films.

What to make of Winterbottom's real Afghani immigrants playing themselves in a "dramatized" underground trek through Asia and Europe? Or Abu-Assad's eternally frustrated passenger van driver, playing the role of a lifetime as himself? Or Apichatpong's desire-struck, nearly mute men and women, who share top billing with jungles and mountainsides, sunlight and flowing water? Or, for that matter, *Joe Millionaire*'s Greg and the bevy of women around him, playing themselves playing out a drama that is supposedly really happening? Who are these creatures? From what universe have they been spawned?

Perhaps a more reasonable question might be: What is the difference between watching *Nanook of the North* in the 1920s, *Paisà* or *Fires Were Started* in
the 1940s, Kent Mackenzie's *The Exiles* or Paul Meyer's *Déjà s'envole la fleur
maigre* in the 1960s (not to mention any number of Godard, Varda, and
Warhol films), and the new crop of hybrids? First of all, aesthetic novelty is
not a characteristic of the current moment—unless you mean novelty *item*,
an apt term for anything from *Dark Days* to a "stunt" film like *Super Size Me*.
No one is "discovering" anything here on the grand scale of the postwar
years—this is not neo-neorealism, despite the fact that there are plenty of
worthy films made in the tradition of that era, like *Maria Full of Grace*, *Rana's
Wedding*, Vincenzo Marra's *Vento di Terra*, or the often thrilling work of Pablo
Trapero and Jia Zhangke. The old Rossellini/Godard/Straub idea of a cinema continually reborn from shot to shot is also alive and well. The films
under consideration here are a different breed, though, more involved with
game-playing than the moral vouchsafing of reality to their audience.

Actors. Performers. Citizens. Individuals. Scrutiny. Attention. Direction.
Talent. Charisma. Honesty. Spontaneity. There many factors at work con-
fusing these categories, moving away from the kind of control for which the
prototypical master filmmaker/actor/writer is known. First of all, there's a
palpable feeling of exhaustion: in documentary, too much allegedly neutral
documentation in the face of too many carefully orchestrated events; in fiction, too many overly exacting and rigorously drilled performers in too
many American commercial films that seem to tell the same story over and
over again, more desultorily each time out. The shift in film grammar and
narrative organization that began with rock videos—and which has multi-
plied exponentially with the shift to digital editing—is also a big factor here,
rendering a sizable chunk of what is now regarded as "classical" film syntax
all but outmoded. Which in turn allows for less need for technical control
and more spontaneity from the performers, particularly when you can shoot
to your heart's content on DV. On top of this, the ascendancy of the DV
image itself has brought about a corresponding ascendancy of nonfiction-
ally based fictions—a conceptual strategy which makes an "imperfect"
image viable. As long as DV is measured against the lush, elegant 35mm
image, it makes a snug fit with amateur impulses (whether feigned or real)
and the casually observed reality of just-plain-folks aesthetics—the diary,
the home movie, the intimate portrait. Other factors at work are the virtual
disappearance of a certain type of technically precise acting, whose last
vestiges can be found in England and France with Ewan MacGregor, Hugh
Grant, Nathalie Baye, Daniel Auteuil, and Jeanne Balibar. Then there are the

multiple forms of fetishizing, and thus intense everyday scrutinizing, conscious or unconscious, of images themselves, an operation which has only stepped up in proportion to the ever-increasing efficiency of the celebrity machine—an ever-more atomized focus on the private personality traits, behavioral standby tricks, and assorted strategies of image control and renewal of people like J-Lo, Johnny Depp, and Renee Zellwegger. There is also the monstrous stylization of network news, morning shows, and, in particular, magazine shows, where ordinary people are locked into melodramatic scenarios of loss, duplicity, or hope against all odds, directed within an inch of their lives to be spontaneous as they amble down a beach or sit on a park bench staring into the sunset for a "private moment." Most disturbingly of all, there's the all-but-complete transparency of the political process, in which the endless tug-of-war between image and reality is renegotiated hour by hour, and in which the focal point is a constant effort at self-refinement (hand gestures, cultural affect, the right smile, the correct timing of a scoff).

The assumption is that ordinary people don't notice this stuff, that it's the exclusive property of film critics and cultural studies professors. Which is, of course . . . pure fiction. When you take two minutes to mull it over, how could anyone not notice? Most of us are fairly adept at reading mood changes, body language, and at noticing when a visual detail in a familiar setting has been altered or moved. How could we not see the titanic effort and corresponding anxiety involved in creating the seamless flow of commercial culture, no matter who we're voting for, no matter what kind of movies we like, no matter what paper we read? And how could it not leave us unsettled?

Take Reality TV. The arrival of these orchestrated ordeals of humiliation feels like the quenching of a collective thirst: instead of watching Katie Holmes or Dylan McDermott going through the motions of some shopworn melodramatic plot, why not thrust some "real" people into a concoction halfway between a game show and an Ulmer movie, with an "inspirational" overlay so half-hearted and shopworn as to be as depressingly hilarious as a Rodney Dangerfield joke? As in pro-wrestling, what's striking are the behavioral details. The dulled eyes and big-shouldered walk of the *Joe Millionaire* protagonist, the not-so-carefully hidden hints that he's not a continental aristocrat but a Virginia construction worker; the absurdly outmoded idea of how things are run in a European castle, which the participants in the real fiction pretend to buy hook, line, and sinker; the aggressive self-presentations of the potential brides-to-be as they get off the bus, between whom the real competition occurs: who will do the most efficient job of hiding her avidity from the audience and present the most appealingly lifelike persona? The announced drama (Who will this schmuck choose, and will she reject him when he "reveals" his true identity?) takes a back seat to the real one: how will these nonpros manage to negotiate the potentially perilous inflation of their images by the TV camera? Essentially, it's the same dilemma that rolls around like a hurricane every campaign season.

Exactly where and how do we ask ourselves these questions? In all likelihood, for most people, it happens privately—call it solidarity in collective solitude. In some odd way, these films and shows are bringing this unease about living in a top-down economically driven world into the open. Obviously, the delicate probing of Apichatpong is a million miles from the craven lust for filthy lucre behind *Joe Millionaire*. Strangely enough, though, they're both playing the same game.

Cinematically speaking, the groundwork was laid in the early 1990s. More than just another biography with occasional guest appearances by the real subject, Hou's *The Puppetmaster* represented something new. Hou's frame—the contact between what we were seeing and weren't seeing was intimate, almost sexual—was certainly a window on the past, but also on the future. The duration of those long takes was dramatic, but it was also historical, personal, perhaps even metaphysical, in a manner that seemed closer to daily life than the elevated durations of Tarkovsky. Hou and his scenarists devised a new form of storytelling, real, fictional, dramatic, and essayistic all at once. Kiarostami's early 1990s work—*Close-Up, And Life Goes On,* and *Through the Olive Trees*—is an obvious milestone. Kiarostami was originally pegged as the new Rossellini by the French, but he was in fact a wholly different animal, bending or torquing reality (the shift to 16mm for the courtroom scenes in *Close-Up,* the sound drop-out at the end of that film) the better to exalt it. The arrival of Kiarostami's unerring eye and ear for natural beauty was a significant event, but so was his hubris, his playfulness, his ability (and willingness) to create artfully constructed versions of real time. And then there was *Goodfellas*. Scorsese's beloved movie certainly has quite a few dramatic winners in its arsenal—a rise and fall scenario, rampant paranoia, a cautionary tale of excessive ambition—but they feel rooted in the exhaustively documented milieu rather than imposed upon it. You may come away from the movie thinking about the dilemma of Ray Liotta's Henry, but you will most likely also be thinking of how garlic liquefies in the pan when you slice it with a razor blade. There's been endless verbiage about the violence in *Goodfellas*, but not enough about its impressive documentary sprawl, the way it disperses our attention across countless characters, locations, activities, and bits of lore. It is also the first in a chain of Scorsese films built around the biggest no-no in Screenwriting 101: the passive hero. In recent Scorsese, the hero is a purposely flat figure over whom history washes, smoothing him out like a stone, like such late Phillip Roth protagonists as *American Pastoral*'s Swede Levov. Many of Scorsese's central figures, like Roth's, are stripped of all heroic tendencies, which squares with a fairly common self-image of the moment and fits the anonymity of the nonactor quite nicely.

Finally, on the level of mass culture, it's impossible to overestimate the importance of the O. J. Simpson "event," simply because it was *understood* as a ready-made dramatic event the very moment the heli-cam picked up the Ford Bronco rolling down the highway. This was the first genuine Reality TV show, complete with a chase, two murders, a cast of hundreds, and enough tantalizing ambiguities and mixed motivations to make Preminger envious. The only missing ingredient was a theme song.

Let's say that these events, taken together, opened a door, and that film-makers have been stepping in and poking around ever since. Atom Egoyan's brilliant *Calendar*, Chris Smith's funny, unnerving *American Job*, Zhang Yuan's unsettling psychodrama *Sons*, the proto-fake documentary *Dadetown*, Michael Glawögger's eye-popping *Megacities*, and even *Blair Witch* seemed like anomalies at the time. Now they seem like markers along a road that ends at the present, giddily disorienting moment.

What do Abu-Assad, Apichatpong, and Winterbottom's *In This World* have in common? They all place themselves within danger spots—Palestine, the transcontinental refugee trail, or, in the case of Apichatpong's movies, the reality/fiction divide itself. What feels new about *In This World* and Abu-Assad's *Ford Transit* is the fluidity, the reactive speed, the ingeniously frontal political attack. In the Winterbottom, the audience knows they're seeing some form of enactment, that the "drama" is in the itinerary and its details (passport checks, menial labor in a variety of locations, bribes for border guards, physical hardships, long waiting periods), that we're never quite watching a simple melodrama enacted by a couple of charismatic, carefully chosen Afghani emigrants trying to smuggle themselves into England. The usual melodramatic hooks are flirted with and abandoned. We get a grace-fully rendered series of representative moments—a nervy exchange with a potentially corrupt border guard in Pakistan, money and clothes-changing and language-coaching in Iran, a trek through the snow into Turkey, and quickly formed alliances with other migrants. Winterbottom elides the details that would have to be faked (deprivation, hunger, depression, physical fatigue) and concentrates on what he can give us, the scope of the journey itself, which is harrowing enough. His purpose is to get as much information as possible into a mobile, fluid form, something neither a straight documentary (too distanced) nor a fully fictional film (too cumbersome) could hope to achieve. The filmmaker elicits just enough identification with his two heroes to keep his film dramatically afloat. What we don't need is another movie with Patrica Arquette or whoever standing by helplessly as yesterday's far-flung cultural tragedy unfolds. But we can do with this fast, pretty, intelligent, up-to-the-minute movie, in which documentary and fiction and West and East harmonize like a well-trained choir.

With *Ford Transit*, on the other hand, the audience is continually sizing things up, guessing about the balance between fiction and reality—basically an intensification of mental operations performed by the average moviegoer on a regular basis, as Raymond Durgnat was always so keen to point out. Abu-Assad's is one tough, nervy movie, and it's gotten him into plenty of trouble ("My films are 100 percent fiction and 100 percent documentary," he's fond of saying, perhaps not loudly enough for either the Jerusalem Film Festival jury or VPRO, his Dutch sponsors, to hear). His movie is almost entirely set in the enclosed space of one of the countless white vans in which, for a few shekels, independent drivers shuttle passengers between roadblocks and checkpoints in the occupied territories. Is Rajai, who was the actual driver on Abu-Assad's previous, more conventional *Rana's Wedding*, the star, the subject, or the center of this movie? What has been staged and what hasn't? There's virtually no way of knowing that the soldier who pulls the driver out of the car is an actor, that the dialogue exchange which prompts his temper tantrum is stolen from Wajda's *Ashes and Diamonds*, that the gunshot fired at the van as Rajai attempts one of his many roadblock evasion schemes is also a staged event. Informed viewers might also question how such local notables as B. Z. Goldberg (Israeli filmmaker) and Hanan Ashrawi (politician) might have found their way into this particular Ford Transit.

And the greater question is: what does it matter? The events we're watching may be acted out, but they are not fictitious. The lack of drama, the "documentary" structure, is precisely what gives this movie its punch. Abu-Assad has found a strikingly compact structure and form here—the endlessly frustrating rounds of the ubiquitous Ford Transits, originally given to the Israeli government as police vehicles and passed down in a worn-out state to the Palestinians, as they make the rounds of checkpoint after check-

point, with passengers almost guaranteed to be arriving late at their desti-
nations. Nothing happens that couldn't happen on any given day. Rajai is
"acting" frustrations ("Another surprise roadblock!"), little victories, out-
rages, kindnesses, freak-outs, and bouts of resignation rather than appearing in some synthesized melodramatic conflict designed to "contain" the
particulars of the situation, because his director knows that the particulars
simply can't be contained. It's hard to think of a more perfect way of exem-
plifying the psychological and political deadlock of the region: the constant
stop-start motion of the van makes for a good workable metaphorical
image, as well as a devastatingly immediate one. Like Winterbottom, only
with even greater cunning, Abu-Assad strikes, guerrilla-style, at a situation
in progress.

Like Abu-Assad in Ford Transit, Apichatpong finds an all-defining form
for each of his films: the exquisite corpse construction of Mysterious Object at
Noon, a daytime journey to a mountaintop for a picnic in Blissfully Yours, and
a delicately acted romance linked to a jungle trek (based on a Thai myth) in
Tropical Malady. Apichatpong's films seem aesthetically rarefied and ethereal
at first glance, but they all have an interesting dimension that one might almost call political, in the sense that it's all about getting the balance between humanity and the material world absolutely right. When Apichatpong is at his very best, this balancing act is breathtaking—what is made up
is so deeply rooted in the actual, from the sense of time to the nonactors,
that you feel like you're getting back to the origins of storytelling. Documentary and fiction both seem to emanate from the same magical/mythical/
cultural source.

At its sharpest, this strain in contemporary moviemaking addresses one
of those moments in history when the comfort of established order (culturally, societally) has given way, however briefly, to the mass acceptance of a
fairly terrifying idea: the realization of permanent change. Interestingly, the
moment was foreshadowed years ago, during a very different time, by earlier hybrid-builders like Jean-Pierre Gorin, Yvonne Rainer, early Chantal
Akerman, the Jean Eustache of Une sale histoire, and the Resnais of Mon Oncle
d'Amèrique. These were the first artists to address what has now become a
burning question: in a world that has neither the time nor the inclination to
see us, how should we see ourselves?

2004

"I love America," says the girl with the curly red hair as she waits her turn through customs at JFK International Airport. She makes the exclamation for no reason in particular, at least none that I can divine. Surely it's not the "neutral" gray (or is it tan?) surroundings or the drone of CNN on the many monitors hanging from the ceiling. I'm sure she got her fair share of American cable wherever she was staying on the Riviera. Perhaps she was in Cannes, and maybe, just maybe, she was there for the film festival. Perhaps, but probably not. Suddenly I find myself thinking: she's not one of us.

Us? Who exactly is "us"? In a sense, I'm referring to the holders of yellow, blue, pink, and white passes—I forgot the intermediate category of the pink pass with the yellow dot, one level below the coveted white. These are the five color-coded classifications for the press at Cannes, and if you are a member of that distinguished body, they are a fact of life for ten days. They are commonly worn around the sweaty necks of journalists, and they must be shown at exactly the right time to the blue-jacketed guards at the various checkpoints and doorways. One becomes acutely aware of the time taken to study the pass and compare it with the face of the bearer. And one discreetly notes the color of those passes—yellow means that the bearer will be waiting outside until the Grand Palais or the Debussy have almost filled up and that they will be obliged to head up to the balcony (it also means that they are all but barred from screenings in the smaller Buñuel and Bazin theaters); blue means that they will get a good seat if they have a friend who is kind (and patient) enough to save it for them; pink (my own classification) means that they're assured of getting a good seat for pretty much everything provided that they arrive early enough; pink with a yellow dot I'm still not clear on; and white means that they can stroll in any time they like, pass through doors that are accessible only to them and their fellow white passholders, and bring their spouses.

Once you know what the various classifications mean, you know the line in which you will find people and what time they will arrive. And you become attuned to everyone's habits: when they visit their press boxes, whether or not they attend press conferences, how long they linger outside the theaters after the screenings have ended, who they know, who they avoid, how desperate they seem as they hustle from one screening to the next. It is a peculiarity of Cannes that the rest of the world tends to disappear as you enter its wholly fabricated world. The configurations and the movies change from year to year, but otherwise it's the same faces, the same screening rooms, restaurants, lounges, hotel bars, and terraces, the same walks up and down stairs, back and forth between the Quinzaine and the main festival, the same screening times (8:30 A.M., 11:00 A.M., 1:30 P.M., 3:00 P.M., 5:30 P.M., 7:30 P.M., 10:00 P.M., etc.). As the festival grinds on, the particular films either fade into the memory or come into sharper focus, the common themes and images and preoccupations among the films start to emerge, shaped by the reactions both predictable and unpredictable of friends and associates, and there is the omnipresent feeling that there's never enough time. Within days, one has entered into a state of mind in which these visual, mental, spatial, and temporal elements comprise your entire universe, and the sun and the sea are simply two more visual touchstones. The Cannes International Film Festival may take place on the Riviera, but it might just as well be in Des Moines or Almaty. For us lucky passholders, that is.

I watched and listened to this girl, I realized that none of us, at this moment in history, would ever publically betray such unqualified enthusiasm for America and things American, with which the microworld of Cannes is always engaged in a curious dialogue—or perhaps a death lock is more apt. In the intense, little world from which I had just emerged physically and from which it would take two weeks to disengage mentally, no remark about America can ever be made without a measure of doubt, disenchantment, or distrust. A collective reflex, as dependable as the rising of the moon, the mirror image of the collective reflex informing this girl's reaction, this girl who addresses her remarks to her friends as if they were all characters in a television show.

Does she know of this other idea of America, the repository of bad faith and misplaced zeal, where every good deed masks a self-interested motivation and where paranoia is therefore eternally justified? Probably not. Perhaps it exists for her as a rumor, a vaguely threatening yet slightly ridiculous fact, real in the same sense that such bygone items as dial telephones or stereopticons or washboards are real. We passholders, who imagine ourselves as models of enlightened thinking as we scuttle backwards and forwards through our little hothouse—consider her America a fiction. But the America of which we speak is just as equally a work of fiction, conjured in opposition to the America of Reagan, Bush II, and the Disney Corporation's "typically American" Celebration USA. In this America, it is difficult if not impossible to speak of September 11 without invoking our aggressive foreign policy and our international covert activities. Is this America closer to the truth? If one considers the country solely in terms of the overall course of action pursued by our elected and appointed officials, then it offers a fairly accurate description of this moment. But if one chooses to see a nation and its culture as more than simply the sum total of the decisions made by its politicians and its CEOs, if one dislodges the reality of a culture from its popular image of itself, then one sees the absurdity of two warring fantasies—the ultimate good vs. the ultimate evil, the land of opportunity vs. the prison of ideology.

And it is in this second America that Lars von Trier's *Dogville* and his new *Manderlay* take place. Seeing *Dogville* in Cannes two years ago was an informative experience. Any hope for a nuanced assessment of the film went out the window the moment the final credit sequence started to roll—a punchy, rapid-fire montage of photos of poverty-stricken American citizens (shot by Jacob Holdt and assorted FSA photographers, uncredited) set to David Bowie's "Young Americans." With this startling transition from implicit to explicit critique, it became clear that *Dogville* was a film designed to be loved or hated. I was part of the "hated it" contingent. On reflection, it was the polarizing posture of the film, partly von Trier's construction and partly a product of Cannes itself, that I hated. *Dogville* the film is a semi-productively annoying object, a literally diagrammatic vision of human behavior with an interestingly self-deluding protagonist and a genuinely shocking melodramatic twist at the end. The film has a perfect arc—an ascent from goodwill and innocence and a corresponding descent into bad faith and experience. Von Trier has genuine insight into the reflexive distrust lurking behind magnanimous public affirmations, and the final reversal, while more of a melodramatic trick than a genuine moral event, put the icing on the cake. My big quarrel with *Dogville* had to do with the precise nature of its Americana. In other words, if this was America, then *what* America, and *why?* To demonstrate how deluded we are about our good intentions? To replace the soft, favorable light in which we insist on seeing ourselves with a harsh, unforgiving one? To simply name and define us "correctly?" Might this story have been set elsewhere? If not, why not?

2005 was the year of *Manderlay.* This time, the subject, or target, is the plight of the African-American. The heroine, Grace (played in *Dogville* by Nicole Kidman and now by Bryce Dallas Howard), is trying (naively, of course) to liberate a group of slaves in the eponymous plantation. The good/bad arc is roughly the same, the heroine is once again debased, there is another reversal in the last reel, and there is another "Young Americans" photo montage, this time of African-Americans in various states of misery, anger, torture, and dismemberment. The narration is once again spoken by John Hurt in a manner that seems meant to evoke Michael Hordern's gently acerbic narration of Kubrick's *Barry Lyndon*. And, once again, the dialogue is oddly stiff, as if it had been written in another language and translated into English by a computer program.

But here's the catch—or the hook. We are indeed in Alabama, but the year is 1933, not 1859. So we begin by thinking that the slaves have been shielded from the various and sundry developments in post–Civil War America. But in the end, we find that this perpetuation of slavery is a joint effort between Mam the plantation owner (Lauren Bacall) and Wilhelm, the elder statesmen among the slaves (Danny Glover). Moreover, they have achieved this apparently impossible task by creating a carefully coded behavioral system and assigning various roles (passive, aggressive, calm, unbalanced) to the inhabitants of Manderlay, thus ensuring the variety afforded by endless conflict and thereby creating a bedrock of social stability.

Von Trier will do absolutely anything to make a grand gesture, and that's exactly what he leaves us with—nothing less, nothing more. How exactly is this homemade program carried out—and who makes it work? How is it that no one, from the invading Union troops of the 1860s to the local townspeople to the politicians, has noticed the goings-on at Manderlay? How could Mam and Wilhelm have possibly anticipated the disaster of reconstruction and "realized" that America wasn't ready for black citizens in 1865?

But wait—it's not a history lesson, as the film's admirers kept reminding me. This is an odd point on which to insist. I have a feeling that for those who have lavished such extravagant praise on *Manderlay* and *Dogville* before it, the supply of films, novels, and plays about the close proximity of compassion and contempt will always be dangerously low. As for the illusion of freedom, the theme has been visited with far less pomp and circumstance by many filmmakers greater than von Trier—Buñuel in particular, who would never have dreamed of couching his musings within anything so pretentious as a cautionary fairy tale about American duplicity. The connoisseurs of the particular frisson around which these films pivot—the sudden reversal of moral sympathies and identifications—have no problem dislodging those reversals from the historical realities that endow them with any credence. And in the end, there's nothing but the frisson. As critiques of Bush II–era nation-building, they are without interest—timely reminders of the delusions behind "liberation" politics to exactly the people who need no reminders in the first place. As studies of human nature, they are remarkably single-minded—*Manderlay* in particular plays like a dramatization of a social work manual ("Chapter 5: The Pitfalls of Doing Good Unto Others"). As a critique of liberal complacency, it seems at least fifty years too late. It's tempting to see it as an homage to Ezra Pound and his endorsement of the institution of slavery. But I'm not sure that *Manderlay* amounts to anything beyond its final reversal. The film's assortment of preoccupations—Grace's delusional do-goodism, her push/pull sexual attraction to Isaach de Bankolé's Timothy, the suggestion that fascism is embedded deep within the human condition—make it finally too weird to be defined or pinned down. I think von Trier imagines he is tossing a hand grenade down the echo chamber of American culture, which has indeed expanded across the entire world. Such are the pitfalls of conflating governments, people, history, countries, and culture industries. Like his heroine, von Trier imagines he is doing a good deed by somehow getting to some kind of truth, and he winds up giving us exactly what we don't need: yet another fantasy version of America.

This is no small point in modern cinema. Just as a bustling, industrially booming, cautious-yet-progressive, dynamic America served filmmakers like Vidor and Frank Capra as well as a couple of generations of studio chiefs, so a floundering, deadened, oppressive America serves a new international generation, and in the end it's just another American export. The nation as poisonous dream factory and/or monolithic hypocritical entity was alive and well in many films other than von Trier's Danish/Pan-European/British/American movie. Carlos Reygadas's *The Battle in Heaven* is a mortifyingly pretentious film that wouldn't even exist without this pseudo-idea of the nation state as evil organism. Reygadas's imagery is never less than vivid, and his soundtrack is impressively assaultive: chunks of time and space are devoted to Mexican soldiers unfolding an enormous national flag, hallucinatory vignettes of soulless, decadent city life, Catholic processions, and miles of human flesh, alternately tempting and repellent. The core idea being that all the various forces at work are crushing the nonentity at the film's center, a lumpen schmuck named Marcos Hernández who is so completely his director's puppet that he makes Herzog's Bruno S. look like Robert Duvall. Amos Gitai's *Free Zone* is similarly crude. We begin with Natalie Portman sitting in the back of a car, crying for an extraordinarily long stretch of screen time as "Had Gadya" plays on the soundtrack. The scene obviously lends itself to the usual reactionary condemnations of modern cinema—movies are too slow, too "self-indulgent," made only for festival consumption and so on. But in Gitai's case, the problem is intellectual vagueness. I wonder why Gitai wants to make fiction films. It seems to me that it affords him a role in life—the one Israeli who bucks tradition and dares to hold a mirror up to his own country. In this scene, and throughout his cinema, Gitai takes this mirror metaphor rather too literally. Portman's Rebecca has "had enough" of Israel because of a failed romance with a young man who admits that he has participated in atrocities during his stint in the army. She hitches a ride to Jordan's free zone with Hanna, played by Hana Laszlo, an Ethel Merman–ish actress who mercifully breaks up the solemn progression of Gitai's filmmaking with a good old-fashioned bravura performance (Laszlo won the best actress prize). During the journey into Jordan, Gitai is on safer ground: he is a better documentarian than a storyteller. He always makes a half-hearted gesture toward Straub/Huillet territory, only to retreat to allegory, and this new film, probably one of his best, is no exception. The final moments of *Free Zone* reach new heights of absurdity. Rebecca is once again stuck in the back of the car. Tired of the bickering up front between Laszlo and Hiam Abass over an unfulfilled payment, Rebecca jumps out and runs through the toughest checkpoint in the world, as the two women continue their nonstop bickering. Just as Portman's ability to cry is taxed in the opening shot, Laszlo and Abass's capacities for improvisation run visibly dry, as the crudest representation of the Israeli-Palestinian conflict in the history of cinema fades to black and from memory.

Haneke's *Caché* also makes use of an amorphously conceived national past, albeit to far more interesting effect. A series of videotapes is sent to Daniel Auteuil and Juliette Binoche, a couple living in the suburbs. The tapes are surveillance images of the outside of their house. They are being watched—for what reason and by whom they do not know. Auteuil immediately remembers a childhood incident with a young Algerian boy that has haunted him throughout his life, and guilt, paranoia, and desperation blend into one harrowing psychic entity. Scene for scene, Haneke's film is brilliant, and its acuity is impressive. The smartest conceptual choice is to make no visual differentiation between the tapes and the film proper (shot digitally), thus blurring the line between reality and psychological projection. If the film is, in the end, not much more that a brilliant exercise in nervous tension—a clever elaboration of *Rear Window*—it has to do with this national past question. At a certain point, Auteuil and Binoche are no longer a bourgeois couple—they are France, and a gauze curtain of national trauma is thrown over Haneke's wonderful intricacies and beautifully engineered variations on privacy and revelation.

For me, the best films dealt in specifics rather than generalities. It's all too easy to imagine Cristi Puiu's Certain Regard winner *Moartea domnului Lazarescu*, the Dardennes's *L'Enfant*, Hong's *A Tale of Cinema*, Hou's *Three Times*, or Cronenberg's *A History of Violence* as different films, each with its own patina of national malaise proper to its own country. For instance, one could easily picture the Dardennes or Puiu moving into Reygadas territory, with montages to preface their narrative, alternating images of poor Belgians/ Romanians with alluring consumer objects. Or Cronenberg incorporating the crude equations of *American Beauty* or *The Sopranos*. In fact, the paucity of ironic Americana in the Cronenberg was held against the film. But with each film, a rich portrait of the surrounding nation is offered by way of the attendant specifics—the real-time journey of a dying Romanian man as he's shuttled through a nonfunctional medical system; the regeneration of a petty criminal after he sells his baby on the black market; the effect of re-seeing a short confessional film on certain friends of the filmmaker; three romances in three time periods, the first gently innocent, the second quietly devastating, the third mournfully blunt; the dilemma of a man who's re-made his life, from murderous Philadelphia hood to quietly upstanding Indiana citizen, only to witness the unwelcome return of what he took to be his buried past. One could, I suppose, argue that I am opposing narrative with nonnarrative: the films I preferred had exceptionally strong narrative backbones, as opposed to the crassly associative Reygadas, the all-but-unformed Gitai or the mixing and matching of clichéd storylines in the von Trier. Even the Haneke, brilliantly engineered as it is, ends with its enigma intact and its central question unanswered. In the end, I believe that it's less an issue of storytelling than of the aforementioned opposition between generalities and specifics. In the first group of films, the idea of national malaise leads to a corresponding absence of vitality in the characters (Laszlo's performance in the Gitai would be an exception—the director's near-ineptitude is, in this sense, a plus). It is as if freedom of movement, choice, and impulse had been removed from the human equation. Meanwhile, the Dardennes's Bruno (played by Jérémie Renier, the young hero of *La Promesse*), Puiu's Mr. Lazarescu, and Cronenberg's average family are vital to the end and their delusions and fantasies believably local rather than pretentiously global. To refine things a little further, let's say that the opposition is really between the directors who do the work and the ones who try to avoid it with strategic shortcuts. All good artists can tolerate complexity and contradiction, and all mediocre artists—i.e., von Trier, Reygadas, and Gitai—knock their heads against the wall trying to find a way of working around them.

I find it bizarre that so many people pounced on *L'Enfant* and *A History of Violence*. The first was deemed repetitive and overly systematic in light of the brothers' post-1996 output (similar complaints were heard about the Hou and the Hong), while the second was tagged as a revenge melodrama/ western redux tarted up with Cronenbergian metaphors. I marvel at a critical establishment that can look at a film as carefully thought out on every level—the relationships between image and sound, mental time and narrative time, the visible and the immanent—as *L'Enfant* and see nothing but repetitions of assorted practices and themes from earlier Dardenne films (when the same critics watch *To Have and Have Not*, do they hear nothing but echoes of *Only Angels Have Wings?* I hope not) or homages to *Pickpocket*. And how is it possible to divine nothing but crude melodrama in Cronenberg's rock-solid vision of everyday psychopathology? Apart from the rapturous concentration of Hou's film (I half-expected to die of Stendahl syndrome during the middle section) and the atonal beauty of the Hong, the two most striking moments in Cannes were delivered by *L'Enfant* and *A History of Violence*. In the Dardenne, where we witness a young man's movement toward redemption via unfolding action and nothing else (no rhetorical gambits— verbal or visual), Bruno and his young accomplice Steve (Jérémie Segard) have escaped from a minor heist. They ditch Steve's scooter and run down to a riverside. They hide under a dock, in freezing water. When they finally emerge, Steve is so cold that he is paralyzed, and Bruno is obliged to keep him warm. Steve emits a screeching, piercing cry, again and again, that cuts through the film—and through Bruno's indifference to others—like a sharp knife through stretched fabric. Like the sound of the table saw that opens *Le Fils*, the brothers lavish incredible care on this cry, finding just the right balance between direct sound and stylization in the mix. And it's clear that it's not designed, as it were, in the manner of a Coen brothers effect, but somehow *found* during the moment of shooting and carefully preserved. In the published script for *L'Enfant*, the indications are minimal: Steve can no longer move, and cries "Maman!" I doubt that Luc and Jean-Pierre made a mental note to themselves that they needed a "special" or "unearthly" sound to come from Steve at that moment, because there's nothing fabricated about it. This is why I can't accept the complaints of systematization. Artists this focused on the life of the spirit usually *are* systematic in one way or another—after all, isn't there something systematic about Bresson's aesthetic? The fact is that all the finely calibrated machinery of the Dardennes' plotting and their ingenious use of action and time are employed to capture moments exactly like this.

138   And then there is the end of the Cronenberg movie. Viggo Mortensen's

Crazy Joey Cusack has just come home to the family who has known him for eighteen years as gentle Tom Stall after wiping out a houseful of Philadelphia gangsters, including his brother. When he walks in the door, his family is eating dinner. They stop. He sits down. His daughter gets up and sets a place for him. His son gets him some food. The mere fact that the hero returns to the family circle was derided by many critics, who saw the scene solely in iconographic terms. But the subtleties and the accents are what count in this remarkable film, and the welcome is not warm but rote. It is as if no one can think of anything else to do. The idea that Joey Cusack and Tom Stall are two different people ("It was Joey who did that, not Tom," says Joey/Tom in an earlier scene to his shocked wife) may be ridiculous, but it is the only idea they have as a family, and they are all too profoundly embarrassed to abandon it for another one. Cronenberg ends with a shot of his hero's face, straining to appear passive. This final shot is a magnificent question mark, as darkly funny as it is tragic. And it speaks, quietly but authoritatively, to the dilemma of modern America more eloquently than anything Lars von Trier or Michael Moore could ever cook up. Here is the dispossessed middle-American evangelical who votes consistently against his own earthbound interests, because he has his eyes fixed on heaven and its rewards. Here is John Kerry, imagining that he can embrace his past as a Vietnam veteran who stood against the war and proclaim the glories of his war record at the same time. Here is George W. Bush, of course, his mind fixed on the invented reality of democracy and free-market capitalism spreading throughout the Middle East, the hellish chaos of the actual war in Iraq relegated to a secondary level of reality. And here, I suppose, is that girl, blithely singing the glories of her native land as she stands under the glow of its florescent lights and the electronic drone of its commercial television.

Not to mention every film critic who imagines that he or she is in touch with reality during those ten days a year spent in the terrarium known as the Cannes International Film Festival.

2005

Leftist Hollywood

Recently there has been a great deal of attention paid to the idea of "left-wing" moviemaking. The idea, which is really no idea at all but in fact a premise for a Sunday paper think piece (such premises now being accepted as ideas), is that these supposed left-wing films will make an "impact" at "the multiplexes." In this case, "the multiplexes" means the great unfathomable area beyond the screening rooms in New York and Los Angeles. I would have thought that this dream of political impact had gone up in smoke with *Fahrenheit 9/11* and the defeat of Kerry, but it is still with us. Meanwhile, the smart people—Robert Greenwald, for instance, with his quickly assembled but well-researched attacks on Wal-Mart or the Fox News Channel—make small, tactically precise moves in the direct-to-video market.

I am not one of those people who see nothing but idiocy and opportunism in what is now called the mainstream press. I can't even blame the writers of these weekend arabesques for seeing so many nonexistent trends and sea changes. That's their job, after all—to generate copy. And while there is a notion of rough equivalence between *Brokeback Mountain*; *Good Night, and Good Luck*; *Syriana*; and *Munich*, to be fair they are all seen as discrete events with their own unique points of view, logic, and, yes, impact. This final word is the one that stings.

There is currently no such thing as real, broad left-wing politics in the United States. Noam Chomsky or Howard Zinn might disagree, and to the extent that there are assorted gestures, sentiments, and longings that qualify as oppositional, they are right. But there is no clear objective, and the enemy is even less clear. There is something called "George Bush," a magnet for any and all hatreds and frustrations, and the usefulness of this Straw Man (easily identifiable as such to anyone of any political persuasion) as a focal point makes a great deal of emotional sense and precious little sense politically. How did they get away with it, we spend our time wondering. We "leftists" are outraged at the breaking of the Kyoto treaty; the invasion of Iraq and the resulting stream of misinformation, graft, and cover-ups; and the New Orleans debacle, and every day there is another log to throw on the bonfire. Which means that the real question is: how long will we keep throwing logs on the fire, and why are there so many? If the supply of fodder is endless, so is the capacity to burn.

There is a limitless supply of markers and flashpoints. There are "Iraq" (and "oil"), "Israel and Palestine" (or perhaps "the Israelis and the Palestinians"), "civil liberties," "freedom of the press," "campaign finance," "global warming," "health care," "education," and, of course, "abortion." All real and pressing issues, if not "issues." In other words, they are easy to handle in conversation or to write about in the op-ed pages, and for that reason they are satisfying, and their subtleties and frames (per George Lakoff) are easily dismissed or ignored by both sides. Emotional satisfaction plays a big part in American politics these days. For this reason, Joan Didion, probably our most brilliant political commentator, was vilified by liberals when she wrote a piece on the Terri Schiavo case that resurrected a number of facts inconvenient to both sides of the argument. She had disturbed the flow of satisfying righteousness, as she had almost twenty years earlier with her brilliant piece on the Central Park jogger case. Didion has always been good at seeing the popular narratives reenacted in the national arena and digging up the facts that have been buried in order to make the narrative play. For the past twenty years, she's been very busy.

Storytelling is always important, but at the moment we have little if anything else, at all levels. The right wing tells one story, the Democrats respond with another story, and the "spectatorial left" (a nice phrase coined by Richard Rorty) responds with yet another. Under the circumstances, it would be a wonder if movies hadn't attained such a high profile in what is known as the national debate. We are reminded, endlessly, that they "matter." But as what? The idea that they can influence votes is as false as the idea that watching them can replace reading as a means of historical education, but this strange desire for relevance persists. I suppose that the psychic mechanism at work is of a piece with "trickle-down" economics: so many movies containing so much political content, which will trickle down into the consciousness of their viewers, as wrong-headed as it was back in the 1950s when HUAC detected subversive messages in the screenplays of John Howard Lawson and Albert Maltz.

Steven Spielberg is the most self-important purveyor of the "entertaining yet informative" idea, so crucial in newsrooms. His discovery of the printed word as a source of inspiration back in the 1980s (if I remember correctly, he started to grapple with the subject on camera for Wim Wenders in his 1982 Cannes documentary *Chambre 666*) has mushroomed into an ongoing, awesomely pretentious project, in which a series of large-scale historical subjects—the Holocaust, slavery, D-Day, civil liberties, now the Israeli-Palestinian conflict, and soon Abraham Lincoln—have been ticked off for posterity (ancient history is farmed out to Ridley Scott). It's striking that Cronenberg is loathe to speak of A History of Violence as anything but an entertaining neo-western, while Spielberg is equally loathe to speak of his recent films on any terms but those of their "ideas " and, presumably, their "impact." The more of these films Spielberg has made, the more transparent they have become as dramas of ideas. On one level, Munich appears to have been designed to generate letters to the editor and discussions on talk shows. On another, it strikes me as a message meant solely for the American Jewish community. On the level of aesthetic satisfaction, it is, to my eyes, Spielberg's first complete failure. Previously unseen forensic details accompany each murder in much the same way that Gene Kelly used to add different flourishes to each new dance number, and the film is structured in an inane manner—murder/discussion, murder/discussion, the details that make up any reasonably satisfying thriller (how passports are forged, weapons are acquired, and information is gathered) jettisoned to make room for more discussions. Thus the Israeli assassins successfully land at fortified beaches, stroll into surprisingly unguarded hotel rooms and apartments. It is astonishing to me that anyone might find it even slightly plausible that a group of paid assassins would spend even a second debating the justice of their cause, let alone that they would spend half a second debating their beliefs with their enemies in a safe house in which they have all wound up as the result of a practical joke.

Truth is stranger than fiction, as the saying goes, but Spielberg is so intent on getting his message across that he provides only a makeshift fictional vessel in which to contain either. On top of which, his grasp of daily human affairs has never been weaker. Eric Bana's chief calls his wife and young child in Brooklyn, resulting in a fairly typical Spielberg moment. "How are you?" . . . "Fine." . . . "Let me put the baby on . . . Talk to daddy." . . . "Da-da." . . . Daddy cries. The entire exchange is timed as perfectly as the evening news and with about as much interest behind the camera in the particulars of being human. As for the penultimate crosscutting between Bana's homecoming orgasm and his mental picture of the Munich killings, it may well go down as one of the worst moments in the history of cinema, but it certainly does hammer home that all-important message. Which is? That revenge pollutes the soul and that violence begets more violence. Unless I'm mistaken, this fact is lost on absolutely no one, from Abraham Foxman to Dick Cheney, from Mahmoud Abbas to Sharon's successors. The real dilemma, so far from the makings of satisfying melodrama, goes all but unacknowledged. Only in a climate in which political debate is so weak would someone dream of making such a uniformly pretentious gesture. As in the late films of Cecil B. DeMille, the cloudy rhetoric of American governmental politics is perfectly translated into audiovisual storytelling.

Syriana and *Good Night, and Good Luck*, from George Clooney's and Steven Soderbergh's Section 8, are vastly superior in every way to Spielberg's official address to the people—ingratiatingly low-key, lovably old-fashioned, reveling in character and the intrigue afforded by politics, the action delivered in quick, semijournalistic vignettes. These have always been hallmarks of Soderbergh's own films as a director, and they have become a sort of house style. The macrocosmic *Syriana* and the microcosmic *Good Night* are eminently likable and satisfying films, and their most politically interesting aspects have been all but ignored by the press: each is devoted to tracing the contours of corporate violence, in which the logic of the free market ensures an absence of accountability. Thus at the end of Clooney's warm, ingratiating celebration of camaraderie and shared commitment in the workplace, David Strathairn's Edward R. Murrow realizes that he and his arch enemy Joseph McCarthy will both be hung out to dry for shaking up the status quo, while Steve Gaghan's film leaves us with a portrait of a Foucauldian world in which treachery is woven so deeply into the fabric of multinational business that corruption is both unheard of and unnecessary, and in which geopolitical power is both efficiently decentered and all-pervasive. As political gestures, they are welcome, I suppose, if only as proof that someone in modern cinema is thinking of modern politics in nuanced terms.

But why waste any time discussing their political impact? Even *Brokeback Mountain*, which has generated the most ink, is not itself a cultural breakthrough, good as it is. Rather, its popularity, which has as little to do with the actual movie as all the would-be wise guys who used to go around reciting Joe Pesci dialogue did with *Goodfellas*, is evidence of the fact that the American public is ready to stop vilifying homosexuality. That the Oscars have "rejected" blockbusters like *King Kong* and championed "small" and supposedly risky movies is celebrated as something like progress, when it is merely a response to what is already in the air. And the popularity of movies like *The Constant Gardener*, *Syriana*, or *Munich* doesn't signal a growing political enlightenment among filmmakers, but is rather a reflection of a growing desire among audiences to see political material in movies. Why left-wing material as opposed to right-wing material? Perhaps because current American right-wing positions are more or less at odds with the flux and variety on which art thrives. There is finally an oddly poignant ring to all this chatter about the leftist politics of this or that film when actual leftist politics are all but nonexistent and everyone is afraid to identify the real enemy. The Berlin Wall may have fallen long ago now, but Americans are still milling in its shadows, afraid to stop celebrating the dubious "triumph" of free-market capitalism: one wrong move into socialized medicine, reinvigorated unions, or increased economic regulation, and we risk losing our already precarious place at the top of the heap. Which is why movies—among many other things celebrations of profligate spending—have acquired so much importance as political gestures. General Motors announces that they're eliminating 30,000 jobs and no one blinks an eye, but the outrage over the fact that *Brokeback Mountain* has yet to screen at the White House rages on.

2006

IV Out of the Fog

A lot of my time is spent thinking about and watching older films, and it always has been. This presented a social problem for me when I was a teenager (it was hard to find someone else my age who was interested in Raoul Walsh, for instance), but the varied beauty of the cinema more than made up for the isolation. Now that so much energy is focused on what's happening tomorrow or next week as opposed to what happened yesterday in film culture, the idea of looking back seems more important than ever.

If the play of memory is strong here, it's because many of these pieces deal with films, some forgotten or neglected, made when I was an adolescent. Many of the other pieces on older films are related in some fashion to my father and my experience of growing up with his not-so-carefully concealed anguish. "If I were to put you or anyone else on a couch and say, 'Tell me your favorite movies,' it would be a way of psychoanalyzing you," Andrew Sarris told me (in an interview at the end of this book). The older I get, the more I realize the truth of Andrew's insight. I was drawn to certain types of actors and movies because they put me on a harmonious wavelength with my loved ones—I realize now that in Borzage's 1930s movies (like *Bad Girl* or *Mannequin*) I saw my grandparents as newlyweds living in tiny walk-ups; that I saw my great aunts in Ida Lupino and Lucille Ball; that for me, Dana Andrews's stiffness and Bogart's stoicism were interchangeable with my father's. The movies may change, but I think the same is true for all of us.

Allan Dwan's comedies for Edward Small and Republic are anomalies in American cinema. At first glance conventional and rather plain, they seem to be (and in many ways are) prototypes for the sitcoms that would soon become mainstays of American culture, with their lighter-than-air tone, "average" heroes, heavily typed supporting characters, and endless store of monetary/romantic predicaments. The films' resilient middle-class characters group and regroup their way through spacious offices, country homes in Connecticut or Massachusetts, or a Vermont inn with the same high-octane inventiveness as Jack Klugman and Tony Randall displayed in their *Odd Couple* apartment, or Lucy and Ricky in their assorted *I Love Lucy* digs.

Moreover, it's easy to imagine Dennis O'Keefe, star of Dwan's Wilson Collison–derived farces and of *Brewster's Millions*, with his own sitcom. As a matter of fact, he had one: *The Dennis O'Keefe Show*, which was on the air during the 1959–1960 season. And the second-drawer actors that Small and Republic were able to attract for the supporting roles—Mischa Auer, Allen Jenkins, Gail Patrick, Joe Sawyer, Jerome Cowan, and Lee Bowman, most of them well past their glory days—endow these movies with the same kind of threadbare ingenuity that, for instance, Peter Boyle now brings to *Everybody Loves Raymond* or that Agnes Moorehead once gave to *Bewitched*—and that's not to even mention *Lucy*'s own Fred, William Frawley, as the by-the-book general in *Rendezvous with Annie*.

The proto-sitcom probably began in the late 1930s or early 1940s, with films like the breezy Gene Raymond vehicle *Cross-Country Romance* or the intermittently hilarious *Obliging Young Lady*—later examples would be the Robert Mitchum/Janet Leigh film, *A Holiday Affair*, the massively popular film version of *The Egg and I* or *Miracle On 34th Street*. All these movies represented attempts to mass-produce the form of romantic comedy that Cukor, Capra, Lubitsch, Hawks, et al., had perfected in the 1930s, in the process creating an altogether new kind of impersonal zip, airiness, and lightness. They threw out the gravity of their betters but retained their speed, and they had a genuinely industrial sleekness—these films were all of a piece with jet planes soaring through the skies, air-stream cars rolling down new superhighways, or the coolly metallic ring of Les Paul and Mary Ford's "The World Is Waiting for the Sunrise." Dwan may have been the only director who knew how (or had the inclination) to harness this industrial beauty. But, very much unlike the aforementioned machine-tooled items, Dwan's movies are inflected with little grace notes—sudden tiny shifts in speed or perspective or visual design that give the films a humming beauty.

The level of anxiety in the Dwan comedies is strikingly high, and it's intimately connected to their speed. Dwan has said (to Peter Bogdanovich) that he rejected a musical number in *Brewster's Millions* because he didn't want to interrupt the flow, and that's a quality shared by all of these films: pure, unimpeded action, with a rhythm that's both exhilarating and a little bit nerve-wracking, like a merry-go-round that feels like it might go off-kilter. The movies also share an interesting quality that seems to have had a special meaning for Dwan: they are filled to the brim with women adored by men who feel downtrodden and worthless. American cinema offers a virtual parade of husbands and wives, but there's something special about postwar movies like *The Best Years of Our Lives* or John Berry's underrated *From This Day Forward*. I'm thinking of Teresa Wright's fondness for Dana Andrews in the former and Mark Stevens's adoration of Joan Fontaine in the latter. In a way, this dynamic is the key to all the Dwan titles: O'Keefe's worry over his fiancée/wife's reaction to an incriminating piece of lingerie in the two Collison farces or his fear that his inability to tell his fiancée about his strange predicament in *Brewster's Millions* will jeopardize their relationship; Robert Shayne's paralyzing sense of inadequacy before his gainfully employed wife (Gail Patrick) in *The Inside Story* (and William Lundigan's worries about his ability to support his beloved Marsha Hunt in the same film); and Eddie Albert's touching pride in his Annie, and his subsequent shame when she believes he's cheated on her. For all their lightness and dexterity, these films share an intense concentration on love, security, and adoration. Dwan has said that he made the two Collison farces with the troops stationed overseas in mind, which perhaps explains the urgent emphasis on an understanding of women's needs in those movies.

Anxiety vs. nurturing, discomfort vs. comfort—they battle for dominance in the overall musical structure of these movies, which might profitably be considered as a suite. Together, the films play in the mind as a series of clean, springing movements forward, all obstacles ingeniously hidden or shunted aside. Dwan's filmmaking craft is consummate on many levels. He gets around his budgetary restrictions with the aforementioned speed as well as an ingenious use of repetition, using certain camera setups (looking up the staircase in *The Inside Story*, from ground level at the open window in *Mabel/Gertie*, or staying tight on Eddie Albert and C. Aubrey Smith in the bomb shelter in *Rendezvous with Annie*) as visual refrains. There's an ingenious moment in *Getting Gertie's Garter* where O'Keefe arrives at the manor house for the weekend that provides a lesson to anyone interested in getting around a restricted budget, but you have to pay attention because it's over in a flash. We start with a standard shot of the grounds, probably from another, more expensive movie. Then we're on the porch, with everyone preparing for cocktail time. We hear the sound of a car pulling up—"Oh, that must be Ken." Before we've had time to blink, or to realize that we've never seen the reverse angle, O'Keefe has bolted into the frame. It may sound simple, but it's important to remember all the movies of the period that spoil their own rhythms with needless expositional, dully functional material. Dwan also gets little visual wonders out of light and shadow that seem beyond most of his peers under such restrictive conditions, and that give the scenes just the extra breadth and pliability they need. I'm thinking of Rochester cleaning the window at the beginning of *Brewster's Millions* and catching Marjorie Reynolds's reflection, or Binnie Barnes and Shelia Ryan sitting outside in the shadows observing O'Keefe and Marie McDonald inside.

Up In *Mabel's Room* and *Getting Gertie's Garter* are twin films, remakes of silent farces (both directed by E. Manson Hopper) in which a bespectacled, absent-minded O'Keefe is a happily married man who spends a weekend in snowy Connecticut/pre-summer Massachusetts trying to retrieve an incriminating piece of lingerie/garter belt he's given to the fiancée of a close friend before his own marriage. Mabel/Gertie decides to hold on to the bit of incriminating evidence and produce it in order to teach O'Keefe a lesson in honesty. Both films begin with brief urban-set prologues and move to the country after about half an hour, in both cases into a spacious central living room, upstairs corridor with adjoining bedrooms allowing for assorted interactions between the various couples, servants, and matrons of the house, and frequent trips under the bed and/or into the closet of the scarlet woman, then outside her window. *Mabel* is the swifter, more grueling of the two; *Gertie* the funnier and more purely deranged, more deeply neurotic yet more ebullient—it's amazing to witness an unexpectedly freewheeling Barry Sullivan (for the first and last time in his career) gleefully throwing his finacée's lingerie around her room in a re-creation of a college "shivaree." Both films feature numerous unconvincing plot contrivances whose sole purpose is to keep the farcical mechanics in working order, as well as borderline-unpalatable "ethnic" work from Mischa Auer and J. Carroll Naish as comically avaricious butlers, and legalistic nightmare sequences. Dwan gets past these potential stumbling blocks with his fast, fluid pace—as Donald Phelps notes in his perceptive Dwan article "The Runners," the comedies are "not so much funny as exhilarating." After a while, the engineering of the various improbabilities and failed double entendres becomes oddly stirring in and of itself.

Dennis O'Keefe in his nonhardboiled T-Men/ Thing mode is a strange guy to build a movie around, with a reedlike body that's almost but not quite pliantly elastic, a long face and bobbing head that aren't quite animated, and a semiaggressive knack for scene-hogging with his loud voice and rolling tones. The amiable thing about O'Keefe is the sincerity of his fear that he could lose his wife. O'Keefe is very good at stumbling into emotion amidst all his neurotic floundering, with a double take or a rhythmic downturn (his best marital sparring partner is the feisty Sheila Ryan in Gertie—as opposed to Helen Walker or Marjorie Reynolds, life with Ryan looks like it might actually be fun). But in these roles, where the inhuman speed of the action and the nonstop farcical dissembling shave away O'Keefe's toughness and circumspection, there's something touching about his sheer ordinariness, the suspicion that his gawky urbanite character in all three movies could have been played by any number of other actors. Mid-1940s Dwan has one striking similarity to Val Lewton's magisterial horror output: the uniformity of second-drawer actors, none of whom are exactly right for their roles, becomes a virtue. The lack of big-star magnetism, the feeling that Charles Winninger could be replaced by Edgar Buchanan or that Gail Patrick is interchangeable with almost any number of urbane, evening gown–toting also-rans of the era only adds to the down-to-earth, strictly life-size quality of these movies made to entertain the troops.

Brewster's Millions, also a remake of a silent (a Fatty Arbuckle vehicle directed by Griffith's Lincoln, Joseph Henabery), certainly has one of the most ingenious ideas in film comedy (in order to earn his eight million dollar inheritance, Brewster must spend a million dollars and have nothing left to show for it within two months). The movie features a less-perplexed, more-driven O'Keefe. There's nothing like the frenzied ballet of opening and closing doors in Mabel/Gertie here—more of a frantic charging back and forth across the spacious living room/office/yacht sets, as one friend after another either walks out of Brewster's money-losing "corporation" in exasperation or joyfully proclaims that he's just made Brewster some more money, which sends the boss into fits of nervousness (his greatest scheme: mounting a stupefyingly bad musical called Girl in a Sweater—à la The Producers—and chartering a yacht to take it on the road, then paying a small fortune to have it towed when it runs aground). Where *Mabel/Gertie* is a series of never-ending zigzags through doors, under beds, and in and out of windows, *Brewster* is a straight line all the way, a race-against-the-clock movie with a very interesting side effect. Excess and impoverishment become kissing cousins as the worry about spending money becomes virtually interchangeable with the worry about never having enough, and the plain fact of money itself amasses a real power, affecting all other considerations: marriage, happiness, freedom—everything. Money worries play a big role in postwar American movies, probably because everyone was waiting for the slump that never came (as a result of an industrial productivity decrease that never happened). It's certainly felt keenly in *The Best Years of Our Lives*, with Dana Andrews's melancholy ex-flyer who can't find a decent job to support his shrewish wife and Fredric March's disenchanted drunkard who finds little if any value in his lucrative banking job. It's also there in *It's a Wonderful Life*, in McCarey's two clerical comedies with Bing Crosby and his later *Good Sam*, and in lesser movies like the 1949 *It Grows on Trees*, another "financial surplus" comedy with an interesting relationship to *Brewster's Millions*.

Brewster has direct ties to *The Inside Story*, made three years later for Republic. As opposed to the earlier movies, meant to reassure G.I.s, this story was meant to caution the citizenry to not hoard money in banks but to let it circulate ("We got a lot of good reactions from the financial world," Dwan told Bogdanovich, "not much from the public, because they never *saw* a thousand dollars"). Dwan actually flashes back to 1933 just to hammer the point home (no one could ever accuse him of subtlety, narrative or thematic). Charles Winninger's near-sighted Uncle Ed tells the story of a thousand bucks in cash deposited in the safe of a hotel where he works behind the desk (by another character actor of yesteryear, Roscoe Karns, more jocosely lecherous than ever), which the owner (Gene Lockhart) mistakenly presumes to be a payment from his supposedly shiftless future son-in-law (Lundigan), and which he promptly uses to pay off the usurious moneylender who runs the hardware store (the beady-eyed and pinch-voiced, apparently omnipresent Will Wright, the last word in crusty self-righteousness in movies—he's also the crustily self-righteous executor in *Rendezvous with Annie*), who has it removed from his hot little hands by his landlady (Geraldine Atherton), who gives it as a retainer to the dispirited local lawyer (Shayne) in order to save his marriage to his adoring wife (Patrick), who uses it to pay the future son-in-law for the portrait he's painted of her, as a gift to her husband, and which the future son-in-law promptly pays back to the hotel proprietor, assuring that the original depositor gets his money, enabling him to pay off a local man who has just had twins. Husband and wife are happy again, father and future son-in-law are able to communicate, and the moneylender gets his comeuppance—thanks to a magical object, not so different on a purely mechanical level from the garter belt or the lingerie or *Annie's* chocolate cake.

For a movie set entirely in a Vermont inn (again anticipating another sitcom, *The Newhart Show*), *The Inside Story* is short on local flavor but long on fluidity, dexterousness, and subtle emotional shading. But the tone is less neurotic, more somber than that of the Collison farces, with a money-generated despair most fully felt in the sequences with Shayne, standing alone in his darkened house and burning with impotent rage over the fact that his wife has to go to the city to work in a nightclub while he can't manage to earn a living as a lawyer. Just as in *Mabel/Gertie*, the improbable farcical mechanics start to take on a life of their own, but the possible outcomes here are terrifying—the already suicidal Shayne mistakenly believes that his wife is having an affair with Lundigan and threatens to bust in on them and kill everybody in the room; meanwhile, Marsha Hunt, Lockhart's daughter and Lundigan's fiancée, is put in the unenviable position of having to stall Karns by vamping him. Other oddities: Allen Jenkins, looking like he's been waiting since 1933, haunting the lobby with his henchman, both in full gangster regalia, ominous reminders of a potentially bad outcome; and a narrator, Winninger, who appears to be the least observant person in the movie. He's so near-sighted that every time someone passes through his line of vision, he officially welcomes them to the inn, no matter that they've crossed his path twelve times in the last half hour.

Rendezvous with Annie, made three years earlier, is the best of these films, probably because it's the one that breaks the rule of second-string uniformity. Picture this movie about a soldier named Jeffrey Dolan who sneaks home from England on a three-day pass, returns home later to discover that his wife has had a baby, and then tries to prove what he's covered up so carefully, with O'Keefe in the lead rather than Eddie Albert—and it becomes apparent exactly how crucial Albert is to its poignance, its sense of longing, its soulfulness. It's easy to imagine O'Keefe in the scene where Jeffrey strolls through his New Jersey home town after he's been discharged, walking on air with the realization that he's a new father. O'Keefe would have turned it into a moment of foolish obliviousness, drawing attention to the incredulous, disapproving looks of the passers-by. Albert turns it into a quiet little rhapsody of a scene, and his endless joy has the opposite effect of deflecting attention away from the scornful townspeople, so rock-solid is his belief in himself and his wife. Similarly, O'Keefe would have turned the scenes with C. Aubrey Smith's diplomat (another excellent piece of casting) into little satires of cultural difference, whereas Albert makes them into moments of terrific, one-on-one cross-cultural camaraderie. With O'Keefe, *Rendezvous with Annie* would have been a movie about a man thrown into one predicament (going AWOL to fly home from England and be with his wife for eighteen hours) that leads to a string of ever-greater predicaments. With Albert, it's a movie about a man who misses his wife so much that he's willing to risk a court-martial to see her and whose love for her and their new child is so great that he's willing to go to the ends of the earth to prove that he's the baby's father, in the bargain securing an inheritance that will take care of his son's education.

Albert is one of those actors who can lay it on a bit thick from time to time, so it's no surprise that he went into television (sitcoms again). But he always maintained an interesting quality as an actor. He would slow down his words and round his tones with a slightly hammy but winning lilt, and he generally worked at a slower pace than his fellow actors, creating the effect of a genial audience member who wandered by accident into a vaudeville skit and became the unwitting straight man. This quality is evident in *Green Acres*, and it's used to devastating effect here, most noticeably in the scenes where Albert is stuck in the cockpit with his double-talking transatlantic chauffeurs or with the fast-talking press agent who gets him into a jam. The "hey fellas, hold on a minute" anxiousness of these scenes gives his moments of peace—communing with Smith in the shelter as Nazi bombs drop over London, singing in his mellow baritone in the cockpit, or rendezvous-ing with his beloved Annie—an extra dimension and rare beauty.

Late 1940s American cinema is short on transcendent moments. What few there are involve sudden strokes of luck—a life's worth of good will boomeranging back at George Bailey at the end of *It's a Wonderful Life* or Eddie Bracken suddenly bedecked in medals and declared a national hero in *The Miracle of Morgan's Creek*. There's a quieter version of this kind of sudden emotional blooming at the end of *Annie*, when Albert walks back into his house expecting to be rejected only to find his old friend Smith there to vouch for him and getting a chocolate cake in the bargain. But Jeffrey Dolan's first meeting with Annie is of another order altogether, on the level of Teresa Wright sponging Dana Andrews's forehead in *The Best Years of Our Lives* and soothing him back to sleep after a flashback nightmare. Jeffrey arrives by train at night and has been careful to alert Annie to the fact that they have to be secretive, that no one else must know he's there. Dwan shoots their reunion across the large expanse of a dark, empty street and puts the couple at opposite diagonal ends of the frame. They walk tentatively towards each other, and when they realize they're once again in the same town, on the same street, after years apart, they run into each other's arms and don't let go. Dwan maintains this beautiful distance, using all his hard-won knowledge of pacing, build-up, and space to create this exceptionally fine moment, which is like a Rockwell *Saturday Evening Post* cover without the all-American mawkishness and saccharine overlay. It's one of the few moments of perfect happiness in movies.

2002

The ideal Orson Welles biographer would have to think as quickly and expansively as Welles himself, and emerge with a book possessing his breathtaking sense of scope and awe—a *real* Mercury Production. Most Welles literature has tended to be too single-minded, either too enraptured by Welles himself or too intent on defaming him.

I suppose that American culture has always turned punitive and deflating when confronted with mercurial behavior from its artists, particularly the flamboyant ones, and few have been as flamboyant as Welles. Which is why, to borrow a phrase from his adaptation of Booth Tarkington's *The Magnificent Ambersons*, he has until recently been the recipient of an ongoing comeuppance, "three times filled and running over." I don't think there's another filmmaker who has had more unflattering books written about him, followed by more impassioned defenses.

Twenty-one years after Welles's death at the age of seventy, the fat jokes are finally wearing thin, and things have started to level out. Simon Callow, who sought in *The Road to Xanadu*, his first biographical volume on Welles, to find out "what went wrong before *Citizen Kane*," has developed a deeper affinity for his subject with his second volume, *Hello Americans*. And Joseph McBride, a marvelous critic and biographer (his *Searching for John Ford* is among the best critical biographies ever written of an American filmmaker) and an ardent Welles defender from way back, has written a lively portrait of Welles-as-independent artist intertwined with a melancholy self-portrait, in which the idolator receives a brutal sentimental education at the feet of his idol. Both books are considerable achievements, immaculately researched and carefully if not painstakingly considered. Taken together, they offer us a picture not of a boy genius who self-destructed at the age of twenty-six, but of a young man of prodigious gifts who developed one of the most distinctive aesthetic signatures in the history of cinema as he gallivanted his way through public life.

Hello Americans covers a relatively short period of Welles's life, beginning with the Los Angeles premiere of *Citizen Kane* in May of 1941, running through the twin debacles of *The Magnificent Ambersons* and *It's All True*, an exhausting marriage to Rita Hayworth, a tempestuous interval in the thick of American politics, and three studio pictures (*The Stranger*, Welles's least favorite; *The Lady from Shanghai*, his most beautifully chaotic; and *Macbeth*, his most threadbare   155 and ingenious). Callow ends with Welles's European exile in 1947 on the heels of a financially ruinous stage adaptation of Jules Verne's *Around the World in 80 Days* and a typically fraught postproduction on *Macbeth*. This is the moment when the Welles of legend solidified—Welles the wasteful, Welles the egotistical monster, with a disregard for discipline and a compulsion to be everywhere at once. The events of these years have been endlessly scrutinized by a parade of axe-grinders, seeing either the betrayal of a great artist by an unfeeling system or a talented wastrel who more or less asked for his films to be butchered and then cried martyr. To say that the truth lies somewhere in between is a rank understatement, and I don't imagine anyone will ever do a better job than Callow of tracking the numerous inclement behaviors and circumstances that converged to create a thunderstorm of disaster.

As everyone knows, *Kane* and Welles's one-man approach to the business of moviemaking did not leave Hollywood in a giving mood, and Welles's man at RKO, George Schaefer, was on the chopping block by the time the *Ambersons* shoot was completed. Since the axes were being sharpened while Welles was in Brazil shooting *It's All True*, the question remains: did he ignore the dire situation back in Hollywood, or was he simply oblivious? Callow speculates but never really renders a verdict, and his nonpolemical approach to this extremely touchy area is admirably cumulative—the details guide the story rather than vice versa. He barely acknowledges what may have been a crucial factor, the possibility that editor Robert Wise might have traveled to Brazil with the *Ambersons* footage in tow. According to McBride, the studio reneged on the allegedly phony grounds of wartime travel restrictions, but given the hectic circumstances I would question how seriously anyone took this possibility, Welles included.

Callow is very good on Welles's steam-roller approach to any and every undertaking bearing his name and on his uncontrollable energies, which often made for some strange aesthetic mismatches between his acting and his filmmaking. "On a purely quantitative level, his productivity is almost impossible to grasp," writes Callow, and he correctly characterizes Welles as suffering from the showbiz malady of "projectitis," of which he had a particularly bad case when he was down in Brazil, while not one but two of his films (*Ambersons* and *Journey into Fear*, a Mercury production directed by Norman Foster) were being eviscerated. The studio certainly indulged in a fair amount of skullduggery—the animus toward *Ambersons* was obviously on the rise well before the infamous Pomona preview, and the joyless Lynn Shores, Welles's production manager on *It's All True*, went a long way toward sabotaging that precarious project ("Almost any human group has its Lynn

Shores, grimly rejoicing in the prospect of disaster," writes Callow, unforgettably). Yet Callow illuminates one deciding factor that has rarely been
discussed or emphasized in previous accounts of the RKO debacle. Pearl
Harbor occurred right at the end of the *Ambersons* shoot, and the sense of
moral rectitude and patriotic fervor that swept the country placed the defiantly egotistical and unapologetically leftist Welles, who had now made two
films rooted in a distinctly American sense of loss and failure, in a suspect
and unflattering light. More to the point, he had made with *Ambersons* a
movie whose "critique of Fordism, potentially a great American theme—
must indeed have seemed bizarrely irrelevant at a time when the United
States was gearing itself up for massive production of mechanized trans-
portation of every kind," as Callow notes. This is no small point. Welles
commentators of all stripes have rightfully derided the studio's actions, but
no one has ever bothered to account for the logic behind its craziness. Callow's insight goes a long way toward explaining why RKO took one of its
biggest investments, ruthlessly cut it down to size, and released it on the
bottom half of a double bill with *The Mexican Spitfire Sees a Ghost.*

Callow also provides a detailed depiction of Welles's adventures in Brazil
among the jangadeiros, *carnival* revelers, and, to the growing consternation
of the Brazilian government as well as the eternally disgusted Shores, the
black favelados of Rio. It has often been asserted that Welles squandered
vast amounts of time and money to no purpose in Brazil, a legend that has
actually outlasted the more complicated truth, not to mention the documentary based on the remarkable footage that was released in the early
1990s. Did Welles have fun in Brazil? Undoubtedly. There were many wasted
days and nights written off to the chaos of *carnival*, the weather, the capri-
ciousness of both the native population and the director, and—tragically—
the drowning of Jacaré, the folk hero of the jangadeiros. And yet, a movie
was being made, a different kind of movie, and exactly *what* kind Welles was
discovering along the way. Callow has a clear understanding of the Brazilian adventure as "a risky strategy of simply shooting until the nature of the
film eventually declared itself." That Welles did so on RKO's dime has never
been forgotten, but it should be, particularly since this method of filmmaking has been adopted by so many filmmakers since—Jean-Luc Godard,
Wong Kar-wai, and scores of documentarians come immediately to mind.
"The luxury of self-discovery readily available to the artist in most other
spheres . . . is unavailable to the film-maker, except on the smallest scale,"
writes Callow, "and Welles was never going to function that way." Welles
recognized the inherently problematic nature of industrial filmmaking

early on and seized the opportunity arising from a set of chaotic circumstances to find another way, a way he would follow for the rest of his career.

McBride's *What Ever Happened to Orson Welles?* takes us through the career, film by film, with an emphasis on the "unknown Welles," the films that are largely unseen or incomplete, along with a trove of fragments—suggestions of films, stray scenes, tests, and sketches, glimpses of which are available in the German documentary *One-Man Band*. David Thomson elected to omit this period of Welles's working life from his entirely expendable 1997 "biography" *Rosebud*—shamelessly so, as McBride reminds us. The fact that any biographer could comfortably do such a thing is indicative of the contempt in which Welles is still held, the overturning of which is the explicit purpose of McBride's book. McBride's singularity of purpose necessarily denies *What Ever Happened* the expanse and wealth of detail in Callow's multi-volume biography, yet along with Peter Bogdanovich's *This Is Orson Welles* (edited by Jonathan Rosenbaum, probably the finest Welles scholar we have), Robert Carringer's books on *Kane* and *Ambersons*, and earlier critical volumes by James Naremore and McBride himself, it is destined to become one of the few genuinely indispensable books on the man and his work.

McBride's purpose being to redeem Welles from his attackers, he does quite a bit of muckraking, some of it to no avail. On the plus side, he proves beyond a doubt that the charges of budget overruns on *It's All True* were simply false. On the other hand, I think he's fighting a losing battle when he draws attention to the positive responses among the largely negative Pomona preview cards (Callow more sensibly paints a portrait of the city itself, and comes to the fascinating conclusion that it embodies "the very form of social existence that the novel [and the film] so eloquently deplores"). McBride also goes to great lengths to portray Welles's exile as political in nature. Welles did indeed throw himself into politics with the same unfathomable energy as he did cinema and radio. He was a fully engaged mid-century American leftist with a deep passion for racial equality, expending a great deal of radio time (and clout) leading the media arm of a campaign to bring to justice the tormentors of Isaac Woodard, a black vet who was brutalized and blinded by a southern cracker cop on the day he came home from the war. Nonetheless, the notion that he fled the country for fear of blacklisting alone doesn't quite add up—the truth seems far more unwieldy. Simply put, he had gone out of sync with the country he loved, politically, spiritually, morally, intellectually, and financially (his tax problems are well known). McBride expends a lot of energy trying to prove this point, but I find Callow's broader perspective more convincing. "The

mood both in the country and in the movie business," writes Callow, as-
tutely, "was dead against everything that had led to Welles's arrival in Hollywood: specifically the New Deal, with its . . . sense of collaborative activity
in every sphere and its wide social embrace." In a word, postwar America
was a disappointment to Welles, and he to it.

The principal value of McBride's book is in its detailed descriptions of
the hidden Welles projects: the long-gestating and proudly unfinished *Don
Quixote*, the fragments of Isak Dinesen's *The Dreamers* shot in his back yard,
and a near-complete adaptation of Charles Williams's *The Deep*. But it is
McBride's accounting of *The Other Side of the Wind*, which took up many years
of Welles's life and which ended in frustration, that makes *What Ever Happened to Orson Welles?* so invaluable. *Other Wind*, as it came to be known to the
army of actors and technicians who worked on the project throughout the
early 1970s, was the story of an old-time Hollywood maverick named Jake
Hannaford (eventually played by John Huston—Welles shot without a lead
actor for some time) who makes an arty movie-within-the movie à la
Zabriskie Point, and, in the twilight of his macho existence, harbors a secret
passion for his young male lead. As the film evolved over the years, the action was meant to alternate between a cocktail party at Hannaford's house
shot cinema-verité style and scenes from his art movie. McBride was drafted
into service by his hero the first time he met him and called upon to play
a variation of himself: a young, nerdy critic armed with questions, pens,
and a tape recorder. "'Is this going to be a *feature film?*'" the naïve McBride
asked. "With the full humorous effect of his rumbling, sonorous voice,
[Welles] chuckled, 'We certainly hope so.'" In this funny yet quietly devastating chronicle, McBride gives us something that Callow largely denies himself
and his readers: Welles's voice. I sympathize with Callow on this count, because Welles's wonderfully entertaining and notoriously unreliable accounts
of his own life are dangerously seductive and meant to throw biographers
off the track—Barbara Leaming's early-1980s biography, for instance, is all
but swallowed up by her subject. Nonetheless, Welles's quicksilver personality is only inferred through the amassing of detail in Callow's books, while
it comes to full-blown life here. Uncomfortably so.

Auteurist hero-worship was infected by polemical excess from the start.
It is the reason that Pauline Kael, in the long run one of Welles's most perceptive and eloquent defenders, wrote the notorious "Raising Kane." For
someone who grew up with Andrew Sarris's *American Cinema* and the *politique
des auteurs* running through his head, there is something deeply moving in
this chronicle of the disciple coming to terms with the monstrousness of   159

his master and realizing that it is all but inseparable from his genius. "It seems clear in retrospect that Welles, in both his personal and professional dealings, often seemed to provoke the situation he most feared," writes McBride, as a prelude to a description of one of Welles's more notorious temper tantrums. "Indeed, there was something in Welles that seemed to set up situations in which people's loyalty was tested under extreme duress and then (almost inevitably) found wanting." Even after his death, this drama of betrayal continues to play on, with Welles's ever-loyal cameraman Gary Graver, his collaborator in life and art Oja Kodar, his friend-turned-chronicler-turned- rival Peter Bogdanovich, his unloved and needlessly litigious daughter Beatrice, and even McBride himself locked in battle over the fate of his film. As the various parties struggle to remain true to Welles's wishes, *The Other Side of the Wind* remains unfinished and unseen apart from a few fragments and rough assemblies shown on various occasions around the world. And those fragments are indeed dazzling, unlike anything made by anyone else before or since.

There is an undercurrent running through these two fine books, of Welles's essential unknowability. Despite the fact that his face and voice were among the most familiar of the twentieth century, I think that he was finally a more resolutely private figure than even Kubrick or Pynchon, guarding the best of himself under the cover of the sacred beast. It's all too easy to go Rosebud-gathering with Welles or to get lost in the brilliantly baroque configurations of his initially explosive and finally peripatetic public life. The key, of course, is the work. As McBride once pointed out of a shot from *Ambersons*, his films are *physically* overpowering. There is a strange sense of softness and immobility in Welles's acting (brilliantly illuminated by Callow) that goes hand in hand with a larger force in the moviemaking: the sense that his characters never move anywhere willingly, that they are always *being moved*, wrenched away by the greater forces of history. Like their creator, they are betrayed, and in *Kane*, *The Magnificent Ambersons*, and *Chimes at Midnight*—his greatest films—they are betrayed by time itself, which arrives in the form of "progress." This is the great modern malady, and Welles suffered from it so powerfully that it animates almost every frame he ever shot and makes his greatest protagonists (Charles Foster Kane, George Amberson Minafer, and Falstaff) into immobilized Quixotes, too stunned by the force of time to pick up their lances and fight. Welles's obsessive preoccupation with betrayal may have cost him dearly, but it gave life to some of the most durable moments in twentieth-century art.

Jack Arnold was no auteur, but he had all-American ingenuity. He was also possessed of a fascinating conceptual bent that now imbues his films with a lot of charm and a measure of excitement for modern audiences. His no-budget 1953 3-D "thriller" *The Glass Web*, a crude but intriguing *Big Clock* knockoff, is mostly a matter of deftly orchestrated dramatic effects, and beyond that it's a triumph of application over inspiration. Arnold was never very interested in his actors, and those fans who feel for him because he was saddled with the likes of Grant Williams or Richard Carlson need only study the ultrafunctional use he makes of Edward G. Robinson here. This is Robinson in his *Manpower/Scarlet Street* wounded male vanity mode, crossed with some of the Machievellian schemers he played in his earlier films. Granted, neither Robert Blees nor Leonard Lee were the equal of Dudley Nichols, but given all the collapsing and foreshortening that's necessary in B-movie writing, Robinson's overly ambitious TV researcher is potentially interesting.

An improbable modern art fan ("What do you think of the Cézanne, Paula?"), Robinson's Henry Hayes is the low man on the *Crime of the Week* totem pole. While the dashing young writer soaks up all the accolades, Henry slaves away for 150 bucks a week, and his meticulous eye for detail goes unheralded. It's familiar territory for Robinson, and he goes dutifully through his paces, loping when he could have been slogging. Henry's sense of ambition is nicely gradated, his hurt feelings allowed to roil just beneath the surface, his murderous rage kept cunningly offscreen. But it's Arnold's failure that the character never really comes alive. Robinson always needed an inventive director to counteract the sedentary side of his humpty dumpty physique, the big head and rounded stomach threatening to keep him pinned in one place. Huston, a genius with blocking and a devil with interior scale, gives Robinson a bantamweight mobility as well as an aura of tabloid mythicism in *Key Largo*. In *Scarlet Street*, Lang accentuates the meek, homely qualities in Robinson's screen character (his compliant smile is pitiful-to-excruciating) and gets at something rare in movies, the kind of weakness that leads to petty domestic tragedies captured so well by Dreiser in *Sister Carrie*.

Of course, Lang and Huston had money to burn compared to Arnold on the no-frills *Glass Web*, with its five cramped sets and two measly exteriors, not to mention the demands of shooting in 3-D. But Arnold possessed none of Ulmer's ability to put his limited sets to claustrophobic and often expressionistic use, or the early Anthony Mann's knack for building netherworlds of menace out of light and shadow (aided in no small measure by John Alton). Robinson, John Forsythe as the adulterous writer Don Newell, and the various characters who fill out the rest of the cast (Kathleen Hughes as the blackmailing actress and murder victim Paula Rainer, Richard Denning as director Dave Markson, Hugh Sanders as the generic plainclothes cop Stevens, and Marcia Henderson as Don's quickly forgiving wife), each one as anonymous as a supernumerary, constantly wind up in awkward stage groupings. They unspool their dialogue in each other's faces as they stand in three-quarter profile, or as they make a move across the set to get to the next static position. From a spatial point of view, this is Moviemaking 101, and that goes for the acting as well. If Robinson is more or less leveled by the lack of invention, Forsythe, a pleasant actor, is never allowed to stretch out. He's very good here at capping his panic, trying as quickly and painlessly as possible to erase his possible implication in a murder he didn't commit in order to return to a bland status quo. He has a very fine moment when he opens an incriminating package at the breakfast table and then quite believably shifts into tense, cover-up mode, his eyes darting across the room and down. But Forsythe is never allowed to let any emotion register before the film hurdles to its next plot point. It's probably not Arnold's fault, but there's a terrible miscalculation when Newell's name tag, which he's removed from the murder site, falls out of his handkerchief, pulled from his pocket by a harpy from the party next door to wipe the lipstick off his face. It drops to the floor (in close-up), Newell fails to notice, and an ominous musical theme suddenly swells on the soundtrack. At a crucial moment, we're wrenched out of Newell's point of view for a cheap music cue.

I'm going to great lengths to point up the shortcomings of Arnold's mise-en-scène, if you could even call it that, in order to highlight his very unusual talents for the conceptual and for reality shock effects that were ahead of their time, predating the likes of Joe Dante and Paul Verhoeven, and even Frank Tashlin by a couple of years. There's a remarkable consistency, intentional or not, between the plight of the *Shrinking Man* and the increasing psychological smallness of Forsythe's Newell and Robinson's Henry, first riding high with wife and kids in tow, then blackmailed into submission by the scheming Paula, an actress on the show with whom he's had a casual affair, then stumbling onto her murder scene and trying to cover his tracks as if he's actually guilty, and finally having to write the murder up as an episode of *Crime of the Week* (and make it good—the show is up for sponsorship renewal). Arnold pushes this sense of smallness by exaggerating everything *around* Don and Henry: the multiple TV monitors and pressure-cooker environment within the control room during a live broadcast and, even more spectacularly, the scene leading up to Paula's murder, where Hughes is nothing but a force field of shrill, conniving bitchery, and a lush orchestral arrangement of "Temptation" keeps playing over and over again on the hi-fi.

The sense of cheapness, flimsiness, and an unfeeling materialist culture, is overwhelming. You'll never amount to anything, Paula screams at Henry, continually pointing out the fact that he makes only $150 a week compared to Don's $500, and meanwhile the record keeps playing. *The Glass Web* has two genuine tours de force (if you don't count its quickly dispatched "3-D" section): the opening coup de théâtre, in which we're plunged into the tackiest B-picture murder scene only to have the camera pull back and reveal that we're watching a broadcast of *Crime of the Week*; and Paula's murder, an extended set piece of cheap maliciousness that's a minor wonder with its manipulation of sound and offscreen space and its very believable sprawl of cheap, shallow, tawdry behavior within an apartment hallway. Hayes knocks on the door, and Paula assumes it's Don, and proceeds to give Hayes the berating of his life. Don walks up to the door but hears voices inside, hesitates to go in, then hides in the hallway from a lumpish, arguing couple from the party next door, their voices drowning out any noise from within Paula's apartment. When Don finally finds a moment to enter, Paula has already been murdered, and he loses no time wiping his prints from the door handles and the chest of drawers, then ripping his name tag from his pajamas, as "Temptation" continues to blare away. Out in the hallway, he's waylaid by a pack of predatory women from the party, eager for a make-out session, one of whom wants to turn Paula's hi-fi off—"This classical music gets on my nerves."

"Here comes the ad, the most important part of the show," exclaims one of the characters in the control booth. The steady, comical undercurrent in *The Glass Web* is the coarsening effect of television with its rampant commercialism, turning its creators into automatons and draining the juice from their souls, drop by drop. It's a humorously high-toned moral position for Hollywood, particularly given the unfriendly rivalry between the two media that more or less began right before *The Glass Web* was made. Nonetheless, it was a fruitful theme from the 1950s onward, from Frank Tashlin through Jack Lemmon sitting in front of his TV after work in *The Apartment*, onto *Network* in the 1970s and the recent *Magnolia*.

Hollywood's antitelevision bent actually found its early apotheosis two years later with *It's Always Fair Weather*, courtesy of a pack of enlightened eastern liberals (Gene Kelly, Stanley Donen, Betty Comden, and Adolf Green). But while *The Glass Web* may seem impossibly crude by comparison, there's a similarly mordant tone, particularly in the scenes with Forsythe's hapless Don, flying high one moment and falling to earth with a resounding thud the next. Before he and his screenwriters are forced to shift into high narrative gear and wrap up the movie in a trim eighty-one minutes (in the process forgetting all about that name tag as well as the looming threat of several witnesses who saw Don in the vicinity of the victim's apartment), Arnold generates a fair amount of deadpan comic momentum around Don's predicament through big, outsized details: the mockingly repetitious song, the arrival of the pajamas in the mail over breakfast, under Henry's watchful gaze ("Your look when you saw those pajamas told me all I needed to know"), and Don's dazed walk away from the murder site, once he realizes he can't possibly retrieve the name tag. How many 3-D set pieces were comically tuned to a hero's woeful psychological state? An oncoming car misses Don (and the camera) by inches, a log at a construction site passes right by his head, and, most hilariously of all, he walks dangerously close to a pile of rocks as it's being dropped from a steam shovel. There's a small-scale conceptual bravura at work here, opening the way to the genuine daring of *The Incredible Shrinking Man* four years later.

And this crude but half-clever murder mystery also has a genuine feel for "thing-ness" (in the Georges Perec sense), the frightening accumulation and insistence of cheap material objects. Logic has largely gone out the window for the film's climax, the broadcast of the Paula Rainer murder episode, but the film stays thematically on target. "Fade in. A California modern house," goes Don's too-detailed script, giving a rundown of the furniture and various objects within Paula's apartment. When the visiting cops get a look at Henry's set, the ante's been upped: it's distressingly perfect. And Henry's passion for detail finally does him in when he instructs the sound man to play just the right recording of "Temptation," over and over. Appropriately, the final confrontation, looking just as much like stock melodrama as the opening episode of *Crime of the Week*, is played out in studio B over a TV monitor.

A droll, media-happy movie made in the long shadow of Welles and his radio-born aesthetic, *The Glass Web* may be more likable artifact today than genuinely exciting aesthetic object. But there's something bracing about its mixture of crudity and conceptual wherewithal, anticipating a key artistic position of the 1970s and 1980s.

2000

Big Wednesday is, among other things, a surfing movie without a single Beach Boys song on its soundtrack. It's also a terrific open-air movie, of which there are precious few in modern American cinema. It's the book that John Milius never wrote—literally. And it's the only movie I know that embraces the form, as opposed to the spirit, of *On the Road.* It's also Milius's version of *The Searchers,* complete with a brief appearance by that film's Mose, Hank Worden; except this time, the mythic search is not for a person or a place, but for a sense of definition, a largely unconscious operation that most of us spend our lives performing, for a moment or an image that will crystallize the pure sensation of existence as it's rushing by, without trying to artificially slow it down or freeze it. Finally it's a work of memory, but one in which the passing of time is neither tragic nor sad, but simply there, impossible to avoid or rail against.

"It was a time of the West swell. A swell of change. A swell you usually rode alone." These are memorializing words, spoken by the film's narrator in a solemn tone. The tone resembled nothing else hitting movie screens in 1978, but was redolent of American movies from an earlier era—*How Green Was My Valley,* for instance.

I remember the late 1970s just as well as Milius remembers the early 1960s, because that was the time when I was coming of age. And just as Milius keeps the Beach Boys and Jan and Dean off his soundtrack because he's filming his early 1960s (and because he doesn't confuse memory with commerce), I don't remember the then-current fashions as much as a particular mental framework, a shared state of mind. And I also remember very well that at the time *Big Wednesday* was released, Milius's tone of memorial solemnity was severely out of step with the moment. This didn't present much of a problem for me, since I'd spent a great deal of my childhood and adolescence immersed in American movies from earlier eras. On a whole other level, it was a problem and not a small one. I was seventeen years old in 1978. As we all know, teenagers spend quite a bit of mental energy thinking about what other people think about them, most of all people their own age. Older movies were as present in my life as they were relegated to the deep backgrounds of my friends' lives. It was difficult, if not impossible, to find anyone with whom I could share my delight over *The Awful Truth* or *Rio Bravo* or *The Crimson Kimono*. And a new movie that evoked older movies presented an even greater dilemma. It wasn't hard to wax enthusiastic over *Dressed to Kill*, which took a nasty spin on Hitchcock. It was harder to root for *New York, New York* because of its anachronistic music and visual scheme, but the movie was powered by the twisty dynamics between Robert De Niro, Liza Minnelli, et al. *Halloween* and *The Warriors* also had their old-fashioned sides, but both movies were also tuned in to a new kind of romantic teenage fatalism. But *Big Wednesday* was different. Here was a movie, made only three years after the troop withdrawls from Southeast Asia, with a relatively becalmed attitude toward the Vietnam War, as well as a scene in which one of the heroes verbally demolishes a caricatured hippie waiter. Here was a genuinely stoic movie, stoic about not just the passing of time but about all misfortunes, at a time that marked the beginning of an overwhelming shift to a youthful "demographic" in the movie business, already signaled by the incredible popularity of *Animal House*. The demand for rectitude that was so central to the student movements of the 1960s mutated into what came to be known as political correctness, and it coupled perfectly with idealized notions of golden youth, the narrative of loss of innocence assuming tragic proportions. Quite a time to make a movie about three surfers who age with stoic grace and look back in tranquility rather than anger or disappointment. Without any Beach Boys music.

As I said, Milius is not a little indebted to John Ford, as were many of the directors who comprised the New Hollywood. But in most cases, the debt was paid visually, or even more commonly, by repeating the central dramatic idea of *The Searchers*—namely, going through hell and losing all reason in the process, in search of someone or something. It's central to *Taxi Driver*, *Hardcore*, *Close Encounters of the Third Kind* (all three of which began as Paul Schrader scripts), *The Deer Hunter*, and, in a roundabout way, *Apocalypse Now*. With *The Last Picture Show*, Bogdanovich did something else: he worked from Ford's gravity, with one of his key actors (Ben Johnson, who would appear the same year as Melvin Purvis in Milius's *Dillinger*), and used it to anchor an elegiac sense of loss quite different from that of Ford's films. Milius was the only one with the temperament to emulate (or attempt to maintain) Ford's stoicism.

In fact, it wasn't just Ford's stoicism, but the stoicism of an entire generation of filmmakers who by the 1970s had reached a venerable old age, at which point their talents were as adored as their values were abhorred. It has often been remarked that the directors of the "pioneer" generation—Hawks, Ford, Vidor, Dwan, etc.—knew a thing or two about other trades before they became filmmakers, whereas for the younger generation, movies were a world unto themselves, not just a profession but a vocation. There is, I think, a profound connection between the relatively recent conception of cinema as a way of life and the idea of innocence lost that came to permeate American cinema in the 1970s. It's a virtual skeleton key for the New Hollywood, a core sentiment behind *Mean Streets* and *The Godfather*, *Badlands* and *Close Encounters*, *Heaven's Gate* and *The Fury*. The extreme love of the film image itself that lies at the heart of these movies is halfway between a prayer and an embrace: a prayer for the recovery of what's been lost; an embrace of the one reliable object left behind.

The spirit of Nick Ray hovers over American cinema from the late 1960s onward. Or, to put a fine point on it, the spirit that Ray anticipated and harnessed to his advantage in *Rebel without a Cause*. And the way that film keeps gravitating toward warm, comforting spaces in which James Dean/Natalie Wood/Sal Mineo can ensconce themselves is echoed in the New Hollywood, in which agoraphobia is a constant. There's a heavy strain of urbanity accompanied by an attitude toward the natural world that's either nervous, distant, or both. Think of Spielberg and his orderly urban sprawl; De Palma and his darkened multilevelled cityscapes, as clean as operating theaters; Scorsese and his poolrooms, bars, apartments, and social clubs; Lucas and his swishing doors and plastic and metallic corridors; Coppola and his dark, sumptuous, comfy lairs. When a New Hollywood filmmaker goes outdoors, more often than not, the landscape and the experience is broken up, charted, and segmented so that it's as close as possible to a good old reliable urban grid, as in *Apocalypse Now*. There's also plenty of aquaphobia, the most extreme version of which can of course be found in *Jaws*. Charlie and Teresa's miserable visit to the beach in *Mean Streets* is emblematic, and Charlie's speech ("I hate the beach, and the sun . . . I like linguine with clam sauce, John Wayne . . .") could serve as a virtual New Hollywood credo (as could Leonard Kouras's miserable running commentary during the walk up the mountain in *Who's That Knocking at my Door?*). The other side of the same coin: a land-locked Matt Dillon's arrival at the ocean, as if he'd just landed on the moon, in the closing telephoto image of *Rumble Fish*.

The disappointed or compromised or traumatized young hero, who gets George Amberson Minafer's comeuppance for life, is another constant. It's the backstory for everyone from *Badlands*'s Kit to *Mean Streets*'s Charlie, from Travis Bickle to Michael Corleone, and from Carrie to Luke Skywalker. Spielberg provides a touching suburban variation on this generational obsession with the shock of disillusionment. There's a sense of endless circling, trying to locate the precise moment when innocence was lost. It's about ten million light years away from Vidor and his pioneering mountain men/industrialists; Hitchcock and his suave, urbane heroes (even the Stewart of *Vertigo*); and Hawks and his pragmatic code of survival. It's impossible to imagine a character in any of the New Hollywood movies asking of another, "Are you good enough for the job?" ("Do you think you can handle this?" is more like it, followed by, "If you can't, don't feel bad, I'll get somebody else"). Walter Hill, with his Hawksian affectations, is an exception, but there is a strange discordance between his heroes' "no-nonsense professionalism" (at least in the early films) and the paranoid spirit behind the camera. But the real exception is John Milius.

There are other great open-air movies in the New Hollywood canon, namely those by Malick and Michael Cimino. But where Malick turns every landscape into a space for ontological/metaphysical inquiry, while Cimino goes for historical pageantry, Milius, perhaps even more than his Old Hollywood masters, has a feel for the outdoors and the way seasonal changes can affect your perception of life. In *Big Wednesday*, Milius knows the seasons and the weather, and he spaces time and change according to the swells and the cold. And his surfing scenes are like no one else's. In most movies, surfing is represented by a cut from an establishing shot of the beach to the action in the water, in which the surfers seem to have been dropped by helicopter—to the sounds of The Beach Boys, of course (or, if the movie has a discerning Music Supervisor, Jan and Dean). As for Milius, he doesn't just get coverage of "waves." He knows what they look like at different times of year. And what it feels like to go out in the spring as opposed to the autumn. And he doesn't just shoot coverage of "surfing," either. He gives you the whole experience—waking up and knowing it's a good day for surfing, going down the beach with your friends, paddling out, standing up and riding the waves, and, in two very special touches, running your hand along the wave "wall" and walking the board.

The film is tied to the elements at every possible level: the lives of the characters, which are lived under the sun; Bruce Surtees's magic hour images, as solid as legend yet as supple as sunlight; the believably bronzed bodies and easy-going affects of Katt, Busey, and Vincent, who are ingeniously cast, an oddly amorphous trio sporting three variations of the Californian overgrown child (Vincent's pout, for once put to perfect use; Busey's ever-present smile of foolish confidence; Katt's dreamy, disappointed solitude); and the narrative, which is structured according to seasonal changes and continually drops the protagonists further and further ahead in time, culminating in Big Wednesday, 1974. Each section ends with a harsh life lesson, a reversal of expectations that is meditated on and absorbed as a lesson. There's a sense of calm that pervades *Big Wednesday*, but I would hesitate to label it "eastern." In a very real way, Milius's position here is an echo of Thoreau's: the only way to properly understand life, the film is saying, is to live under the sky and, in this case, by the ocean, as the seasons change.

Milius never leaves his movie in the hands of any one character. At times, it seems as though everything will center around Katt's Jack, the most responsible of the three. But when he bravely goes off to war, he returns a quiet man, and he disappears from his friends, his family, and, more or less, from the movie, until the final scene (the same is true of Busey's "Masochist"). At other moments, Vincent's Matt Johnson seems like the film's lynchpin, perhaps because he's the "baddest" of the trio, drinking himself into a stupor and playing matador on the highway. In fact, for a time, Matt seems like he's going to be a Southern California variant on either De Niro's Johnny Boy, Martin Sheen's Kit, or Mickey Rourke's Motorcycle Boy, destined to ride off into oblivion. Then, at a certain bend in the becalmed sprawl of the narrative, thanks to a trusting woman (Lee Purcell's supercool Peggy is one among many trusting women, in this film and in Milius's body of work in general), Matt becomes as responsible an adult as Jack was a teenager. And while his is the character who weathers the most onscreen changes (in and out of friendship with Jack, beating the draft by faking a knee injury, seeing his favorite burger joint converted into a hippie crunchfest, and realizing he's been reclassified from Golden Boy to Outmoded Pioneer without knowing it at a screening of an *Endless Summer*–type documentary), Matt is also the only one of the three who actually comes to accept his own limitations as a man. One might suspect that this is one of those movies with a "secret hero" located in the supporting cast—Bear perhaps, the rough hewn maker of boards with a poetic appreciation of the beauty of surfing, played by that old *Gunsmoke* veteran, Sam Melville. But Bear is actually a maudlin, self-destructive drunk, who loses his business, his wife, and his home. And while he is the only one who keeps the faith and hands Matt the hallowed board he's saved for him alone to use on the big day, he never quite feels like a grand guiding spirit: the realization of his dream, to see Matt, Jack, and the Masochist surf on Big Wednesday, is finally a personal satisfaction, while the triumph is theirs. In Milius's universe, everyone is ultimately responsible for himself. Actually, it's best to look at *Big Wednesday* as a movie about a place, the Point, which makes Matt the de facto hero simply because he's the only one who sticks around.

The more I think about it, the more I admire the feat that Milius pulls off in this movie. He follows Kerouac's form of an epic narrative, with the rambling disorderly sprawl and the apparent randomness of remembered reality. But he films each of his set pieces—the first surfing episode, the party at Jack's mother's house (in which the tall tales from every party of Milius's youth seem to have been packed into one extended scene), the disastrous trip to Mexico, Bear's wedding, the pre-Vietnam induction hall (which contains an ingenious piece of casting: Joe Spinell as an army psychiatrist) and the subsequent farewells, and not to mention Big Wednesday itself—with a feel for the weight of gestures and the beauty of faces as they bear up under the pressure of time, inherited from the Ford of *They Were Expendable* or *Fort Apache* (the party scene or moments in the induction hall also recall the raucousness of *The Quiet Man* and *Donovan's Reef*). He leads the way, ever so quietly, to some heartbreaking moments: Bear's tearful speech to Jack and Sally (Patti d'Arbanville) about the destruction of the pier and his henceforth land-locked existence, inflamed by a golden-red sunset; Fly's (Robert Englund) heartfelt goodbye to Jack as he goes off to war; and Waxer's funeral (which, at first glance, seems to be Jack's). Milius never isolates anyone or anything in a golden nostalgic glow, either visually or thematically. He removes his characters from the flow of experience only once, when he heroically frames the trio banding together once again on Big Wednesday and marching down to the water with an apparent knowledge of their own timeless beauty and grace. I think it's a mistake, though not a costly one, because it soon gives way to some beautifully rendered surfing. I wish that each character had hit the water separately, in search of his own moment, trying to reclaim his own wonder, and found one another as they were riding the waves as opposed to striding into the water as one valiant team.

In the political reality of 1978, John Ford was deemed a reactionary scoundrel. Now, it's the rhetoric of that moment, which required a veritable laundry list of affinities and predilections of any artist before they were deemed politically acceptable, which seems dated. It's Ford's work that seems alive now. And Milius, who once seemed like a throwback—and a reactionary to boot—now seems like an independent artist who chose his masters well. In many ways, *Big Wednesday* is the signature work of a stoic countertradition of which Milius and John Carpenter are the only remaining members.

2002

There's a lot that's wrong with The Driver, at least by Hollywood standards—
the incongruousness of smooth-skinned, self-pitying Ryan O'Neal as the
world's greatest getaway driver; the portentous namelessness of the principal characters (The Driver, The Detective, The Player, The Connection); and
the unrelenting funereal coolness of the enterprise, like a Melville caper
stretched out to ninety-one minutes. Yet, like many Walter Hill films, it has
a near-primitive physical power and an itchy brand of existentialist dread.
Not to mention an assortment of odd discordances that break the flow of
Hill's "exercise in style" in unpredictable ways.

Almost three decades after the fact, The Driver seems like a striking pre-
cursor to Tarantino's the-world-is-a-genre cinema as well as Michael Mann's
L.A.-specific crime stories. In 1978, Hill did indeed seem like the last man
standing, devoted as he was to Americanizing the "mythic genre movie"
genre originated by Melville and raised to operatic heights by Leone. With
only a handful of scripts and the excellent, winningly modest Hard Times
under his belt, Hill made a bold move with such a stylized undertaking, particularly in cruddy 1978 Hollywood. At a time when old-guard genre filmmakers like Siegel and Karlson were still working and extreme stylization
was customarily reserved for subjects of corresponding heft (or for horror),
the film barely made a dent, at least in this writer's memory (apart from a
glowing mention from Pauline Kael in her celebrated return to The New
Yorker). It would be Hill's next film, The Warriors, which would hit just the
right pitch of mythicized stylization and teenage anomie and make the box
office registers ring.

Among the many differences between Hill and Tarantino, the sense of
physical environment as key dramatic player is one of the most striking. In
Tarantino, no apartment/street/bar/restaurant appears without being pre-
formatted into its generic place—the films are as verbally free as they are
physically uptight and regimented. Hill, on the other hand, is always threatening to move away from his drama and let the landscape take over—
the bayou of Southern Comfort, the dusty, acrid border town of Extreme Pre-
judice, and the teenage dream New York of The Warriors. Hill manages
the same kind of cold, tough look at the downside of L.A. that Huston did
in The Asphalt Jungle, a Melville favorite and in some ways the prototype for

all mythicized genre movies. But this L.A. is as depopulated as the post-apocalyptic landscape of *The Omega Man*. Hill's film has the acrid flavor of William Friedkin's *To Live and Die in L.A.* as well as Huston's mean streets, but where those films offer us picturesque tours of antipicturesque industrial landscapes, *The Driver* gets down to basics: coldly glittering asphalt under dull streetlights and believably homely rooms and apartments emptied of everything but the bare necessities. Meanwhile, there may be more than a few similarities between Hill and Mann, but we're a million miles from the latter's lush pictorialism, though perhaps a little closer to the Chicago of *Thief*.

The funniest aspect of *The Driver* is the global disillusionment of its characters. Whenever anyone has money in their hands, their affect is so disenchanted that they seem to be already anticipating the moment when it will slip through their fingers. Unlike Sterling Hayden's Dix and his band of small-timers in the Huston film, no one here is dreaming of that elusive last big score, and there is no honor among thieves à la Melville—this is jungle morality, survival of the fittest, all but interchangeable with *Southern Comfort*'s swamp pursuit or the bare-knuckled fighting of *Hard Times*. It's as if Hill's characters were trying to beat each other for top spot in a none-too-promising purgatory. The only illusions here are small ones—the semipro thieves think they can wriggle their way past the cops and the driver, Ronee Blakley's "connection" (she seems more like the proprietor of a vegetarian restaurant than a fence with nerves of steel) thinks she can talk her way out of certain death, and Bruce Dern's cop thinks he can outwit O'Neal's driver. The parallels between the Dern/O'Neal relationship and the Pacino/De Niro standoff in *Heat* are striking, but Hill's antagonists have no extravagant dreams or lofty desires for a better life. They've long since resigned themselves to the fact that they're stuck in nowheresville and battling for nothing much—king of the bus depot, lord of the parking meters.

This lack of a romantic dimension is at once oddly disconcerting—you wonder why the film's population doesn't just retire to their rooms and wait for the chill of death—and what gives the film its oddly hypnotic quality. As in *Southern Comfort*, the emotional tone of *The Driver* is undifferentiated, and the only variations are supplied by the actors—Dern's maniacally animated facial expressions, monotonously twangy tenor, and overly studied unease within his own body (as in many of his performances, he seems to have something unpleasant on his mind that has absolutely nothing to do with the movie he's in); Blakley's southern homeiness and grace; Joseph Walsh's skuzzy intelligence and desperation (his is probably the best performance in the movie); Adjani's ghostly, doll-like presence; and O'Neal's sadly arcing eyebrows and eternally disappointed half-smile. I'm not sure if Hill intended his movie to be quite this uniformly blunt and straight ahead—I wonder if he was looking for the exquisitely timed emotional shifts of *Le Cercle rouge* or *Un Flic*. And yet, the uniformity of *The Driver* is quite striking: this is a truly all-action movie. There are no Hawksian asides or nods at camaraderie in the manner of Carpenter, no romantic entanglements like the Richard Crenna–Catherine Deneuve–Alain Delon triangle in *Un Flic*. If Hill was counting on a delicate play of feelings between O'Neal and Adjani, it certainly didn't happen. The Player sides with The Driver simply because he is the most reliable and self-assured figure in the movie.

This straight, single-track action endows the film's justly celebrated car chases with a great deal of their considerable power. Since the emotional conflicts are so simple, the movie plays like a carefully gradated index of physical exchanges, with the conversational transactions on the low end and the car chases at the high mark. The car-chase-as-set-piece was well past its early peak when *The Driver* came out (having matured into its "decadent" phase the year before with *Smokey and the Bandit*). It is a strange phenomenon, always promising a surge into the stratosphere as the narrative and the expressive apparatus suddenly become one and gel into pure unadorned motion. Chases are notoriously tricky, though, often becoming monotonous (*Ronin*), ridiculous (*The Rock*), or utterly predictable in the alteration of points of view from windshield-looking-out to tires-on-asphalt to pursuing-car-in-rearview-mirror to long shot and so on. What is so unusual about the chases in *The Driver* is the way they're tied so completely to the film's global, dog-eat-dog conflict. One could say that they function like musical numbers, but that's not quite right. They don't move outside of the spare, laconic action as much as they crystallize it. Words and idle behavior are of no use behind the wheel, only reflexes and mental dexterity, and this is where Hill's car chases have it all over everything from *Bullitt* to *The Rock*. What O'Neal lacks in grit and focus (he's the dreamiest getaway driver in the history of movies), Hill makes up for with his tough, alert editing: mind, body, and automobile become one finely tuned working instrument, and Hill is careful to fudge as little as possible. Most chases don't bear up to close scrutiny—they are usually made up of carefully concealed ellipses culled from second-unit footage, a succession of well-timed kinetic thrills engineered by the editor, diverting the viewer's attention from the absence of spatial coherence. In *The Driver*, every twist, every swerve, every tire screech is the result of a reaction to either the pursuers behind, the oncoming traffic, or the grid of L.A. at night. These sequences are exciting as pyrotechnical feats, doubly so as instances of character in action.

One of the most fascinating aspects of Hill's work is the way his films tend to take on a kind of second unconscious life, a spilling over from the making of the movie and, no doubt, the individual temperaments of the actors into the movie proper. *The Long Riders*, for instance, has quite a bit of shaggy, nondescript time-wasting among the assorted brother acts, which seems almost but not quite at odds with the "greenery western," as Tom Allen called it, in which they're starring. *48 Hours* has a lot of broad, skuzzy standoffs that threaten, but never quite manage, to send the buddy movie, the action flick, and the romantic sparring comedy off-kilter. For a filmmaker who has always been discussed in terms of control and authenticity, Hill has a decidedly modernist penchant for jamming disparate elements together and seeing what results from the collision, most spectacularly in *Wild Bill*, where Pete Dexter's novel and Thomas Babe's play are (sort of) fused into a grand, deliberately messy phantasmagoria.

It's fairly easy to discuss *The Driver* in terms of its hypercontrolled elements but a little more difficult to nail its strangely neurotic tone, which is finally what separates it from the myriad paint-by-numbers exercises in fanatically "controlled" genre filmmaking cluttering the multiplexes today (Mike Hodges's *Croupier* and *I'll Sleep When I'm Dead* are two of the most lavishly overpraised examples). *The Driver* is indeed the sparest, driest, and most dramatically concise of Hill's movies, but its three principal actors and their respective "acts" are about as far as you can get from a neo-Hawksian exercise in professionalism and grace under pressure. Dern's needling, self-aggrandizing cop is very close to his vain *Coming Home* husband or his psychotic blimp pilot in *Black Sunday*—while almost any other actor would have accented the procedural aspects of the role and made The Detective a study of hubris gone awry, Dern offers yet another portrait of wounded machismo. Meanwhile, O'Neal, with his *very* 1970s male sensitivity and pampered jock good looks (this is before the filled-out, weathered O'Neal of the 1980s), plays his role like the cool guy in a romantic comedy, waltzing into the frame and claiming the beautiful woman without even trying. This dynamic of warring male psyches—the self-actualized sensitive man vs. the outdated, unfeeling man of integrity and action—was already present in Hill's earlier comic script, *The Thief Who Came to Dinner* (also starring O'Neal, with Jacqueline Bisset in the Adjani role and Warren Oates as the pursuing cop). It was also a staple of countless romantic dramas, comedies, and sitcoms of the period—it was, after all, what powered M*A*S*H for eleven years. Yet rarely, if ever, did it lie at the center of a movie devoted to getting at "the muscle, the sinew, the tissue, the very nerve center of a getaway driver," as Hill put it in the press notes. The tension between the dolefully attractive O'Neal in his stylish jackets and open-collared shirts, an otherworldly Adjani adorned in sleek late-1970s couture, and the jumpy, beady-eyed Dern with his off the rack drip-dry suits is closer to Paul Mazursky than to Howard Hawks. It's what finally gives *The Driver*, which has the chassis of a somnolent Alan Alda triangle and the body of a no-frills action movie, its own very special charm.

2005

Sorcerer

Two men, filthy, sweating, and exhausted, are flying in a helicopter over the meanest stretch of South American jungle. They approach an oil fire—an angry torrent of orange, yellow, and black, overtaking an already uninviting gray sky. One turns to the other and says, "I've seen worse."

If there's one moment that epitomizes the strange sensibility of William Friedkin, this is it: two lumpen actors surveying an industrial accident in the middle of nowhere from the vantage point of an expensive helicopter shot. Friedkin is one of the oddest of Hollywood moviemakers, the man who has it both ways: an insider fully enjoying all of the attendant luxuries of big-time moviemaking and a scornful maverick offspring. As was the case with John Frankenheimer, another all-pro with an attitude, the good films come at odd intervals: you never know what you're going to get when you walk into a Friedkin movie. Yet, while his aesthetic is often cruder than Frankenheimer's, he is capable of some of the more remarkable passages in contemporary Hollywood moviemaking, crossing into emotional/psychic territory that the older director never approached. It has to be admitted that roughly half of Friedkin's oeuvre is drudgery to sit through, a collection of exhausted genre exercises unredeemed by their director's documentary interest in locale or penchant for cruelly orchestrated action (*Rules of Engagement*, a fashionable exercise in "moral ambiguity" for which Friedkin's $2 + 2 = 4$ approach to life is especially unsuitable, is probably his worst film, but there's stiff competition from *Jade* and *Deal of the Century*). But on a half-dozen occasions—more than most filmmakers get in a career, when you think about it—Friedkin has found or cultivated material that is in perfect harmony with his dog-eat-dog notions about existence. The end product is a movie so deeply immersed in pure action that it becomes hallucinatory. I'm not sure if Friedkin is much of a philosopher, but he does have an admirable and dogged devotion to showing people at existential extremes with the reality of obliteration hanging over them like a rain cloud about to burst. If anyone could nurse the nuclear Armageddon scenario back to life, it's Hurricane Billy.

There isn't much in the way of character in a typical Friedkin film, which is less terse than blunt—motivations are shorn of subtleties and ambiguities, and human interactions are stripped to the marrow, the quicker to plunge into a purely physical conflict tied to the most terrifying landscapes: the least-picturesque sections of New York City in *The French Connection* and *Cruising* (like Abel Ferrara, Friedkin films only in places that Woody Allen would never dream of visiting), sterile urban wastelands in *To Live and Die in L.A.* and *The Hunted*, the inside of a D.C. townhouse in *The Exorcist*, and that South American hellhole in *Sorcerer*—to my mind his crowning achievement and a vastly superior film to Clouzot's extravagantly overpraised original. Perhaps the only Friedkin hero who comes close to being a fully fleshed-out character is Jason Miller's *Exorcist* priest. Where Hackman, Pacino, and Tommy Lee Jones in *The Hunted*, the *Sorcerer* trio, and William Peterson in L.A. are accumulations of tics, postures, states of exhaustion and indignation tinged with cynically bemused detachment, Miller is a good actor whose brooding sensibility finds an objective correlative in the heavy psychological conflicts cooked up in William Peter Blatty's novel (a disbelieving priest trained as a psychiatrist, feeling guilty over the death of his mother). Unlike Popeye Doyle or even Pacino's sexually perplexed undercover cop in *Cruising*, Miller's Father Karras actually percolates on an interior level. Beyond that early peak, it's one long parade of sinewy physicality, wisecracking revenge, obsessiveness, world-weariness, which at times is so graphically overvisualized (you wonder if Friedkin ever grows tired of sweaty bodies and worried eyebrows) that it borders on the laughable.

Friedkin may be the least-convivial sensibility ever to step behind a Hollywood camera. Even Carpenter is more captivated by the beauty if human affairs. It's fascinating that he's stayed so enmeshed within the Hollywood machinery and kept pursuing his own curious brand of punk action cinema. *Sorcerer*, *To Live and Die in L.A.*, and *Cruising* are pretty strong medicine, close to bursting out of their generic pulp forms into a potentially terrifying nihilism. In *Sorcerer*, for instance, the film proper ends with an overly pat irony, but the images of the trucks getting over the bridge and a pale Roy Scheider wandering through a hollowed-out, lap-dissolved landscape have already left their impact. Friedkin seems to have neither the inclination nor the imagination to make a *Raging Bull* or an *Apocalypse Now*. He always stays strictly within the boundaries of up-to-date pulp formulae. The supposedly anachronistic *The Hunted*, for example, is a member of the currently popular genre of government-trained killing machines run amok.

Even in the most low-down Friedkin project, like *Rampage*, the element of luxury (top cinematographers, the most fashionable musical scores, a massive team of technicians, multimillion dollar equipment, geographically complex action) is present. Yet in all other ways, he's a direct link to the pulp sensibility of a Jim Thompson or a Cornell Woolrich. While it may be true that he's quite a canny operator—keeping his movies geared to pure action and never risking an eccentric position (Friedkin doesn't quite tip his hand the way that, say, Tourneur does toward the supernatural or Aldrich does toward the anarchic)—there are intimations of something deeply unsettling in his best films, moments where he works so hard to represent the forces threatening mankind that he gives us a glimpse of sustained disharmony, the blackest terror.

With rare exceptions, Friedkin has set his films within heavily proletarian, task-oriented milieux. In his best work, there are long stretches of men hard at work, performing complex, inhumanly difficult tasks under extreme pressure. The justifiably famous *French Connection* car chase remains a stunning piece of work because of the way it stays so grounded in reality. Far from the usual cool contest of skills enacted before dumbstruck pedestrians, Hackman's Eddie Egan is trying to outrace a Brooklyn el train while steering clear of oncoming traffic and the occasional bystander. Most car chases, including the prototypical *Bullitt* maneuvers through San Francisco, are lyrical events, with images of the coolly silent driver (as in Frankenheimer's preposterous *Ronin*) juxtaposed with the ecstatic motion of the cars. In this case, the standard rhetorical effects are blunted by Hackman's precise sense of desperation, his mixture of anguish and impatience when he almost kills the woman with the baby carriage. In most American movies, professionalism equals cool. In Friedkin, it equals anxiety, fatigue, anger. There's very little in the way of grace or gentility in a Friedkin movie—the exchanges between Miller and Max Von Sydow in *The Exorcist* are about as close as he gets. At times Friedkin seems like a champion of the working class—every aspect of the drudgery of labor is ticked off in his punishing, larger-than-life universe, where even the *Exorcist* priests and Pacino's undercover cop in *Cruising* are hard at work.

In the late 1970s, Raymond Durgnat and Judith Bloch wrote a fascinating, overlooked piece for *Film Comment* called "Attention: Men at Work" about the inflation of physical rhetoric in movies at the expense of genuinely realistic action. Interestingly, the man who devoted a lengthy climactic stretch of his Academy Award–winner to the disassembling of an automobile never comes up. Perhaps Friedkin represented a reverse of Durgnat and Bloch's ideal: rather than building a movie around tasks (as in Siegel's *Escape from Alcatraz* or Olmi's *Tree of the Wooden Clogs*, two of their key examples), Friedkin always finds a way to tie task performance to suspense, and jump cuts his way through the details. But unlike a Melville, who capped

his career with Un Flic's brilliant helicopter/train set piece, there's never anything magical in Friedkin. It's always drudgery—alternately nerve-shredding
and time-consuming for the people performing the action yet hypnotic for
the spectator. At times, the discrepancy between Friedkin's conventionally
breathless pacing and his fascination with realistically complex and exhausting tasks is gaping—there's something weird about marrying the hot
pursuit mechanisms of The Hunted to something as time-consuming as
searching for a piece of iron, starting a fire with sticks and stones, and
smithing your own knife. In Sorcerer, the sleek pace and velvety Tangerine
Dream score are fascinatingly mismatched with the grungy slog through a
wet, reeking jungle. And To Live and Die in L.A., the meanest of all neo-noirs,
wears its Wang Chung score and modish aspects (Willem Dafoe's ambi-
sexual villain, a druggy, sybaritic ambience) with more than a little ambivalence: how much is Friedkin trying to soak the movie in L.A. decadence and
anomie, and how much is he trying to tart things up with fashionable ac-
coutrements? On the other hand, The French Connection works a little too
perfectly, the most expertly calibrated and well-oiled suspense machine in
Oscar history. Nonetheless, the discrepancies tend to produce an interestingly discordant effect, the sense of a director at once upping the suspense
ante and pushing the punishing physicality, as if to say to his audience: okay,
you're going to get the thrills, but you have to earn them.

The French Connection car search, those hard-working and elaborate exorcisms, Cruising's fascination with the lore and codes of the late-1970s leather
underworld, Sorcerer's truck reconstructions and elaborate explosion of a
fallen tree, To Live and Die in L.A.'s concentration on the procedures of an expert
counterfeiter, the details of The Brinks' Job, and the survival lore and tracking
procedures of The Hunted are all eye-openers, less ordinary than they seem at
first glance. Tools and gadgetry have been a proven winner in movies and
TV, from the docudramas of the late 1940s to the safe-cracking set pieces of
The Asphalt Jungle, Rififi, and The Killing. What's so unusual about the Friedkin
movies is the absence of elaborate gadgetry as well as the leisurely concentration and solitude afforded both Siegel's meditative, relaxed Alcatraz prisoner and Bresson's resistance hero in A Man Escaped. Friedkin puts an extravagant Hollywood frame around a back-to-basics approach to existence,
in which man is pitted against himself and/or nature, and the advances of
civilization are just so many distractions and oases. In the Sorcerer truck
preparation sequence, we get to see the insides of a truck in the most elaborate (and hitherto unseen) detail, and the painstaking construction of believably indestructible supertrucks from the workable guts of old ones (most

interesting of all is the way that nothing is made of the fact that Scheider, Bruno Cremer, et al., know every spare part and how to instantly size up its usability). The pace, set by those Tangerine Dream synthesizers, goes sleek but the detailing stays earthbound throughout. And in *The Hunted*, a conventional exercise in psychological thriller-making, large portions of the action are given over to the banal, functional details of an urban tracking exercise. We've seen hundreds of moves like this in contemporary action films, where the specifics are fudged and the supposedly expert, hyperacute hero tracks down his prey by magical, editorial sleight of hand. There's a strange excitement about Tommy Lee Jones, a bundle of grim determination, vs. Benicio del Toro's maniacally focused assassin gone awry in the wilds of Chicago. Friedkin edits as always for maximum speed, but every time Jones divines del Toro's whereabouts, the director is careful to give us as many of the telltale signs and as much of the methodology as the high-impact storytelling will allow. There are no laptops, pocket radar devices, or night vision goggles—just a human being putting his intelligence and his senses to work. Perhaps the most astonishing of such moments is the destruction of that fallen tree in *Sorcerer*, which involves not just the use of the explosives but a primitive timing device that enables the drivers to get far enough away that they can shield themselves at the moment of impact. This intricate set piece is genuinely masterful, a textural tour de force—Friedkin keeps us so absorbed in the Crusoe-esque action that the climax of the scene, rather than the explosion itself, is a sharpened stick puncturing a box of explosives, from which liquid nitro leaks out onto a rock set in the middle of the offending tree.

There are a few instances in Friedkin's cinema where the impossibility of the man vs. task conflict is felt so deeply—pounded home in the action and visualized with such exquisite care—that it achieves a supernatural power. Friedkin has some very sharp visual instincts, whether he's working with Owen Roizman, Dick Bush, or Robby Müller behind the camera, and his documentary sensibility sometimes leads him into a rarefied sphere of stylization—the supernatural undercurrent of some of his films is never imposed on the realistic details but grows directly *out of* them. When Von Sydow steps into the cold purple light of Linda Blair's room and shivers with Miller at his side, the quiet inside the room, the mixture of dread and awe between the actors and the inhuman texture of the air itself make for a uniquely haunting vision, at once more solid and yet more suggestive of some dread province in the ethereal beyond than almost anything in the horror canon. For me, the most impressive moment in Friedkin's cinema comes with the two precarious trips over the rickety bridge in the midst of a pounding rainstorm in *Sorcerer*. The image of a massive, beaten-up truck swaying on the bridge in the center of the frame amidst a swirl of trees and water, the human figures almost disappearing in the vari-colored tangle of mist, jungle fauna, earth, and sky, is held to the point where it becomes a real *vision*, like something out of J. M. W. Turner but with a demoniacal power.

Friedkin, like Jim Thompson, harbors sentiments and notions about the world altogether too dark to be contained by any form *other* than pulp fiction. Both of them have an ability to create moments so powerful that they can't be elaborated or enlarged, only *happened upon*—that truck swaying on the bridge or that cold purple room where the devil has set up camp are kissing cousins to the double ending of *A Hell of a Woman* or the hallucinations in *Savage Night*. This Academy Award–winning master entertainer's greatest contribution to the cinema is a small collection of moments containing intimations of unfathomable dread.

2005

With *Unforgiven*, Clint Eastwood's urge (or perhaps desire) to explore the reality of violence bloomed like a hearty desert flower, and it came as a genuine shock. The poster indicated something else, another hard-nosed, physically exacting mythic genre piece, like *Pale Rider*. But *Unforgiven* took violence, broke it down, and patiently laid out the distinctions between intent, action, and aftermath, a rarity in American movies. Many critics pounced on the ending, upset that Eastwood had stayed within the conventions of the western genre, as though the entire movie was nothing but an elaborate excuse to bring the Man with No Name back to life. But *Unforgiven* had left its mark long before its final, and powerfully muted conflagration. The film contained scenes the likes of which Eastwood had never filmed: Little Bill's merciless beating of English Bob on Independence Day before the disgusted townsfolk, the terrible moment when Munny and his team gutshoot a man and watch him die, and most unforgettably of all, the scene where The Schofield Kid confesses that he's never killed anyone as Munny takes a revivifying swig of whiskey, man and boy framed against a heavy silvery sky as a rider approaches on the horizon. "It's a hell of a thing to kill a man," says Munny. Eastwood and his editor Joel Cox cut the scene in a slow rhythm, and they're very careful to let us hear those words, words that stayed in the mind during the summer of the Rodney King riots. Eastwood wasn't merely commenting on his own past, he was speaking to a country whose national profile had been tainted by the righteous postures of self-defense and hubristic bullying and whose commercial images were brimming over with violence. *Unforgiven* was immediately transformed into a "classic" western by critics and multiple Oscars, but to my eyes it was something else, a terrible, mournful elegy for good intentions clouded by vengeance, a hard look at America's addiction to decisive action at the expense of meditative thought. Just like *Do the Right Thing* in 1989, Eastwood's movie spoke with poignant directness to what was happening in America at that very moment.

A *Perfect World*, Eastwood's like-minded and even tougher follow-up, already felt like a rare bird in the summer of 1993, and it still does. It's a strange feeling to look at a film that speaks to a moment already past, particularly when it was misunderstood during that moment in the first place.

Why couldn't people embrace *A Perfect World* in the way that they'd embraced *Unforgiven*? Was it the jokey, formulaic banter between law enforcement authorities cross-cut with the far more soulful drama between Kevin Costner and the little boy he's kidnapped? Was it the failed slapstick interlude, out of *Sullivan's Travels*? Was it the extended farewell between Costner and the boy at the end? Or was it the film's brooding urgency itself, which takes precedence over its generic aspects fairly early on?

I recently interviewed a French director who had a plan to take Hollywood by storm. The Hollywood film is just an appearance, he explained to me, a gaudy house that can stand on a rigorous foundation. In this case, rigor is defined as: following through on your ideas, impulses and intentions, and not cutting yourself off at the knees with the various "winning" formulae that have been afflicting American cinema since the runaway success of *Ghostbusters*. The director was correct but hopelessly naive, because this kind of freedom is harder and harder to come by in the high-venture capital phase of Hollywood history (two recent examples: *Casino* and *Starship Troopers*). According to the old auteurist model, a Nick Ray or a Jacques Tourneur made their own secret, internal film buried within the film proper that sophisticated viewers might then divine through their sensitivity to the subtleties of mise-en-scène. The adventure, and the duty, of auteurism was to supply the missing piece and complete the "intended" film. The result was the fully coherent work it would have been had it been made under the Utopian conditions of unlimited artistic freedom.

Hollywood is no longer based on the factory model of production, so the old subversive paradigm no longer functions. In fact, it's become a construction: the very idea of a conventional storyline with built-in subversive undercurrents is a pretty popular package these days, in so-called indie films (*Happiness*), Hollywood superproductions (David Fincher's films), and TV shows (*The X-Files*). Today, everybody's an auteur, by virtue of either their "subversiveness" or their "style." But the real auteurs, the proud, the few, are the ones with the intestinal fortitude to stick to the courage of their convictions on someone else's dime. "To make a movie, all you need is not to be afraid of anybody or anything," said Cassavetes years ago, and it's truer than ever now. Provided that it's the movie you want to make, as opposed to the one that will make you.

It's commonly imagined that there are a select few filmmakers working in Hollywood who have control over their own artistic destiny, Spielberg, Lucas, Cameron, and Eastwood among them. In the case of the first three, I would say that the degree of commercial calculation built into their goals and their intentions instantly disqualifies them, unless you want to replace the word "artistic" with "financial." In Eastwood's case, he has not only worked frugally, but he's also stuck to the "one for me, one for them" strategy. In two cases he's lucked out, making films that seemed to satisfy everyone: *Unforgiven* and *The Bridges of Madison County.* But judging from the evidence of *True Crime,* an unsuccessful attempt to combine both tendencies into one project, things haven't gotten any easier for Clint Eastwood in Hollywood.

Eastwood is and always has been a popular artist. Not exactly a red-hot insight, but it's something that both his admirers and his detractors take for granted. The illusion of freedom in modern Hollywood allows critics to sidestep the extraordinary financial pressures that Eastwood has always tried to contain before they contain him, not unlike Kubrick, which in turn skews the vision of Eastwood's work. On the one hand, his admirers can inflate something as flawed as *Midnight in the Garden of Good and Evil* into a masterpiece, while his detractors can degrade *Unforgiven* for lacking the melancholy sweep of, say, Tarkovsky. And it makes *A Perfect World,* with its odd mixture of delicacy and ferocity, particularly problematic. Ironically, the film raises all kinds of objections simply because it isn't . . . perfect.

It's best to throw out ideals of perfection where American cinema is concerned, where the bottom line is higher and harder than the Rockies. You'd do better to focus on the gestures and maneuvers made within and around its multitude of restrictions. Filmmakers can steel themselves against the barrage of enticements and terrors and make exactly the movie they want to make (Scorsese, Malick, Jarmusch, Wes Anderson), they can keep a low genre profile and work on the margins with increased freedom (Carpenter, Hill), or they can convince themselves they're auteurs as they're selling themselves down the river (take your pick). But they also have the choice of sparring with audience expectations, incrementally stretching the limits of the permissible, from film to film, laying the groundwork for moments like the profound shock at the end of *A Perfect World.* For filmmakers like Eastwood who've adopted this bob-and-weave strategy, it's inevitable that artistic tensions generated by their unstable place within the industry work their way into the movies—metaphorically, unconsciously.

Thus, *A Perfect World* is filled with odd little lessons, built around the way we want things to be and the way they are. "In a perfect world, Miss Gerber, we'd all lock arms and thrash the bushes until he turned up," says a good ole' Texas Ranger to Laura Dern's criminal psychologist Sally Gerber—he's talking about the escaped convict they're hunting down. "In a perfect world, this wouldn't've happened," she ripostes, in the actress's trademark semi-

Southern drawl, which suits the bantering rhythm of the law enforcement scenes, set in a cozy, teched-up trailer with movie-movie snugness. What's perfect, the world where trouble can be contained or where it doesn't exist at all? The world where good movies can be made by stealthily escaping the gaze of the bean counters or where they can be made freely, without any interference or restrictions whatsoever?

Critics complained about the unevenness of A Perfect World, but the sequences with Eastwood's Red Garnet and his team out searching for escaped convict Butch Haynes and the little boy he's abducted (T. J. Lowther) operate at the same level of execution, depth, and even-toned charm as about 95 percent of American cinema, just like the similarly maligned brother/sister scenes in Madison County. It's as if Eastwood were saying, "Here's what you expect, and now here's the way things really are." In both cases, the perceived blandness (which Eastwood, consciously or not, accentuates with the breezy acting and execution) matches the complacency of the characters. As the brother and sister in Madison County read through their mother's diary, as Garnet, Gerber, et al., discover that Butch has killed his own fellow escapee and allowed the boy he's kidnapped to live, their entire frame of reference is thrown. Are they surrogates for us? In fact—again, whether by design or by accident—I think they're actually surrogates for "the average viewer," a phantom creature asked to participate in polls, marketing surveys, focus groups, and test screenings, for whom the world is a perpetually happy, stable place. The contrast between the perfectly regulated world of consumerist myth and the terrifying human impulses and compulsions excluded from that myth—this theme crops up again and again in post-Bird Eastwood, and it manifests itself in a raw, poignantly extra-aesthetic fashion in these two films. Beyond what the top-heavy dramatic constructions tell us about Eastwood the artist, the core conflicts of both movies are enhanced by their parallel conflicts and given an extra resonance and dimension in the process.

In 1993, when he was at the peak of his stardom, the casting of Kevin Costner added another dimension to A Perfect World. As an actor, Costner has always oscillated between amiability and bombast. When he takes on a role like this one, where there's plenty of disenchantment to tamp down his quest for populist nobility, he comes alive as an actor. The disenchantment sparks him and puts bite into his line delivery and his tense, swaggering walk. "That ain't a threat, it's a fact," warns Butch's unsavory fellow escapee, a gun in his hand. He's mad enough to kill. "In two seconds I'm gonna break your nose," announces Butch, in Costner's characteristically flat, all-American accent, with his trademark pedantic tone—he often sounds like an insecure math teacher in a Midwestern high school. "That's a threat." Then he deftly turns the guy's nose into a bloody pulp and snatches the gun from his hand. "And that's a fact." "I'm gonna kill you for that," announces the wounded convict. "And that's a threat," counters Butch. "Beginning to understand the difference?" Costner's never played a character like Butch, before or since.

This terse, Brechtian exchange is the first of many lessons for Phillip, which are quite different from the standard life lessons in American cinema ("Follow your heart"; "Life is short, so grab for all the gusto you can"). "I'm askin' you—I ain't asking your mother, and I ain't asking Jehovah," Butch tells the dumbstruck Phillip, who's been brought up in the cloistered, pleasure-denying atmosphere of the Jehovah's Witnesses. In this movie where a wizened law enforcement officer realizes that he's effectively destroyed the life of a young man he'd thought he was helping (Red had sent the adolescent Butch to "the toughest juvie farm in Texas" to get him away from his abusive father), there's a penetrating sadness, a sober realization amongst all the characters that people are nothing but the sum total of their actions, and that they can never get any real help choosing the right ones. The point is reiterated, restated, and reenacted throughout the movie, and it hits us with pulverizing force during the film's climax. The car is a time machine, explains Butch to Phillip—behind them is the past, around them is the present, ahead of them is the future, and in a car you can travel into the future as fast as you want. In other words, there's no refuge; there's only action.

Eastwood is often portrayed as a filmmaker of "classical" virtues: narrative economy, understatement, self-effacement, and balance, which is true to a certain extent, particularly in terms of the way he visualizes action sequences. But he's entirely modern in his sense of duration, the way he allows action to develop slowly, play out until the right chord is struck, a matter of mood, character, environment, and the moment: Whitaker and Venora restlessly roaming through their suburban house in Bird, until their discomfort becomes palpable; Eastwood and Streep's slowly building attraction in The Bridges of Madison County, played out in a loping rhythm across chance meetings in town or at the bridges themselves, a mingling of summer heat and delicate emotional reticence. In A Perfect World, there are many scenes devoted to Butch's absorption in preparing for the next move forward: the small-town shopping episode where he simultaneously stocks up on supplies, flirts with the girl behind the counter, and keeps the suspicious owner at bay or the lovely moment where he picks clothes off the line at a

farmhouse before he steals the farmer's Ford.

For a classical filmmaker, Eastwood's feeling for landscape can be variable: he has a tendency to slide into mythic vistas, and he often settles into one standardized look, usually cold and clear (in a way, he's more at home indoors, where emotional and physical vectors merge). But he does wonderful things with distances and placements within open spaces: that approaching rider in *Unforgiven* and those surpassingly beautiful scenes at the Madison County bridges, where Eastwood and Streep communicate across diagonals from meadow to bridge. The site of that Ford theft is green, rolling (as are many of the film's landscapes, the opposite of the standard vistas of Texas in movies). Butch sends Phillip off to pee while he sizes up the place, calculates how long it will take to drive away before the farmer can get off his tractor and run two hundred yards, then starts yanking the clothes off the line, giving the farmer a cunning wave just before he begins. It's a funny gesture (perfectly acted by Costner), as if to say, "I'm stealing from you and now you have to catch me—that's the common currency of life." And instead of the standard build-up/pay-off structure of most movie scenes (like the ones with Red and his Texas Rangers, for instance), these scenes work towards nailing the sense of Butch's damaged spirit and the peculiar spectacle of an amoral man imparting moral lessons to a sheltered boy. There's a peculiarly beautiful sense of time in the movie: unreal and elastic, idyllically stretching into infinity. As opposed to most "life education" movies, the affinity between Butch and Phillip remains tentative, less important than the strange immediacy of the situation, in which a charming but near-sociopathic career criminal temporarily assumes the role of father figure.

It's common in American movies to fudge emotional, psychological, and physiological realities, and this fudging runs the gamut from Julia Roberts as a streetwalker or Carol Kane as the "homely woman" to retarded people with variable IQs (depending on what the drama requires of them from moment to moment) and psychopaths with hearts of gold. It's a line that Eastwood's always been able to walk, from the sexual "deviance" of *Tightrope* to the frank perspective on societal outsiders in *Bird* to the angry desperation of being all but banned from normal life in *A Perfect World*. For those who have difficulties with *A Perfect World*, who find it excessive and awkward or who have a "Kevin Costner problem," I would urge them to think through the many sorry portrayals of psychopathology throughout the history of American cinema, so that they might appreciate the terrible grandeur of Eastwood's achievement here.

It's a difficult thing to show someone who's been driven to kill due to circumstances as opposed to pure malice or revenge, to maintain audience sympathy and stay true to your subject at the same time. Eastwood is very smart here. He begins by setting up the classic good convict/bad convict opposition—Butch objects to Phillip's kidnapping in the first place, saves Phillip from rape and murder by murdering his escape partner, and treats the kid to a liberating vacation from the joyless, restricted life of the Jehovah's Witnesses. But along the way, small details, verbal, psychological, and physical, are sifted into the action, like Butch's remorselessly tough wisdom, according to which all illusions must be terminated on sight. When Phillip tells Butch about his mother's promise that his wandering father will come home one day, Butch's response is, "She's lying to ya, pure and simple." He also makes mercenary use of his own charm and good looks with women. The toughened guardian asking the tender ward to look the other way while he makes a sexual conquest is an old saw in movies, from *Little Miss Marker* through *Alice in the Cities*, and the scene where Butch tells Phillip to eat his sandwich outside so he can be serviced by the waitress at a roadside diner is one of the least surprising in the movie. But it's enlivened by Butch's elemental explanation after the fact—it's purely a matter of biology, nothing to do with love or affection.

Most troubling of all is Butch's trigger finger, not exactly itchy but primed for action the minute the time machine threatens to stop moving forward. T. J. Lowther's Phillip is one of the least tricked up child performances in movies, ranking with Danny Lloyd in *The Shining* and the children in Maurice Pialat's oeuvre. Basically it's a deft editorial collage of scrunched-up eyes, drawn breaths, and a tense scrutiny of Butch's every move and reaction, coupled with a polite child's withdrawal (one of the neatest things in the movie is the moment where Phillip stubbornly fixes his sights on the Casper the Friendly Ghost costume at the small-town general store, as all hell breaks loose around him: there's a funny internal war going on, just barely visible on his face and in his tensed body). Eastwood doesn't make dramatic turning points out of the instants where Phillip observes Butch resorting to violence—they're always keyed into the forward motion. "If Bob'd put up a fight, I mighta had to shoot him," Butch explains to Phillip. They've just stolen a station wagon from a family man and left him by the roadside with his wife and kids. Phillip has already saved a farmer from having his face shot off by biting his hand in order to force him off of his own car. He's learning that every action must be decided immediately and that each decision is irrevocable.

By the time Butch and Phillip arrive at the home of a black sharecropper,

Eastwood's already established a very unusual tone: amiable, a little melancholy, shot through with uneasiness, anxiousness. He builds slowly, quietly to the wrenching climax, a genuinely shocking event, on a par with such ground zero turnabouts as David Bowie kissing Ryuichi Sakamoto in *Merry Christmas, Mr. Lawrence* or Jesus's descent from the cross in *The Last Temptation of Christ*. There's a cliché in play here—Butch's murderous rage at the sharecropper, his wife, and his grandson is triggered when the man slaps the boy across the face. In an echo of Freddie Steele's mother complex in Sturges's *Hail the Conquering Hero* or Tippi Hedren seeing red in *Marnie*, Butch goes ballistic whenever he sees an adult hitting a child. But Eastwood dissolves the cliché by upping the ante and increasing the agony by degrees—repeating the slow Cajun waltz that Butch and the woman have danced to, its drone as ironically appropriate to murder as it had been to joyful release just a moment before; multiplying expectations, from a beating (in order to force the sharecropper to tell his grandson he loves him—"like you mean it") to a murder to the methodical destruction of an entire family. Costner handles the scene well by keeping it simple, refusing to play his character's madness, letting his blinding confusion mount with the momentum. When Phillip picks up Butch's gun and shoots him in the gut, it's painful and bottomlessly sad. The lesson's been learned and absorbed—everybody's alone.

I have a feeling that *A Perfect World* was unpopular most of all because it leaves its audience in a state of emotional disequilibrium. Butch and Phillip have a tearful, protracted farewell beneath a tree at the bottom of a rolling pasture, as Texas Rangers gather around them with guns drawn. Butch's gift to Phillip is finally a sad one: knowledge of the world's imperfection. In this film set in Texas, November of 1963, the week before Kennedy's arrival in Dallas (Red Garnet has requisitioned the teched-up trailer from Governor John Connelly, who sat next to Kennedy in the limo and was himself shot through the hand), the last chicken comes home to roost as a loudmouthed FBI marksman shoots Butch in the chest, reasonably assuming the postcard he's pulling out of his pocket is a gun. When Red punches the marksman's lights out (Gerber knees him in the groin for good measure), it's a futile gesture, a vain attempt to slow down the time machine and retard the speed of life for just an instant.

This is an extraordinarily clear-eyed movie, as mindful of circumstances as it is of actions, as tragically true to American experience as any movie in the 1990s, and it's prophetic as well. The postcard could've been a gun, but it also could have been a wallet, met not just with one shot but with forty-one.

The Big Red One: The Reconstruction

I was once told, by Jonathan Rosenbaum, that Sam Fuller had no use for *Full Metal Jacket.* When Rosenbaum expressed his enthusiasm for the Kubrick movie, Fuller would have none of it: "It's a recruiting poster." I can't agree with Fuller's assessment, but I love him for making it. And I love him even more after seeing the reconstituted version of *The Big Red One,* painstakingly assembled by Richard Schickel, someone else who cares a great deal about the way war is represented onscreen. Chopped down to a stately (for Fuller), elegiac, relatively old-fashioned 113-minute war movie in 1980, it is now, at 2 hours and 40 minutes (not the 4-and-a-half hours of myth), a very different experience. This is a movie about the hell of being at war, the tedium of it, and the callousness shown by the charmed living toward the soon-to-be-dead. Crassness aside—and what would a Fuller movie be without crassness?—it now lives up to the words that served as both its original tagline and its final voiceover: "The real glory of war is surviving."

When *The Big Red One* was released in its truncated form (with the director's blessing, I've been told by a reliable source), it was a movie caught between two eras: an artifact of the old studio-bred approach to filmmaking following the onslaught of Vietnam rock 'n' roll extravaganzas that threw the old spatial/narrative/thematic decorum out of whack for good—basically, a 1959 movie in the middle of 1980. The Coppola/Cimino epics featured near-psychotic protagonists who made the very idea of Lee Marvin watching over an ethnically balanced squad of young Stars of Tomorrow seem hopelessly quaint. That the male ingénues were the callowest actors imaginable was no help—Robert Carradine as Fuller's alter ego still looks and sounds like he's just emerged from a Ralph Meeker/Gene Evans double feature in an air-conditioned screening room.

Over twenty years later, the "Vietnam era" of moviemaking has acquired its own patina of quaintness, and the Good War has re-emerged as a national obsession. And just as our new triumphalism is in the process of falling apart, Fuller's movie seems more impressive than ever, a shoestring memorial epic (shot on the cheap in Israel and Ireland) as simple and unimpressed with itself as a tale told by your father. The spirit of the film seems right, in a way that Malick's and Spielberg's self-important World War II films don't, their obvious virtues aside. The sense of becalmed resignation shared by Fuller and his lead actor; the sudden eruptions of crazy sexuality; the slightly fabulous aspect of the storytelling, as if every event had been filtered through years of repression, trauma, acceptance, and then hardened into personalized legend; the macho swagger carried over from the *Dirty Dozen* era, which once seemed so repellent and which now seems like a reasonable defense mechanism for any young man afraid of being sent home in a body bag—it all rings true. Even the callowness of the actors, now the forgotten men of yesteryear, rings true: after all, it's always just a bunch of kids who are sent off to war.

Fuller, with his just-the-facts reporter's point of view, knows something that Spielberg and Kubrick and Malick and Coppola don't. For Fuller, war, real war, can never be encapsulated or reduced to its essence and that when you try to "balance" the insanity of the enterprise with fire-lit discussions of Emerson or interior monologues about the duality of human nature—when you give it a form of its own—you are according it more reverence than it deserves.

"See, there's no way you can portray war realistically, not in a movie nor in a book," writes Fuller in his posthumously published autobiography— every word reads as if it's been barked over the phone from the scene of a crime. "You can only capture a very, very small aspect of it. If you really want to make readers understand a battle, a few pages of your book would be booby-trapped. For moviegoers to get the idea of real combat, you'd have to shoot at them every so often from either side of the screen. The casualties in the theater would be bad for business."

That's from someone who escaped Rommel in North Africa, suffered through the hell of Omaha Beach, and was present at the liberation of a death camp in Czechoslovakia, all re-created here. Of course, as is true of all subjects, there is no one, irrefutable way to represent war. If it *seems* as if there should be, it's simply because the gulf between those who have experienced it and those who have not is so wide and because the nature of the experience is traumatic at best and physically ruinous at worst—if you're lucky enough to have lived through it, that is.

Saving Private Ryan, probably one of the most influential films of the last twenty years, is the obvious point of comparison. How does Fuller's D-Day stack up next to Spielberg's? Spielberg certainly comes out on top in terms of sheerly physical impact, thanks to his consummate skill at handling set pieces with multiple fields of action and criss-crossing motion and sound. The Fuller version is far less spectacular, the "you are there" quotient is lower, the moments are blocked out *as* moments in the best old Hollywood manner as opposed to instants seemingly grabbed from an ongoing flow of reality. Yet the Spielberg scene works more as an abstract experience than anything else, a kind of maximalist audio/visual installation that could be called "Omaha Beach" or "Pinned Down on All Sides." As a piece of cinema, it's brutally single-minded, while the Fuller has a motoring dramatic logic, as well as a greater concern with the more mundane but no-less-crucial details. We understand that the American shells have fallen too far inland, that the Germans up above are not "combat rejects" as had been suspected, that an antitank barbed wire trap has to be blown through before the soldiers massing onto the beach can move. Fuller settles on a trenchant device for showing the passing of time, which survived the first cut: a wristwatch on a dead soldier's arm, floating in the increasingly bloody Normandy surf. The scene is then centered around the bangalore torpedo and the men getting cut down one by one before Mark Hamill's Griff makes it through, under fire from both the enemy and, when Griff freezes, from Lee Marvin's Sergeant.

In the 1980 version, the scene has a simple, solemn power. In the reconstituted version, Robert Carradine re-enacts Fuller's run down the besieged beach to alert his commanding officer that the trap has been destroyed. Just before he makes it to the colonel's position, he hits the dirt. There's a dead soldier lying next to him. The camera pans down and we see, for a brief instant, that his stomach has been blown open and that his intestines are exposed. Which is followed by the oddest detail: Carradine spots a good cigar by the soldier's side, grabs it, plants it in his mouth, and gets up to finish his run. Just as odd is the moment when the colonel gets the news. He stands up and screams, "There are two kinds of men out here—the dead and those who are about to die! So let's get the hell off this beach and at least die inland!" So much for the satisfaction of breaking through.

Fuller doesn't try to re-create the event, the way Spielberg does. The most traumatizing details are more often than not left out of the stories told by veterans—they're so far beyond comprehension that they're almost unrecountable. "Heads, arms, fingers, testicles and legs were scattered everywhere as we ran up to the beach, trying to dodge the corpses," writes Fuller of landing on Omaha Beach, committing to paper what is at once too arresting for casual conversation and too mortifying to be rendered visually with prosthetic trickery. Unlike Spielberg, Fuller doesn't try to convince us that we're watching a real event. He knows that the minute you show something, you're not only begging the audience to question its reality, you're also putting a cap on the horror, giving it a shape and a finitude it can't possibly possess when it's witnessed in reality. So he allows us to share his own convulsive horror by giving us single, almost ideogrammatic images—a dead man's arm, a corpse with exposed intestines—that suggest a wealth of associations.

Where the 1980 cut was a relatively staid film, the new version is continually surprising. Nearly every scene is now thrown into some kind of spin by a believably off-kilter detail, from the Legionnaires who slice off the ears of dead soldiers (at the climax of a wonderfully intricate battle scene on horseback) to the old German farmers defending the fatherland from American invaders, only to recoil at the first shot from Marvin's rifle. There's now a scene with a young sniper, a direct corollary to the *Full Metal Jacket* climax, and it ends very close to the *Private Ryan* episode in which the squad agonizes over the fate of their German prisoner. The Fuller scene is less grandiose than either. What to do with this unrepentant Hitler Youth, on whom no one can bring himself to pull the trigger? Marvin cuts the conversation far shorter than Tom Hanks managed to and decides to give the boy the worst spanking of his life, which has him screaming for his daddy. It's funny in a way, close to the kind of bluster you find in older World War II pictures, but it also has a crazy logic: what else do you do with a boy?

Fuller supposedly had *The Big Red One* project set up at Warner Brothers in 1959, with John Wayne in the lead, and both Richard Brooks and Dalton Trumbo wisely advised him against it. Lee Marvin's scarred soulfulness did wonders for Aldrich and Boorman, but I don't think they ever found a better setting than this movie. At this late point in his career, Marvin had lost that Liberty Valance jangle and acquired his weary authority, and in a smart move, Fuller set the entire picture at the actor's loping tempo. "Lee did get drunk a couple of times, but, for cryin' out loud, he was carrying the entire picture on his shoulders!" writes Fuller, who claims that he and Marvin didn't have to do much talking. Small wonder. Marvin saw action in the Pacific theater, where he was the only surviving member of his squad at Saipan, and he's buried at Arlington. Which is no doubt why this performance is such a quiet miracle.

In the new version of *The Big Red One*, children are drawn to Marvin throughout—a Tunisian girl, a Sicilian boy who thanks him for seeing to it that his mother is buried, and a girl who decorates his helmet with flowers and who is later shot when she runs to kiss him goodbye. He lets the children sit quietly by his side, neither welcoming them nor brushing them off, acknowledging their presence with a turn of his head or a shrug of his shoulders, allowing them to stay within his protective aura without risking affection. Which makes the already devastating final episode with the dying boy at Falkenau that much more so. Three minutes of cinema at its most eloquent—the boy is carried by Marvin, deposited on a bed, beckoned out of the shadows, brought to the riverside and hoisted on Marvin's shoulders for a few seconds in the sunlight before he gives out. The rarest tenderness, the most brutal simplicity.

If you want to quake in your boots, watch the first twenty minutes of *Saving Private Ryan*—but remember, it only works once. If you want to ponder the question of whether evil is within or without, watch *The Thin Red Line*. If you want to hold the concept of war in your hand, like a perfectly formed, elegant black diamond, watch *Full Metal Jacket*. Not to take anything away from those movies, but *The Big Red One*, in its current state, might be the one movie that takes in the full measure of the experience of battle. It gives us a sense of why men like my father, fifty years after the Good War came to an end, still break down in tears when the memory of what they went through comes rushing back to the surface.

2004

v Two Critics

There's very little to add by way of explanation here that isn't already contained in the following pieces. I suppose I would only add that I would never
have written a word had it not been for Andrew Sarris and Manny Farber,
and I know many other writers who feel likewise.

After the New York press screening of a revived *Mickey One* a few years back, a certain critic was heard to remark, "I guess that's what you'd call Strained Seriousness."

And I guess the remark is what you'd call an inside joke. *Deep* inside.

For those of you who don't get the joke, and I expect many of you will not, it is language learned from a sacred text, officially dated at 1968. Strained Seriousness is the name of a category, which appears between two other categories, Lightly Likable and Oddities, One-Shots, and Newcomers, in much the same way that Corinthians appears between Romans and Ephesians. Each category contains a list of movie directors and a corresponding sublist of their films, the important ones italicized, and the entire enterprise is appended by a series of hierarchical yearly lists, the top four or five also bedecked in italics. This is an all-American affair. True, there is a smattering of foreigners (Fringe Benefits) and the odd Brit (Carol Reed, David Lean), and the one called Renoir was so great, it is said, that he made it into heaven (the Pantheon) with only five American films to his credit. But the particular spiritual discipline embodied in these revelatory lists and rankings is as fundamentally American as Emerson or Hawthorne. And just as the specter of original sin turns the tables on Young Goodman Brown, so The Book sends John Huston, William Wyler, Fred Zinnemann, and William Wellman wandering through the world with the legend Less Than Meets the Eye emblazoned on their foreheads.

"I can't get those fucking categories out my head," a friend once complained, like the woman who hears the ticking bomb in the opening shot of *Touch of Evil*. Small wonder. Consider the descending order, from the transcendentally whole to the prosaically piecemeal ("He has created more great moments and fewer great films than any director of his rank" rings an especially alarming note) or the cursory texts that are not so much defenses as cryptic stabs at illumination (for instance, "Cukor's cinema is a subjective cinema without an objective correlative"). *The American Cinema* has the monumentally timeless authority of an originary text—it does not appear to have been written but handed down from above and received by its readers. Of course, there is writing, very good writing, in the preface, the introductory essay, and, in recent editions, in the afterword. But these feel like scholarly notes, somewhat removed from the transfiguring object that is The Book itself. An alternative history of American movies? Of course, given the fact that a multiple Oscar winner (*Ben-Hur*) sits sadly unitalicized at the bottom of 1959. But it's more than that, and it had a type of impact that was altogether different from the signature pieces of James Agee or Farber or Kael, in which readers heard sympathetic voices validating sentiments or confirming intuitions theretofore unexpressed in the greater culture. If you received *The American Cinema* at the right moment in your life, and many of us did, it came with the force of a cinematic Great Awakening. I suppose that makes Andrew Sarris the Jonathan Edwards of film criticism.

It has often been pointed out that many English language film critics before Sarris invoked the director in their reviews—in fact, it's been pointed out most often by Sarris. Yet the fact is that no one except Manny Farber had looked long and hard at the question of what direction actually was. They had done pretty much everything but—ontological observations, theoretical prescriptions occasionally illustrated by actual movies, or critical observations such as the following: "He has come back from the war with a style of great purity, directness, and warmth, about as cleanly devoid of mannerism, haste, superfluous motion, aesthetic or emotional over-reaching, as any I know." That's Agee on Wyler, and while it's all very lovely, it doesn't even begin to address the topic of what Wyler does for a living. For Farber, and for no one else, this was part of the job, and he approached the task from his own stubbornly particular viewpoint—so particular that almost no one noticed at the time.

It was Sarris who took it upon himself to overhaul American film criticism by facing what everyone else had either avoided or backed into, with and without cultural alibis. He accomplished this with a few simple, elegant moves. First of all, there was the ranking, from most to least personal. Whether or not you agreed with his choices, it was clear that somewhere in the world, priorities had been reversed from content to form, from outside to inside. Sarris took a postwar French idea—the Politique des auteurs—and sold it as The Auteur Theory, which he later (correctly) admitted was not a theory at all but "a collection of facts, a reminder of movies to be resurrected, of genres to be redeemed, of directors to be rediscovered." It's been said that he simply took a French notion and Americanized it, which isn't untrue, but this minimizes the daring. To embrace American movies and moviemakers in Paris was one thing. To embrace those same movies and moviemakers in the country that had made and marginalized them in the first place was a riskier proposal. This was a systematic destruction and re-

198

construction of the standard view of American cinema and by extension all of cinema; an insistence that cinematic beauty did not come from without (the right subject, actors, set designer, cinematographer, etc.) but from within; and an assertion that where the matter of authorship was concerned, all signs pointed not to the writer or the performers but the director. Putting it another way, to fix one's sights on the actors or the cinematography or the dialogue was like staring at mouth, knees, and navel, whereas contemplating a film through the framework of direction was more like looking at the whole person. Bazin, the *Cahiers* and *Positif* critics, and the Brits at *Sight and Sound, Sequence,* and *Movie,* were already there, but it was Sarris who shepherded this new way of seeing into American consciousness, the toughest job of all.

His smartest move was parachuting two French terms into the American critical language—auteur and mise-en-scène. Auteur was a brilliant choice, because it killed two birds with one stone: on the one hand curbing the then-prevalent literary bias in criticism by finding an alternative to Author, on the other hand solidifying the concept of personal creation with a term that went well beyond the term "director." Mise-en-scène was necessarily more mysterious, and neither Sarris nor Alexandre Astruc ever adequately defined it. "We might say that *mise-en-scène* is the gap between what we see and feel on the screen and what we can express in words," Sarris wrote in response to a request for a definition from a Maryland doctor. Fair enough, but a little too tricky. "*Mise-en-scène* is the shaping of an objective core. Take away the objective core, and you have pure personality without *mise-en-scène*." Not bad, but perhaps an overly fancy way of saying that filmmakers manipulate their raw material the way sculptors mold their clay. "What *mise-en-scène* means is perhaps less important than what it implies." I wonder if the doctor was satisfied with that one.

The point is that mise-en-scène is, or was, a necessarily indefinable and eminently malleable term, which ultimately came to stand for a kind of alchemical magic in the happy meeting between artist and material. This type of purely aesthetic thrill had remained in the shadows of serious film criticism—cinema had been pegged as either a modern, theoretically-driven marvel in perfect sync with the ongoing ascendancy of the proletariat ("When Eisenstein demonstrated that anything goes as far as temporal distortion is concerned, the actor was completely forgotten as the intransigently counter-revolutionary agent operating against the smooth flow of dialectical montage," wrote Sarris, brilliantly), a purely sociological phenomenon ("As soon as we identify an entity called 'Marilyn Monroe' as an iconographical element of *Niagara*, we incorrectly limit a variable element with an invariable name"), a twentieth-century entertainment machine, or nothing more than the sum total of its various parts. Among many other things, Sarris was saying that magic in cinema was a question of sensibility rather than visual, verbal, or aural splendor, and mise-en-scène came to denote the crucial evidence that human intelligence, as opposed to efficiency or self-importance, had been present behind the camera. If you insisted on a strict translation, the term applied more to métier than magic, but it seemed ridiculous to describe the mise-en-scene of Joseph Pevney or Delbert Mann. Ultimately, the term as Sarris put it to use is a kissing cousin to Farber's negative space, Sarris's "personality" jibing with Farber's "experience." The difference is that where Farber's language and orientation as a critic were always resolutely private, Sarris's were public and explicitly polemical. And they did the trick. The next time you browse through the Vincente Minnelli section at Kim's Video on Broadway or watch a TCM tribute to Raoul Walsh or read an appreciation of Park Chan-wook in the *New York Times*, think of Andrew Sarris. And think of the many critics who imagine they're scoring points by insisting that film is a collaborative medium, only to return to the director as organizing principle without missing a beat.

"Americans can't resist a good revival meeting," Jean-Pierre Gorin said of *Fahrenheit 9/11*, and Sarris whipped up a remarkable amount of fervor among his cinephilically inclined countrymen in the 1960s and 1970s. Once he realized that he had fans—which came with the realization that he had enemies—he was quick to point out that fanaticism was a two-way street. "I would be the first to concede that any critical theory carried to extremes is absurd," he wrote in 1970. "When you become too addicted to the *politique,* you wind up listening to visiting Frenchmen whispering into your ear that Edgar G. Ulmer has just directed a nudist film anonymously . . . The point is that in America we are always overcompensating for the extremisms, real and alleged, of others, thus becoming extremists ourselves." In retrospect, the venomous extremism of Sarris's avowed enemies is notable for its underlying anxiety, not to mention its evasion of the subtlety and intricacy of his arguments. On the one hand, Dwight MacDonald and John Simon (immortalized by Sarris as "the greatest film critic of the 19th century") were taking Sarris to task for legitimizing the most vulgar impulses in cinema and thus betraying the original promise of the medium; on the other hand, a certain critic at *The New Yorker* was trying to have it both ways, tipping her hat to MacDonald and Simon's aesthetic conservatism and then wheeling around to accuse Sarris of turning the ecstatic rush of movie-going into a slow, somber trek to the museum, with multiple stops along the way for genuflections and incense burning.

It's one of the odd quirks of history that, at least at this moment in history, the name of Pauline Kael is unavoidable if you're discussing Andrew Sarris. They go together like Petruchio and Kate, Zeus and Hera, and Bobby Riggs and Billie Jean King. Despite the fact that they shared certain predilections and preferences (for Godard in the 1960s, Altman in the 1970s, and *The Earrings of Madame de . . .* now and forever), they remained bitter antagonists between 1963, when Kael tossed a grenade into the auteurist cell with the lively but ridiculous "Circles and Squares," right up to Kael's death in 2001, commemorated by Sarris with a deflating obituary in the *New York Observer.* "Not that I have any desire to continue playing good old Charlie Brown to Miss K's Lucy," wrote Sarris in 1970, "but I can't really discern any overriding moral issue involved in the conflicting tastes of two movie reviewers." Perhaps not, but just as Godard defined the tracking shot as a moral affair, so one might say the same of a critical stance. *Pace* Renata Adler, Kael was an electrifying prose stylist. And yet, it's Sarris who has had the more positive and lasting effect on the way we look at movies.

Sarris met every challenge head on, and Kael sidestepped many of them—Resnais, Malick, Fassbinder, late Bresson, late Dreyer, post–*Dr. Strangelove* Kubrick, post–*Last Waltz* Scorsese, *Shoah*, and, last but not least, the classical American cinema that was getting such a spirited revision from both sides of the Atlantic during her ascendancy. Moreover, she had a very pretty way of encouraging her readers to sidestep right along with her, by providing them with snappy alibis that jangled in the brain like Top Forty hooks—*Hiroshima, mon amour* was "an elaborate masochistic fantasy for intellectuals"; *Barry Lyndon* "says that people are disgusting but things are lovely"; *The Merchant of Four Seasons* is "an art thing, all right, but perhaps not a work of art." No question about it: you can't "get drunk on" the aforementioned films and filmmakers. You *can* fall in love with them, but it's quite different from the type of love you might feel for *The Godfather* or *Dressed to Kill*—a communion rather than a crush. Sarris often shared Kael's ambivalence over art cinema, but he almost always tried to come to terms with it—for him, the uncrossable line of viewer tolerance that Kael watched like a hawk was nonexistent. As long as filmmakers didn't lose their nerve or cop out, Sarris reckoned that the ideal, sympathetic viewer owed them their best. One could say that for Kael the artist is guilty until proven innocent, while for Sarris he/she is innocent until proven guilty.

"I suppose . . . I am a revisionist in the most restless sense of constantly revising myself," Sarris wrote in the introduction to *Politics and Cinema.* "Consequently, every movie I have ever seen keeps swirling and shifting in ever changing contexts." This open-hearted stance before the wonder of cinema, the polar opposite of Kael's famous one-viewing/one-judgment credo, is crystallized in Sarris's return visits to Kubrick. "It's not that I have seen the light," he wrote in 1975 of *Barry Lyndon,* "but that I have come to appreciate Kubrick's particular form of darkness." But he had started with 2001, and a little remarked report on a second re-viewing of a film he had vilified in *The American Cinema* ("The ending . . . qualifies in its oblique obscurity as Instant Ingmar"). It was two years later when he took this "enhanced" look, resulting in one of the most charming passages in American film criticism. "I must report that I recently paid another visit to Stanley Kubrick's 2001 while under the influence of a smoked substance that I was assured by my contact was somewhat stronger and more authentic than oregano on a King Sano [cigarette brand] base. (For myself, I must confess that I soar infinitely higher on vermouth cassis, but enough of this generation gap.) Anyway, I prepared to watch 2001 under what I have always been assured were optimum conditions, and surprisingly (for me) I find myself reversing my original opinion. 2001 is indeed a major work by a major artist." I'm not sure what I love most about this passage—the fact that it's impossible to imagine anyone else writing it (in 1970! in *The Village Voice!*), its complete lack of guile, or its corresponding lack of self-consciousness. A few sentences later, a kind of peak is reached: "I don't think that 2001 is exclusively or even especially a head movie (and I now speak with the halting voice of authority)."

Sarris's disarming candor and his complete lack of concern with being hip have always been his trump cards as a critic and his *bêtes noires* as a journalistic player. The old Voice probably could have tolerated an attention-getting firebrand like Stanley Crouch forever, no matter how reactionary, if he hadn't tried to smash up the joint; but its patience wore thin with this "instinctively" Christian centrist (whose political acumen could have given any of his fellow staff writers a run for their money) with an unapologetic love for old movies and a curiously formal prose style in the best belle lettrist tradition. Despite the fact that his arch enemy's dizzying virtuosity is often stood in opposition to the style of every other film critic before or since, it's Sarris with his restless intelligence and his Proustian proclivities who is finally the more penetrating writer. What is winning in Kael—moving, in fact—is the urgency of her need to communicate her immediate emotional responses to films and, especially, actors, in a style so breathlessly intoxicating that it haunts film criticism to this day. Her best pieces shimmer and throb like a great Tommy James single. And that's always been the rub, for her and for her devotees. Anything that carried more than a hint of premeditation or intellectual mediation was anathema. Unfortunately, a high percentage of art and a higher percentage of criticism smacks of both premeditation *and* intellectual mediation (out of necessity), which is why she had more or less painted herself into an aesthetic corner by the time she retired. Meanwhile, Sarris, in the tradition of Bazin, Daney, and Farber, was and still is a critic/theorist—in other words, his immersion in the medium is so total that he generates theory through his practice. While he may not have a defining essay like "The Ontology of the Photographic Image" or "White Elephant vs. Termite Art"—or, God help us, the unfathomable "Fantasies of the Arthouse Audience" (reduced to ashes by Raymond Durgnat)—he does have fifty years' worth of remarkably trenchant and insightful criticism, in which the cinema itself (as opposed to the reader) stands at the center, valiantly protected by Sarris as if it were his queen and he its knight.

Flip to any given page from any one of his anthologies, long out of print and overdue for a fresh look (come to think of it, a few more anthologies of uncollected material are in order), and you will find a restlessly inquisitive and extraordinarily supple mind at work, joyfully tying together an assortment of elements—historical antecedents, contemporary political realities, and personal memories. On the whole, Sarris's valentines to the very best (Ophuls, Mizoguchi, Hitchcock, Ford) are less exciting than his investigations of the flawed or failed: sublimity, in this case, tends to be a great equalizer, while imperfection comes in a tantalizing array of seemingly limitless variations. "On the whole, most movies tend to be more complex than profound," Sarris wrote in The Primal Screen, "but this makes them all the more difficult to pin down, describe, and categorize for all time." No one aside from Farber worked harder at pinning down, describing, and categorizing (always provisionally).

Sarris, a winningly improbable blend of William Hazlitt and Howard Cosell, was at his very best when confronted with an especially knotty problem, and the aesthetic and political convulsions of the 1960s and 1970s provided him with a bonanza of paradoxes, delusions, and hypocrisies to deflate and dissect. "I think Nixon can be beaten in 1972, but not by reluctant virgins and pure ideologues," Sarris wrote of The Candidate, seeing through the beguiling surface to the core of pure bullshit. "At the very end of the movie . . . all McKay can do is ask, 'What do we do now?' Well, for one thing, Senator-elect McKay can go to the Senate and vote against the confirmations of Renquist, Powell, Burger, and Blackmun." One of his finest moments came when he took not Gillo Pontecorvo but the Lincoln Center audience to task for cheering the café bombing in *The Battle of Algiers:* "All right, you say you believe in indiscriminate violence. Then squeeze Robert Redford, Paul Newman, Jane Fonda, Jeanne Moreau, Catherine Deneuve, Marcello Mastroianni, Laurence Olivier, Vanessa Redgrave, Jean-Paul Belmondo, Peter Finch, George C. Scott, and Diana Rigg into a crowded café in Algiers. Then let the bomb go off five minutes after the picture starts, and show all our cameo stars as shattered corpses . . . Is it still an occasion for cheering? I think not." Sarris was not a bandwagon jumper—needless to say, he did not equate the first New York showing of *Last Tango in Paris* with the inaugural performance of *The Rite of Spring*. Nor did he see anything so new about the New Hollywood: for him it was just a group of talented filmmakers operating under a different set of conditions than the ones under which their studio-contracted forefathers had slaved. If Sarris tended to underrate Coppola and early Scorsese, he also did a far better job than anyone else of positioning them within the totality of film history and then stuck by them once the heat of youth had cooled into the contemplative distance of age.

Sarris was always bracingly honest about his prejudices, and his greatest was for the avant-garde. "Live and let live has been my motto," he wrote of his reluctance to attack non-narrative films in print, "and since most American avant-garde film artists have tended to be as poor as church mice, it seemed unduly cruel to heap abuse atop neglect." I will never forget the hair-raising moment when he took fellow *Voice* writer Jim Hoberman to task in print for "freaking out on the arthouse acid below 14th Street." In retrospect, while I can't abide the notion that narrative is the only package in which moving images should be wrapped, I have to commend and even envy Sarris for his candor and, even to a certain extent, his unapologetic alarmism—most of his colleagues would have hidden behind layers of rationalization or obfuscation. And yet, Sarris is always surprising. He owned up to missing the boat on Cassavetes at the time of *Shadows* and fought hard to get *Faces* into the New York Film Festival even though he didn't much care for it; when he took a good look at *The Chelsea Girls*, he admitted that he saw a work of great gravity and beauty. Sarris always had a problem with youth culture, but he balanced his graybeard griping with passages that reflected the most generous and enlightened point of view since Bazin's. "We are simply too close to the popular cinema of today to read it correctly," he wrote in his *Easy Rider* review. "If American movies today seem too eclectic, too derivative, and too mannered, so did they seem back in the twenties, the thirties, the forties and the fifties . . . Out of all the mimicry of earlier times emerged very personal styles, and there is no reason to believe that the same thing will not happen again and again. Hence beware of all generalizations, including this one, perhaps especially this one, because it is just remotely possible that after all the false cries of doom, the cinema might actually be racing to the creative standstill so long predicted for it. But I doubt it. It is not the medium that is most likely to get old, tired, and cynical, but its aging and metaphysically confused critics. This particular critic has never felt younger in his life."

Sarris has become a more becalmed and solitary presence in recent years, dropping the mantle of head "cultist" and regarding the games of moviemaking and moviecritiquing from a benign distance. Younger readers complain that he is overly content with covering only the latest commercial releases, as if we should all aspire to write for an audience of all-region DVD player owners. I can't begrudge his failure to grapple with Apichatpong or Omirbaev—the distance from *Three Comrades* to Fassbinder is already far enough. And his voice remains one of the most penetrating in film criticism. I recently had the shock of my life when I opened the *New York Observer*, where he's had a berth for the last sixteen years, to find his review of Godard's *Notre musique*. Midway, he segued into a reminiscence of his youth spent in a "casually anti-Semitic household." For him, the effects of his upbringing were dispelled only when the footage of the death camps appeared on American screens. This bracing honesty was a prelude to lowering the boom on Godard's "evasive paradoxes," with one stinging sentence: "Mr. Godard hasn't earned the right to take the mantle of Jewishness upon himself as if it were some sort of Halloween mask." *Notre musique* hasn't been the same since for this reader.

"I never argue with people about movies," Andrew told me when I visited with him at the cozy Upper East Side apartment he shares with his wife Molly Haskell. "We all see different movies. We all go to the movies and see our friends, our family, our loved ones. Brothers, sisters, fathers, mothers. Lost loves. Failed loves. People we hate. Movies are as old as psychoanalysis. So if I were to put you or anyone else on a couch and say, 'Tell me your favorite movies,' it would be a way of psychoanalyzing you." Our conversation ranged and rambled across a lot of territory in two hours—Billy Wilder ("When *Sunset Boulevard* played Radio City Music Hall, I saw it about twenty-five times. I was a great enthusiast. And then Truffaut talked me out of it"), the Pope's then-impending death ("I'm suspicious of how long he's taking"), showing *Citizen Kane* to students at SVA ("The lights came up and one of them raised his hand and said, 'They certainly wore strange clothes back in those days'"), the political problem of landing on the right-to-die side of the Schiavo case ("You can't just stand up in the senate and shout 'Pull the plug!' It wouldn't go down well with your constituents"), and Clint Eastwood ("I find people all the time now saying things like, 'I *agree* with you about Million Dollar Baby—I didn't like it either.' Their not liking it is a much more sweeping thing than anything I've said. They feel it's not big enough, important enough, overwhelming enough. And I suppose it isn't, but what is?"). The theme that we kept circling was the practice of film criticism, on which Sarris has spent a lifetime of reflection. "I've always said to people that auteurism is nice, but it's hypothetical, and gradually you learn how much or how little influence different directors had. You can see that Hitchcock had more influence than someone like Stahl. What it really is, is first you see something, and you like it, and then it's a mystery, and you go into the mystery—and that's what's interesting. And the test of criticism is: can you make a case for it."

"Do you think we've wasted our lives?" Andrew asked as he walked me to the door. A joke, of course, but with a poignant ring. People are always implying that movies, and the hours spent watching them, are wastes of time. When you're young, it's "Why do you want to sit in the dark on such a beautiful day?" When you're older you feel it in the flip tone of movie journalism or in the cultural credence afforded cinematic illiterates like Gore Vidal. You even feel it in such supposedly sympathetic terms as "cinephilia" or "movie love," which carry the taint of affliction. Andrew, with his honesty and his grace, has always made such objections seem utterly irrelevant.

As I walked home through the park, I remembered the last time I had visited Andrew and Molly's place, when Andrew's right-hand man and my mentor Tom Allen died of a heart attack at the age of fifty. I remembered the weekend that Tom, a Jesuit monk, went away on retreat, the Voice almost went on strike and Andrew came down with what became a year-long life-threatening illness. I remembered my mercifully brief stint in the early 1980s as Andrew's personal secretary, at which I was an unqualified disaster. And I remembered getting my first copy of The American Cinema from my mother's friend when I was twelve years old. It was a loan, and it got so much wear that she made me buy him a new one. Thirty-two years later, I still can't get those fucking categories out of my head. Not that I've ever tried. That I like Huston or Wellman more than Andrew does, or did, is beside the point, and it always has been. He gave me and many, many others, a framework, a way of seeing and understanding an art form that was and still is culturally disreputable. I owe him a lot, and so does anyone else writing about cinema in the English language.

The Throbbing Acuity of Negative Space

Given the number of people who claim to admire his work, the constant attempts to reduce Manny Farber's writing to a comfortable soundbite singualrization are pretty disconcerting. Too often, he's been tagged as "hard-boiled" or "macho," the Mitchum of film criticism. Never mind that this man's man spent his final stretch as a working critic concentrating on the likes of Roeg, Fassbinder, Akerman, and the Straubs, in collaboration with his sharp, perspicacious wife Patricia Patterson. It's a surpassingly stale image of a writer who properly belongs in the company of Melville (Herman, not Jean-Pierre), Dreiser, and Roth, artists who exhaust every possibility as they pursue mysteries right to their ends, so doggedly and intently that "the thing becomes filigreed," as Farber himself once put it. No doubt Farber's status as a gaudy noir wish fulfillment has a lot to do with *Movies*, the mid-1970s reissue of his collection *Negative Space*, with its colorful nostalgia-crazed portraits of Bogart, George Raft, and some Lauren Bacall/Ida Lupino hybrid on its cover, and its midsection of sumptuous stills from the likes of *Railroaded* and *Each Dawn I Die* (nothing from *Wavelength* or *Le Gai savoir*). But the urge to pin everyone and everything down to a single, flat, one-sided image has become almost second nature in America, as though it was a necessity of modern life: let too much specificity slip into our prose or our conversation and the machinery of kul-cha, high and low, might grind to a halt. What to do with this world of "nothing but winners," as Manny himself put it to me recently. He was referring to cinema, but he could just as well have been talking about politics, journalism, publishing, the art world, or the classroom.

It was a copy of *Movies* that this nostalgia-bit fifteen-year-old first got his hands on back in 1975. In the lobby of a movie theater in western Massachusetts, specializing in revivals and unusual new foreign cinema. It was the sort of place that doesn't exist anymore, anywhere, whose particulars— uncomfortable rows of used seats asymmetrically positioned around the theater, a rock-related rather than film-related ambience—are so gone that it's hard to even remember why or how they came to be in the first place. Somewhere in the lobby there was a bookshelf, with a few dust-covered paperbacks for sale: *The Bonnie and Clyde Book*, Classic Film Scripts for *The Blue Angel* and *Ivan the Terrible*, *Groucho and Me*, and, with that corny cover that caught my eye, *Movies*. The know-it-all, first-year-grad-student type behind the counter took my $5.95 plus tax. "Manny Farber, he's cool." Do you know how old he is, or if he's still writing? "I don't know. Hey Tom, you know how old Manny Farber is?" "Manny Farber? I think he's dead."

Of course, at fifteen what got me excited was Farber's prose. As Jim Hoberman put it recently, when he introduced Farber to the audience of New York film critics who had given him a special citation for Da Capo's expanded edition of *Negative Space*, you'd read his work and think, "Who is this guy, and how did he get to write like this?" To say that the tone comes out of another era is to put it mildly—it seemed like quite a sparkling throwback during the mellow days of the New Journalism, and now, in the age of so much word-processed dribbling and do-it-yourself facetiousness, it's positively startling. And very much the opposite of the hard-boiled style, much closer to a Johnny Carson monologue than a Horace McCoy novel. Farber worked up a rhythmically intricate prose, where the film in question comes to life in bright, vivid swatches, the insights like "the sharp, clean thrust of the chisel as it slices through the wooden strut," to borrow his evocation of a prized moment in Huston's *The Asphalt Jungle*. A personal favorite: "Even at his worst, in reviews where he was nice, thoughtful and guilty until he seemed an 'intellectual' hatched in Mack Sennett's brain." This is from a 1958 piece for *The New Leader* about Farber's old friend James Agee, that he now regrets having written. "He didn't deserve that at all," he said, as we sat and talked recently in the tea room of an Upper East Side hotel. "So much of writing is involved with the time it's written in, combating something or going with something. When that piece was written, all my friends in the world were idolizing Agee, and it just seemed so slumberous. So I decided I should reverse it."

I insisted that the piece was a good one, and very important to me personally ("You like *everything* I write!"). I read Agee quite carefully when I was young, and there was always something about his criticism that bothered me, no matter how gorgeous the prose. Simply put, he was forever writing about the film he *wanted* to see as opposed to the one he *did* see, and that unfortunate tradition in which the critic's prose competes with the film in question begins with him. "I know what you're talking about. He wasn't that way himself. I've never seen anyone who loved movies so much, taking them apart and putting them together again. Maybe . . ." At this point, the lady playing the harp in the back of the room broke into "My Way." "I knew she was going to do that," said Manny. "It just figures. You get the feeling that when she's finished, they'll have to drag her out of here." Throughout our conversation, he kept returning to the problem of that damned harp, trying to match the somnambulant sound with the lugubrious action. "Obviously the instrument takes so long to . . . there's a pluck, and then you hear the sound . . . so there's a waiting period. You keep wondering: when's she gonna get to the next note?" It's this kind of persistence, of refusing to rest until he's absolutely nailed the object in question, that's at the heart of his writing.

And the more carefully I read Farber's pieces throughout the years—well over twenty-five at this point—the more I realized that this persistence was what made his work so thrilling (and lasting: how many film critics do you find yourself going back to over twenty-five years?). Every adjective and every reference point opens up new territory, as opposed to the common tactic of coordinating everything to one fixed meaning or judgment: the reader might just have the ecstatic feeling of gazing up at a meteor shower. The words are there to place the movie through what Farber calls "surface excitement," which makes him diametrically opposed to the critic with whom he is most often lumped together, Pauline Kael, another old pal. As a prose stylist, Kael may well be as exciting as Farber, and my preference for his homegrown vernacular, forged in the great sportswriting era of the 1920s and 1930s, to her muscular matron urbanity is purely a matter of taste. Farber is just as judgmental as Kael, but he never felt her need to stay perched outside of the movie or to fill his pieces with so many directives and shoulds/shouldn'ts ("you" feel this, "you" wish that). With Kael, *you're* always aware of the fact that she's writing for a very particular audience: whoever agrees with her.

Whereas Farber burrows himself so deeply into whatever movie he's dealing with that hierarchies and judgments—"derelict appendages," as he once put it—are beside the point. The most crucial aspect of his writing is its mobility, the way that it implies that every point is connected to every other point, that contexts and positions are constantly shifting and mutating, that nothing is fixed and everything is fluid. "This will sound silly," he told *Cahiers du Cinéma* back in 1982, "but criticism is a mode of writing that always lags behind its era . . . *The Man Who Shot Liberty Valance* . . . is an exciting film . . . I know I now think about it in very contemporary terms: today, at this particular time. I know what these films said to Andrew Sarris . . . but what about right now?" It's a point that's often lost on Farber's acolytes, who scour the landscape looking for examples of termite art when his most important lesson is to find oppositions that speak to the year 2000 as directly as White Elephant/Termite Art did to 1962. For instance, the distinction between aesthetics that are handmade (*Rushmore*) and those that are rented for the occasion (*Three Kings*).

Farber went the deepest when he had Patterson for company. In their remarkable 1977 *Film Comment* piece on *Taxi Driver*, "The Power and the Gory," their take may be more negative than positive, but the piece is so exhaustive, looking at the movie from more angles than you might have thought possible, that the attentive reader is bound to find it satisfying no matter what his/her opinion. "It's a good piece," said Manny. "It took an enormous amount of work. Believe it or not, it went from San Diego to Chicago and back—I don't know what I was doing in Chicago. I spent a good half day getting to a theater in the suburbs to see something in that movie. Why? I don't feel safe unless I see things over and over again . . . I don't think I'd ever do it again, see a movie that many times. Every *frame*." After Patricia joined us, she also expressed relief, tinged with a little sadness, at being through with the hard work of writing. "This was before the word processor, and we did so much cutting and pasting that when we were through we had produced these incredible *objects*—you should have seen what the final pieces looked like."

But when they see something that really grabs them, they have the urge to get back to the typewriter—*not* the computer ("We're incapacitated by modern technology"). Manny's curiosity in particular was boundless— what were people writing about, who won the *Film Comment* poll, what was the last good film I saw, what were Hou Hsiao-hsien's films like. "We never get to see things, unless it's five years from now when it'll run for about three days. And San Diego is deadly on movie magazines.

"Actually, the things I've liked are all foreign, and they're almost all duplicated by everyone else. I mean, if you asked Hoberman what he liked, he would say pretty much what I liked." Like many people around the world, he's fallen in love with Kiarostami. "One of his I liked a great deal was the one with the little kid [*Where Is the Friend's Home?*]. The last fifth of the movie, where the kid goes looking for the notebook: his mother is putting away the washing, and suddenly Kiarostami switches to a night shot. He does the same sort of thing in *Taste of Cherry*, where the guy drives up to his apartment. The camera doesn't take you inside the guy's house, which is quite wonderful. It's possible it's just an accident that he got that effect. It's a double transition—in lighting, and in what he's showing you about the person. Through the whole movie, you're right on this guy's shoulder, you're with him, and suddenly you're taken away from him in space. There's something very exciting about it—what is he *doing* in that room? It's funny that he even goes back to the house. It seems unusual. He's a funny director."

I asked him how he thought the seemingly modest earlier film stacked up against the grander newer one. "About even. I think the kids' movie is less sentimental, less cosmetic. The other movie is sort of troubling because . . . everything works. It's a little rich. I think it's tremendous for metaphor, for doing various forms of digging a grave or burying somebody. He keeps playing around with the idea of shoveling dirt on top of a casket: sand coming down, a little guy coming down the hill. A guy going upstairs to a lookout station, with a funny ladder shot, at the mine. And the soldier running away from him. It's a little bit of a shift. The whole first part of the movie is exciting for being inside of the car and looking out. It's the most common movie shot, and it's one thing they never get right. The scale is very exciting. When you're in car scenes in movies, the things that are passing are much smaller than he gets, the *aspect* of them. He gets the laborers walking past, much closer and larger."

But the movie that's excited both Farber and Patterson the most over the last few years was barely a bleep on the radar screen of American criticism, Maurice Pialat's unsung masterpiece *Van Gogh*. "That's one of the things that kills me about getting away from criticism, that we were never able to do *Van Gogh*. And God knows, we've seen it thousands of times."

"We own very few videos, but we got that one," said Patricia.

"He is *some* director," said Manny. "The thing about his movies—he gets low shots. His focus is closer to the ground than other people's, it seems to me. So he gets some very intimate things. Like in that whole scene of the picnic. And he did beautiful work with that actor [Jacques Dutronc]. Using his back—he has this funny back that projects a little bit. And Pialat gets measurements that intrigue me. The spaces that he goes through with a railroad car, and the people walking alongside, the way he spaces them, the way that Van Gogh looks at a painting—it's not too different from Bresson, the way he breaks up action. You get a kind of staccato move. We first saw it in Paris . . ."

"We knew so much of Van Gogh's history that we pretty much knew what was going on," added Patricia. "It's funny. Pialat Frenchifies him so much that he has to become a libertine: he spends more time at the whorehouse than he does at his painting. But I just found it so exciting that they didn't go down the usual routes. There's no reason to try a closer image of Van Gogh. We already have it through his writing and the painting. To do something close, a step by step kind of mimicking, wouldn't work." We had a good laugh over the way Pialat references every painter in the *impressionist* canon—Bonnard, Renoir, Degas—but barely gets around to Van Gogh himself. "He never really does Van Gogh," said Manny. "Ever! And at the end, it's as if he says to himself, 'Wow, this is a movie about a painter! I'd better get to work!' Suddenly he starts brushing the canvas. It's very funny."

So what does Manny Farber do now, at the age of eighty-two? He paints, which he's been doing since he was a young man—contrary to popular belief, it isn't something he took up after he "retired" from film criticism. He doesn't show often in New York—"The only place I score is in San Diego. Which is fortunate, because that's where we live"—so I haven't been able to keep up with his work the way I've wanted to. The last show I saw was five years ago, made up of large boards that featured handwritten notes (a constant), vegetables from Patricia's garden and stray household objects thrillingly splayed and scattered across an indeterminate surface with a constantly shifting perspective (another constant, as anyone who knows his movie paintings can tell you): your eye is continually being oriented and reoriented, and, just as in life, hierarchies are continually being thwarted, overthrown. The overall tone? Organic. A field where space stretches off the canvas, and where the contrast in objects and colors, which always seem to edge or blend into one another, suggests that everything under the sun emanates from the same source. I went back to the show three times, and each time I was more wonderstruck by the time Farber took, the patience he displayed, with the rendering of ordinary, everyday, unenhanced *vision*. "Did you like the paintings? Did they interest you?" Manny asked me. I said I loved them. "Truthfully? Because they go nowhere." Characteristic self-deprecation. As with his criticism, which all together adds up to an ecstatically engaged, bracingly immediate history of the cinema, it's not that Manny Farber's paintings don't go anywhere—it's that they never end.

1999

These pieces appeared in a slightly different form in the following publications: "Tangled Up in Blue," "Life Goes On," "Family Romance," "Young and Innocent," "Airtight," "A Niche of One's Own," "In the Thick of It," "American Movie Classic," "In the Mood for Love," "Beau Travail," "In Praise of Love," "The Wind Will Carry Us," "Sunshine State," "Magnolia," "The New World," "Walking the Line," "The Big Red One: The Reconstruction," "Hail the Conquering Hero," and "The Throbbing Acuity of Negative Space," in Film Comment; "The Actionist" (© Bookforum, Feb/Mar 2006, "Human, All too Human," by Kent Jones) and "The Betrayed" (© Bookforum, Sept/Oct/Nov 2006, "Rio Divorce," by Kent Jones) in Bookforum; "Waking Life" (© Artforum, September 2001, "Dream Whirl," by Kent Jones) in Artforum; "Some American Comedies" and "Digital Cinema" in Cahiers du Cinéma; "A History of Violence" in Cinemascope; "Cannes 2005" in Trafic; and "Leftist Hollywood" in Les Inrockuptibles. The piece on A Perfect World was written for a catalogue that accompanied a retrospective of Clint Eastwood's films at the Venice Film Festival. The piece on Allan Dwan's comedies was written for a collection of writings occasioned by a Dwan retrospective at the Locarno Film Festival. The pieces on The Driver, Big Wednesday, and Sorcerer were written for catalogues that accompanied retrospectives of the films of their respective directors (Walter Hill, John Milius, and William Friedkin) at the Torino Film Festival. The piece on The Glass Web was written for the collection Jack Arnold: L'étrange Créateur, edited by Charles Tatum, Jr., and published by the Cinémathèque Française.

About the Author

KENT JONES is Editor-at-Large of *Film Comment* and American correspondent for *Cahiers du Cinéma*. He is also a regular contributor to the film journals *Trafic* and *Cinemascope*, as well as *The Village Voice* and *Bookforum*.